# THEIR
# WAR
## FOR
# KOREA

# Also by Allan R. Millett

*A War to Be Won:*
*Fighting the Second World War*
with Williamson Murray

*For the Common Defense:*
*A Military History of the United States*
with Peter Maslowski

*Semper Fidelis:*
*The History of the United States Marine Corps*

*In Many a Strife:*
*General Gerald C. Thomas and the*
*U.S. Marine Corps, 1917–1956*

# THEIR WAR FOR KOREA

## AMERICAN, ASIAN, AND EUROPEAN COMBATANTS AND CIVILIANS, 1945–1953

### ALLAN R. MILLETT

BRASSEY'S, INC.
Washington, D.C.

**Library of Congress Cataloging-in-Publication Data**

Millett, Allan R.
    Their war for Korea: American, Asian, and European combatants and civilians, 1945–1953 / Allan R. Millett.—1st ed.
      p. cm.
    Includes bibliographical references and index.
    ISBN 1-57488-434-4
    1. Korean War, 1950–1953—Biography. I. Title.

DS918.A553 M55 2002
951.904'2'0922—dc21

                             2002010228

Printed in Canada

Brassey's, Inc.
22841 Quicksilver Drive
Dulles, Virginia 20166

First Edition

10 9 8 7 6 5 4 3 2 1

# Contents

# Acknowledgments

This book represents a decade of study of the Korean War and Korean politics and culture. However, ten years is not long enough to research this absorbing subject, and my interest in Korean history will continue as long as I do. Because this book represents that expanding, if incomplete, education in a way none of my earlier writings on the Korean War do, I want to use it to acknowledge the contributions of all the people and institutions who have helped me to understand and appreciate Korean history. It is a long list, and I have omitted military ranks and academic titles in the interest of brevity. My mentors have ranks and academic titles and institutional affiliations past and present that justify my complete confidence in their advice. They are, of course, not responsible for what I did not understand or wrote inaccurately.

My journey toward the heart of the Korean War included my wife, Martha E. Farley-Millett, and my daughter, Eve Millett, full partners in a family enterprise: learning about the Korean people in their language in their land. Both of them have been limitless in their encouragement, enthusiasm, and advice.

Without financial support and the gift of time, no scholar can write the "perfect" book, and I have been generously supported by the Mershon Center at The Ohio State University; the Korea Foundation; and the Korean-American Educational (Fulbright) Commission. I want to thank especially Charles F. Hermann, Richard Ned Lebow, and Raymond E. Mason Jr. for their patronage.

As with my other books and articles of the last decade, this work profited from the keen intelligence and skill of Beth Russell at the Mershon Center, who has shared and supported our Korean experience from afar.

I have been especially fortunate to enjoy the advice of two American veterans of the war, Edwin Howard Simmons and Horace G. Underwood, who have been ready to share with me their keen historical judgment, memories and documents, and evaluation of people. Horace and his wife, Dorothy, have been generous hosts in Seoul, and they are the best summer landlords one can imagine, as well as expert interpreters of Korean life and culture. Horace's adult children—Nancy and Horace H. Underwood and Peter Underwood—also provided good company and more wise counsel. Another early mentor was Fred C. Carriere, executive director of the Korean-American Educational Commission in 1991.

Although I have always avoided conscripting my graduate students for my projects, I have been blessed with willing, timely, and able support from a group of exceptional research assistants at some time in my work on the Korean War: Huh Nam-sung, Kim Kook-hoon, Donald M. Bishop, Charles J. Gross, Park Il-song, Lee Choon-kun, Kim Taeho, Cho Duk-hyun, William B. Feis, Andrew J. Birtle, James G. Hogue, Mark R. Jacobson, Jon McIntosh, Katherine Becker, Peter Schrijvers, John M. Stapleton Jr., Richard B. Meixsel, David R. Gray, Kelly C. Jordan, Thomas E. Hanson, Bryan R. Gibby, C. J. Horn, and Leo J. Daugherty III.

Several of my colleagues in the Department of History at The Ohio State University advised me about aspects of their expertise in Japanese, Chinese, and American history: James R. Bartholomew, Phillip C. Brown, Samuel Chu, David L. Stebenne, and Peter L. Hahn.

My education in Chinese history depended upon my academic colleagues in the United States, contacts in Beijing, and former members of the American diplomatic mission to the People's Republic of China: Yu Bin, Li Xiaobing, Chen Jian, Timothy Long, Song Zhongyue, Karl W. Eikenberry, Roy D. Kamphausen, John Louton, Donald M. Bishop (again), and the anonymous colonels who enlivened one of my afternoons at the PLA (People's Liberation Army) Academy of Military Sciences by avoiding open discussion.

I have been educated in different but helpful ways by an international community of students of Korean history whose reputations are safe from my errors: Carter J. Eckert, Donald N. Clark, the late Donald S. Macdonald (one of the great ones), William Stueck, James I. Matray, Bruce Cumings, B. C. Koh, John Merrill, and James H. Grayson. My understanding of the experience of the South Korean army was enhanced by my participation in translating and editing the revised official history, *The Korean War* (Ministry of National Defense,

ROK), arranged by Cho Sung-kyu, Chae Han-gook, and Choi Sang-jin. I am especially indebted to Suh Yong-sun, who served with constant commitment to my work when he was at the Korean Institute of Military History, since renamed and reorganized for reasons that escape easy explanation.

During my many trips to Seoul, I enjoyed the hospitality and assistance of two offices located on the U.S.-ROK (Republic of Korea) military base in Yongsan-ku. The first is the combined and joint history office that serves Combined Forces Command, U.S. Armed Forces in Korea, and the U.S. 8th Army. During those years of imposition (1991–2000) I tried the patience of several command historians: Thomas Ryan, Richard A. Gorell, and Robert Collins. My fieldwork and a great deal of my "street knowledge" of Korean military affairs I obtained from Ronney V. Miller and Kim In-hwa, my companions on many a "staff ride." Karl Swanson helped with access to the library and photographic archives. I appreciate the help of two Air Force historians in Korea and Hawaii: John Sullivan and Deryl Danner. My ability to travel and operate with discretionary temporary duty orders issued by several Commandants of the Marine Corps permitted me to impose upon my fellow Marines of Marine Forces-Korea, who gave me invaluable administrative support and enthusiastic encouragement and their comradeship. Semper Fidelis! I want to mention one of them by name, William P. Eshelman, who with his wife, Pat, provided crucial help upon our first arrival in 1991 with our seven-month-old daughter. Bill was a great officer when he and I were lieutenants in 2nd Battalion, 2nd Marines, and he remained that way until his honored retirement as a major general.

My understanding of the South Korean army could not have been possible without the tutoring of Korean and American officers whose experience extended to 1945 and whose interest is alive today: Paik Sun-yup, Lim Sun-ha, Kang Moon-hoon, Kim Ung-soo, Lee Chi-op, John K. C. Oh, Harold Fischgrund, Stephen M. Tharp, and Jiyul Kim. In another book I will attempt to do fuller justice to the Korean Military Advisory Group and the South Korean officers with whom they labored to create a new and victorious army. In addition to Lim Sun-ha, whom you will meet in this book, the late James H. Hausman Jr. provided me and many others a balanced and candid account of the problems of forming the South Korean army. I received sound advice as well from Chi Kapchong, George Kim, and John Nowell, longtime observers of the Korean military scene in Seoul. Stephen Bradner, a current political advisor to Combined Forces Command, was equally generous with his advice. I also want to thank the officers of the Neutral Nations Supervisory Commission for their hospitality during my trips to the Joint Security Area, Panmunjom.

Since 1991 I have profited by my association with the Korean National Defense University (KNDU) and the comradeship of its faculty, principally the faculty of the Research Institute for National Security Affairs (RINSA) and the National Defense College. In addition to Huh Nam-sung, now the director, RINSA, these colleagues include Yoon Jong-ho, Jung Byong-ho, Rhee Kang-suk, Chung Joon-ho, Hwang Byong-moo, Lee Chang-hoon, Kim Soon-nam, Kim Hyun-ki, and Mun Hwei-mok. Although they have different affiliations, Baek Jong-chun (Sejong Institute) and Lee Chung-min (Yonsei University) have also been generous with assistance.

Among the other historians who have helped me with special problems related to finding documents and interviewing subjects, I want to recognize Edward Marolda (Naval Historical Center) and Thomas Fairfull, former director, U.S. Army Museum of Hawaii, and Judith Bowman, current director of the same museum, for their help.

I hope this book will reflect its international dimension since it attempts to represent the perspective of other nations serving in United Nations Command. My tutors on Commonwealth military affairs are Anthony Farrar-Hockley, Michael Hickey, Jeffrey Grey, and David J. Bercuson as well as all the participants in the Korean War history conference (2000) sponsored by the chief, Australian army. My Continental assistants are: Luc de Vos (Belgium), Piet Kamphuis (the Netherlands), and André Bach (France). My guides into Russian military history are: Mark A. O'Neill, Katherine Weathersby, Alexandre Mansourov, and Victor A. Gavrilov. During a week's visit at the Japanese National Institute of Defense Studies I learned a great deal about the Japanese perspective on the war from Ishizu Tomoyuki, Jun Yasuda, Sakata Yasuyo, and Hayashi Yoshinaga.

I especially appreciate the help of John Toland, the late Roy Appleman, and the late Clay Blair for their generosity with their own sources and insights. The interviews and documents they left behind will benefit all historians of the Korean War. Conrad C. Crane and I studied the air war together, with the support of Lt. Col. Duane E. "Bud" Biteman, USAF (Ret.), the historian of the 18th Fighter-Bomber Wing.

Many of the individual chapters in this book could not have been written without the gracious cooperation of the principals themselves or their friends and families, who provided photographs, correspondence, documents, and invaluable recollections about the principals and the Korean War. Those people who contributed to a specific vignette are identified in the source notes for each chapter, which may be found at the back of the book.

The documentary sources for Korean War history may be found around the world, although the number of people who do research in Moscow, Beijing, and Pyongyang are limited, and I am not one of them. (However, some of my friends are.) The archives, collections, and repositories I searched provided the material that gives the texture of truth of historical writing on the Korean War. I cannot thank everyone who assisted me at these institutions, but I want to name the repositories and indicate a few of the people who provided timely and important assistance: The Harry S. Truman Presidential Library, Independence, Missouri (Dennis Bilger); the Dwight D. Eisenhower Presidential Library, Abilene, Kansas (David Haight); the Douglas MacArthur Memorial Library and Museum, Norfolk, Virginia (William J. Davis and James Zobel); the U.S. Army Military History Institute (Richard Sommers, Dave Keogh, and Louise Arnold-Friend); the George C. Marshall Library (Marti Gansz); the Air Force Historical Research Agency, Maxwell Air Force Base, Alabama; the Hoover Institution on War, Revolution, and Peace; the National Security Agency; the Central Intelligence Agency; the U.S. Army Center of Military History; the National Archives and Records Administration (Timothy K. Nenninger and Richard Boylan); the Korean Language Institute, Yonsei University; the Franklin D. Roosevelt Presidential Library, Hyde Park, New York; the Defense Prisoner of War/Missing Personnel Office; the Naval Historical Center; the Marine Corps History and Museums division (Dan Crawford and Robert Aquilina); the Citadel Archives and Museum; the Princeton University Library; the U.S. Military Academy Library; the U.S. Naval Academy Library; and the U.S. Air Force Academy Library.

I also want to thank Mr. Fred H. Rainbow, editor, *U.S. Naval Institute Proceedings,* for permission to use an adapted version of "Waging War on Germs in Korea," *Proceedings* (March 2001), 78–79.

To all of you, a heartfelt *kamsa hamnida.*

ALLAN R. MILLETT

# Preface

all me Ishmael and join my search for a war. With apologies to Herman Melville and Joseph Conrad, one looks for a war in the sea of the past—turbulent, shifting in aspect and color, relentless in its tides—and the darkest heart of mankind. I do not remember when I began my search for the Korean War. Was it in December 1950, when I and my fellow Boy Scouts of Troop 27, Leonia, New Jersey, manned a winter camping display, which no one visited, and our feet froze? Gone were allusions to Valley Forge, even in New Jersey. We were now Marines attacking in a different direction from the Chosin Reservoir. Did my search begin in 1960, when as a real Marine lieutenant I trained at The Basic School with Korean Marine lieutenants and wondered why they worked harder than we did and never smiled? I remember my first trip to the Republic of Korea in 1986 and the excitement of seeing the battlefields of Seoul, Inchon, Tabudong, Osan, the Naktong River, and Taejon, already rebuilt and reforested to such a degree that it was hard to imagine these places as the bleak, treeless ground frozen in 1950 photographs.

Even as a Fulbright visiting professor at the Korean National Defense College in 1991, I had not yet committed myself to a serious search for the Korean War. No doubt a second trip to Panmunjom worked its subliminal magic, as did a tour around the 5th Marines battlefield on Yonhui ("Smith") Ridge on Seoul's western outskirts. Dr. Horace G. Underwood, who saw the September 1950

battle there as a Navy intelligence officer and interpreter attached to the 1st
Marine Division, gave us the grand tour. The battle destroyed the Underwood
family home at Yonhui College (renamed in 1957 as Yonsei University), founded
by Horace's grandfather, the first Presbyterian missionary to Korea. During
those busy months in Seoul, I often visited Tom Ryan, historian of U.S. Armed
Forces, Korea, and an avid student of the Korean War. Tom's enthusiasm for
battlefield staff rides was as infectious as the plague, and he also introduced me
to General Paik Sun-yup, the moral equivalent of meeting Ulysses S. Grant.

By the time my family and I returned again to Korea for the fourth time, in
1993, I knew I wanted to write a book about the Korean War. Now I will write
two, having already published twenty-two edited books, essays, and articles. On
the evening of August 25, 1993, my wife and I dined at the officers club of the
Ministry of Defense with three of my special graduate students: Colonel Huh
Nam-sung, Colonel Kim Kook-hoon, and First Lieutenant Park Il-song. Today
Kim is a general, Park is a major, and Huh Nam-sung is still a colonel, but close
to sainthood for his leadership as former dean of faculties at the Korean
National Defense University. I asked them all one question: What do you want
Americans to know about the Korean War? Their advice was unanimous: Tell
them that our war was total, uncompromising, and bitter. It brought unimaginable suffering to all the Korean people, which continues fifty years later. Americans, they said, do not understand such a war and its impact on the people who
survive and their children. My wife, Martha, and I, whose families fought in the
Union and Confederate armies, quickly asserted that Americans had once
fought themselves, but the Koreans countered that fewer than one-third of the
American population had families in the United States when the Civil War was
fought and that the pain of a war almost 150 years old could no longer be sharp.
Besides, the Confederacy was gone with the wind, and the Democratic People's
Republic of Korea showed no signs of fading away. (Even when Kim Il-sung
died the following year, the North Koreans showed surprising survival skills for
a nation on the verge of starvation and bankruptcy.) All three of our hosts that
evening knew their own civil war, and they believed the people of the United
States did not.

Colonel Kim pointed out that his family was unusual, since in 1950 his parents lived in Kwangju, Chollanam-do (South Cholla Province), and were able to
avoid the purges that followed the occupation of the city by the North Korean
6th Division in August 1950. A month later the Communists were gone, and
although the province had its problems thereafter with Communist partisans,
it became a backwater in the continuing war. Lieutenant Park's family had
not been so fortunate. His grandfather, a merchant and landowner, had been
betrayed and executed by the local Communists in Chollabok-do (North Cholla

Province). We already knew a similar fate had befallen Huh Nam-sung's father, a landowner and prominent Catholic lay leader in Chunchon, capital of Kangwon Province, and only a few miles below the 38th Parallel. The Huhs came originally from Wonju, and they had been well-to-do as long as family tradition could recall. The Huh family, early converts to Catholicism in the days of the martyrs, saw wealth as a means for pursuing learning and artistic skill; the Huhs were teachers, religious leaders, poets, writers, scholars, and artists. When the Communists came to Chunchon in July 1950, Mr. Huh went into the hills to organize some sort of resistance—in fact a plan for community preservation, not guerrilla warfare. Betrayed, he became a martyr on August 27, 1950, when he was shot with fellow Christians in a cave near Yanggu. In the meantime, Mrs. Huh and her eight children trekked south to Pusan, starving, frightened, and confused. Huh Nam-sung, age three, rode to safety on the back of an older brother. Two of his sisters did not survive the journey, dying of starvation-fed respiratory infections. A widow at thirty-six, with six surviving children to save, beggared, without skill or family ties in Pusan, Mrs. Huh told the children that the war was God's punishment of the Korean people, but she was confused about just what sin the people had committed. As Colonel Huh finished his story, the other two officers nodded. Yes, they agreed, the Americans should know that the Korean War was a total war.

Dedicated in 1995, the Korean War Memorial in Washington, D.C., is a monument to American confusion about "the forgotten war." Eighteen oversize military statues walk through a "paddy" of arbor vitae and black marble, which by no stretch of the imagination represents any field I have ever seen in Korea. At least the statues look confused and unhappy in the name of realism, and they are draped in ponchos, which is supposed to imply that Korea is deluged in tropical rains, when in fact the rainy season lasts only about six weeks in June and July. Korea is not Vietnam. Memorial artwork and inspirational inscriptions grace two sides of a marble wall that has already suffered from weather damage. The patrol marches toward a central stone, which reads: "Our nation honors her sons and daughters who answered the call to defend a country they never knew and a people they never met." Another memorial slogan—"Liberty is not free"—is a ringing banality. The two national presidents who dedicated the American Korean War Memorial dramatized the war's clouded reputation in the United States. Once viewed by many of his countrymen as a dangerous subversive and regarded by his own army as a Communist appeaser or worse, Kim Dae-jung shared the dedication with President William Jefferson Clinton, whose own lack of enthusiasm for military service and weak self-discipline had aggravated even his most forgiving follower-believers. It was not a memorable event except that Kim Dae-jung spoke with graciousness about how Americans had saved his country and then saved him from the assassins of his own government.

Four years later the Korean War Memorial became the site of a rededication, since the original memorial had not survived four sets of Washington seasons and some shoddy construction. The linden trees around the "pool of remembrance" had died, which would not have happened if they had been sturdy Korean pines or the Korean national flower, the unconquerable *mugunghwa*. The pool had sprung a leak and drained away all but a film of green scum. The walkways had become dangerous as the paving stones split. Why not add some mines, I thought, to get some real ambiance, reproducing the fields of rusting explosives that border the paths up Heartbreak Ridge. The same contractor who built the original memorial—the U.S. Army Corps of Engineers—did the repairs. When Senator Paul Sarbanes presided over the reopening of the memorial, he expressed his wish that more veterans would visit the memorial. Those who had, Sarbanes told his audience in July 1999, should be heartened that Senator Strom Thurmond had sponsored legislation that officially made Korea "a war" and not "a conflict."

The *Washington Post* story about the rededication, "Korean War Memorial Marks New Beginning," noted that "the war" had begun on June 25, 1950, and ended with an armistice on July 27, 1953. "Historians say that more than 54,000 Americans were listed as dead and that South Korea lost approximately 47,000. The 15 other United Nations countries involved suffered more than 3,000 deaths." The article did not mention that the enemy forces came from North Korea and China and that these nations probably endured two million war-related deaths, military and civilian. The identities of those "historians" who so carelessly misreported the fatalities of United Nations Command are unclear. What is certain is that for almost forty years the Department of Defense misrepresented Korean War deaths in the American armed forces by erroneously reporting that "deaths, other" for the "Korean conflict" numbered almost 20,000, when the actual figure for the same category in the Korean theater of operations was 3,249. When the Department of Defense finally held a press conference in January 2000 to announce its mistake (some unknown "clerk" had lumped all deaths worldwide into "deaths, other"), the press did not bother to ask why "deaths, other" outside the war zone had reached such catastrophic proportions—a rate per thousand service personnel higher than that of World War II. With such brilliant coverage of American losses, why would anyone expect the United States government to report the devastation of Korea accurately?

War memorials speak as much for living memories as they do for dead soldiers. The war memorial of the Republic of Korea gleams in all its massiveness behind a plaza and two reflecting pools in Yongsan-ku, Seoul, on property that once housed a Japanese military base. The style of the memorial might be called Greco-Korean, influenced by the architectural styles of the Soviet Union and the French Second Empire. There is nothing subtle about the style or the message. Within the grounds there is a round building especially dedicated to the Korean War, dramatized by a statue of two embracing soldiers. One is Park Kyu-choll, a South Korean master sergeant, and the other, Park Yong-choll, is a private in the Korean People's Army. They are brothers who found each other alive on a forgotten battlefield.

The displays and exhibits of the War Memorial Museum offer the visitor a complete military history of Korea for almost three millennia, but two struggles share the place of honor: the resistance to the Japanese (1905–1945), and the war between the Republic of Korea and the Democratic People's Republic of Korea, the two Koreas known to the rest of the world by convenient geography, "South" and "North," respectively, which is especially easy for Americans to understand. Two wings in the museum focus on the history of various elements of the South Korean armed forces. In each service wing one discovers that "the Korean War" seems to have begun before 1950 and continued past 1953, extending the war against Asian Communism with the deployment of a Korean expeditionary corps to Vietnam.

The real story of the Korean War starts outside the museum in a colonnade, which runs along the war memorial's western side and which then extends along the entire face of the memorial. This L-shaped structure is probably six hundred yards in length. Along three walls—two of the western colonnade and one along the memorial's face—the Koreans have placed one hundred memorial plaques bearing the names of those Koreans who died in the service of the Republic of Korea (ROK). Each obsidian plaque, 255 centimeters by 100 centimeters in size, can hold the names of eighteen hundred Koreans. The plaques are organized by unit and chronology and include not just the armed forces, but also the Korean National Police, the Korean Constabulary, the Railway Police, and special units of paramilitary volunteers. The first names are those of three members of the National Police: Kang Shin-ok, Kim Shin-ong, and Son Hang-chin. They died in September 1945, three years before there was a Republic of Korea.

When the original plaques were dedicated in 1994, they bore the names of 141,113 service personnel. After a review of the status of South Korean "missing in action"—totaling 43,472 officers and enlisted men—the Ministry of

National Defense announced on June 25, 2000, that South Korea's wartime military deaths now numbered 187,712 and that new plaques would be added to the Roll of Honor corridors, not just for Koreans but for all the fallen servicemen of United Nations Command. The plaques for the period 1945 to 1950 bear the names of 7,235 members of the Korean National Police, the Korean Constabulary, and the Korean army and coast guard (navy), all killed in a partisan war with the Communist insurgents who fought the creation of the Republic of Korea in 1948. The South Korean armed forces suffered more combat deaths than the Union army in the American Civil War, the ROK soldiers drawn from a male population smaller than the Union's. The number of civilian deaths for both of the Koreas is variously estimated between one and two million, for which there is no relevant American comparison: "Please tell all Americans that for us it was a total war."

All the fatal statistics cannot hide the fact that ultimately the Korean War, like all others, is about the lives and deaths of individual human beings. Occasionally they are even memorialized in statuary, though I doubt that the real soldier ever looked quite like his statue. On Cheju-do, an island province off Korea's south coast, there is a memorial in Sogwipo to Second Lieutenant Kang Sung-u, born in the village of Sihung-ni. Cheju-do is now a resort, where honeymooners and failing Russian presidents go to commune with nature, other vacationers, and Korean politicians. I wonder what Lieutenant Kang would think of all the Russian vodka one can now buy in Cheju-do convenience stores along with the island's famous tangerines. From 1948 to 1950 the island was aflame with terrorism, reprisals, atrocities, and wanton destruction, a ravishment so complete and devastating that the islanders prefer not to remember it at all. It is not difficult to guess which side Lieutenant Kang joined, since his occupation, according to his memorial, was youth and rural development specialist, which could be a euphemism for paramilitary antipartisan gang leader. Kang's memorial says he died in the Battle of White Horse Mountain (Paektusan) on October 12, 1952, in an action in which Kang and two sergeants stormed and captured the last Chinese stronghold on the mountain's peak. Lieutenant Kang perished in the action. The monument does not mention that a Chinese counterattack the same day recaptured the position and that it took three more days of battle and two more Korean infantry regiments to hold the peak. The Korean 9th Division suffered thirty-five hundred casualties in nine days of combat, the Chinese 38th Army ten thousand soldiers. I have seen White Horse Mountain, and it is not a big place, yet tens of thousands of Asian soldiers fought back and forth across this modest ridge, which changed hands seven times. A local boy who died well, at least Lieutenant Kang has a statue near his hometown.

Cheju-do and White Horse Mountain are thousands of miles from Upper Arlington, Ohio, both geographically and culturally. In what was once the town center of Upper Arlington, a bedroom suburb of Columbus, the city fathers erected a war memorial to honor the city's veterans and wartime dead since World War II. Although cynics claim that Upper Arlington is a city built on golf, football, The Ohio State University, and *Wendy's* hamburgers, the city began its existence in 1916 as a mobilization camp for Ohio National Guardsmen called to duty to police the troubled border with Mexico. Despite its development as an upper-middle-class, affluent, and white residential community, where the worst violence occurs on its many athletic fields, Upper Arlington has sent its best and brightest off to fight America's wars, even the one in Vietnam. The war memorial, two stone cenotaphs garnished with the predictable plaques, honors those who served in World War II, totaling 596 in the last count by the Upper Arlington Civic Association. Fifteen died in service, which indicates some relationship between socioeconomic status and survivability in the American armed forces. On the other hand, nine Arlingtonians died in the Vietnam War; their names are inscribed separately on a small plaque on one of the monuments. The twin stone has a plaque for Korean War deaths. It is blank.

In terms of the collective memory of the American people, the Korean War is not just forgotten. It was not remembered in the first place, and if it is, the war is misunderstood and wrapped in a mythos rivaled only by American's other "foreign wars" in Mexico, Cuba, and the Philippines.

The best way to start America's reeducation on the Korean War would be to walk every critic of America's continuing alliance with the Republic of Korea down the long colonnade of the war memorial in Seoul and to read the thousands of names on the plaques.

This is a book of war stories. It is impossible to imagine how the people I met in person or in research could have had the experiences they endured except within a war. Some of the war stories are also soldier stories, but even soldier stories can vary, since the forces in which soldiers serve can be radically different in their demands and expectations. Sometimes the enemy is really one's own army. War stories, however, attempt to say something about the unique experiences that men and women have when they find themselves caught in a world defined by primal instincts and emotions: survival, fear, desperation, exhaustion, hunger and thirst, wounds and sickness, rage, the urge to kill, the urge to die, absolute hopelessness, ecstasy, callousness, brutality, tenderness, selflessness, and a great deal of boredom, however punctuated with terror. War, as Carl von Clausewitz insisted in arguments that marched in circles, was not like anything else. He chose to define war in terms of its violence and the management and purposeful use of violence, but Clauswitz was a general, not a humanist.

Although war as a human phenomenon has essential elements that have repeated themselves from the dawn of recorded history, every war is unique unto itself. It is the business of historians to sort out the continuities and changes in the history of warfare, and indeed as much ink as blood has been spilled in the cause of explanation: Wars demonstrate technological determinism or the lack thereof; wars reflect the evolution of society; wars dramatize the evolution of armies, navies, and air forces as social institutions and the direction of those forces by a professionalized officer corps; and wars are an audit of the strengths and weaknesses of the nations that fight them. Wars changed history or, conversely, did not change history, at least not very much. Under such scrutiny, the uniqueness of a specific war can be leached out of the event, and the human experience—unique or not—blown away like so much thin gun-smoke. Yet no war in its meaning as part of the history of human experience is just like another.

This book attempts to find the meaning of the Korean War through the experience of individuals and small groups of people caught within the third bloodiest conflict of the twentieth century. Almost fifty years after the most violent phase of that war ended on July 27, 1953, its effects still shape the daily lives of more than sixty million Koreans and might—through a relatively few number of miscalculations—once again involve the lives of millions of Chinese, Russians, Japanese, and Americans. The Korean War is unfinished in the terms of international law and diplomacy; the relations of the two Koreas and their foreign partners are determined by a cease-fire agreement, not a peace treaty. Millions of Koreans of advanced age still show the signs of malnutrition, illness, and wounding. The psychological scars are deeper and pass as surely as genetic traits to at least one successor generation, if not two. To assert social trauma is not, however, to explain it.

The Korean War from first to last pitted Koreans against Koreans. It did not begin on June 25, 1950, but sometime years before, perhaps in the 1920s, perhaps in 1945, perhaps in the spring of 1948, when an insurrection organized by the South Korean Labor (Communist) Party failed to prevent the creation of the Republic of Korea under the sponsorship of the United Nations. The Korean War reflected the development of two diametrically opposed political visions of a modern Korea, released from the Japanese colonial exploitation that began in 1905 and ended forty years later. Neither revolutionary vision—one embodied in several exile and internal Communist parties, the other represented by even more fragmented groups of Western-inspired modernizers—could claim a preponderance of legitimacy. Neither had played a critical role in driving off the

Japanese; neither had a monopoly on Korean nationalism or freedom from the stain of foreign patronage; neither could produce a national leader of unquestioned authority and popularity. Neither could reach into the past to make an irrefutable claim on the future of the Korean people.

In addition, the two revolutionary visions left no room for compromise. The Korean version of Marxism-Leninism had passed through the gauntlet of Maoism and Stalinism and emerged as doctrinaire and murderously tyrannical as its Chinese and Russian variants. The stillborn spirit of political accommodation in Korea reflected a worldview that recognized the evil of Marxism-Leninism. To some degree, the Communist vision had been polluted in Korean eyes by its association with two traditional enemies of Korean independence, China and Russia. By itself, however, Korean nationalism would not have rallied the anti-Communist opposition throughout Korea. This opposition had to be ruthlessly crushed by the Communists for more than a decade before they could claim that the Democratic People's Republic of Korea (Pyongyang) represented the will of the people. The struggle for the soul of the Korean people was a war between two religious faiths, Marxism-Leninism and Christianity.

Western and Korean historians have difficulty in dealing with the role of Christianity in shaping Korea. The easiest way to dismiss the impact of religious conviction is to argue that Christianity was a convenient way to enlist American help in mounting a nonviolent resistance movement to Japanese colonialism. Another rationalization is to argue that Christianity excused the excesses of capitalism and traditional landholding rights enjoyed by an exploitative Korean gentry, the *yangban* class. A third explanation is simply that Christian commitments reflected a political conspiracy of a favored, educated political elite of mandrinal instincts that used a Western religion to hoodwink their native competitors into believing that the Korean Christians occupied a higher moral ground than pure nationalists and Communists could ever attain. Christian Koreans—certainly no more than 5 percent of the population in 1945—were part of the problem, not part of some truly "Korean" solution, usually framed as a kinder, gentler form of postcolonial social democracy managed by a secular elite. This position is almost as ill-considered as attempting to tell the story of the Thirty Years War without acknowledging that Catholicism and Protestantism might have had some competing interests in the conflicts that scourged Middle Europe.

Our own first insight into the influence of Christianity in shaping modern Korea came during our visit in 1986. After a week of attending an international military history conference in Seoul, held at the Sheraton Walker Hill Hotel, which is akin to introducing Koreans to America by holding a conference at Caesar's Palace in Las Vegas, we spent a week in Taegu with old friends Jemma and Don Bishop. We had first met the Bishops when Don came to Ohio State to do graduate work before becoming a faculty member at the U.S. Air Force Academy. As an Air Force base defense officer in Vietnam, Don had gotten to know some of the members of the Korean expeditionary force, and his interest took him on a subsequent assignment to Korea. There he had met and married Jemma through their association at a Catholic church near Don's post, Kunsan Air Force Base. When Don left the Air Force for a new career in the American Foreign Service as a cultural-public affairs officer, he and Jemma returned to Korea with their three young sons to manage the U.S. Cultural Center in Taegu. During the week we spent with them, we saw that much of their considerable local influence came from their religious commitment, not their association with the U.S. government. Even at dinner one night at the officers club at the Taegu air base, we learned that the waitresses had been among Jemma's latest converts to Christianity as they trooped by to "make their manners." I mused that Jemma's married name, Bishop, might be more appropriate than her Korean family name, Kim. In Taegu I also noticed for the first time the red neon crosses that blazed away at night to mark the spires of the Christian churches. The city was a forest of red crosses.

The struggle of Christianity against Communism in Korea should require no explanation. We know, for example, the role of the Catholic Church in Eastern Europe in the opposition to native Communism and Russianization in Poland, Hungary, and Czechoslovakia. We know about the role of militant Islam in the disintegration of the Soviet Union and the Peacock Throne in Iran. In part, the problem is the cultural-geographic setting. Europeans and Americans cannot believe that Asians can leave behind the world of Buddha and Confucius for the world of Jesus Christ. In fact, one can count on one hand and with one finger the number of Asian nations that have made that transition—but the exception is Korea. Filipino Catholicism is an entirely different matter on both religious and cultural grounds. I make this point because any serious understanding of the Korean War must deal with the Christian resistance to Communism in Korea. I chose vignettes with Christian content not as a form of religious proselytizing, but because the Korean War was to a large degree a religious conflict.

The Korean War was also an internationalized conflict, and the experience of non-Koreans is also essential in understanding every dimension of the war. Again, the Thirty Years War offers some useful parallels since it might have been a German civil war with deep religious overtones, but it cannot be explained without dealing with the impact of Swedish and French intervention. If one dates the war's first stages to the Russian and American occupations of 1945, the international context is essential from the very earliest days of this irreconcilable conflict. To deal with these events is not just a way of dealing with "the causes" of the war. It explains why the North Korean invasion of 1950 represented only a change of strategy, not a redefinition of political goals, which had always been an independent Korea from the Yalu River to the Straits of Tsushima. It was the social and economic structure of this liberated Korea that was at issue. The implications of an independent, modernized Korea had serious meaning for China, the Soviet Union, and Japan, which meant that Korea also became a foreign policy problem for the United States of America.

This book attempts to reflect the international dimension of the Korean War whether that influence appears in the lives of Koreans or in the experiences of non-Korean, non-American soldiers who served in United Nations Command. The experiences of Chinese and Russian participants are underrepresented not because I am insensitive to the importance of their participation, but simply because of the limitations of time and the technical and legal problems of using foreign-language sources. In fact, I made repeated efforts in two trips to Beijing to interview Chinese veterans, but instead I have relied upon already-open sources to provide some exposure to the perspectives of the Chinese and Russian participants. The North Korean perspective is even more difficult to provide because the North Korean concept of *juche* or self-determination translates into misrepresentation and fabrication of the North Korean role in the war. Even the Chinese and Russians find the North Koreans unwilling to deal with the war in anything but propaganda terms.

In sum, this book of human experiences in the Korean War should be regarded as a journey still in progress, but a journey worth taking through the lives and deaths of uncommon people who had no idea how exceptional their lives might look after the passage of time. The common theme for many of them, especially those I interviewed personally, was to deny any claim to exceptionalism. "What happened to me really wasn't much different from what happened to thousands of other people." I heard this disclaimer from not just Koreans, but soldiers of every nationality. I did not really believe all the demurs, but I can honor the survivors of the Korean War by stressing exactly what they say. These stories represent essential truths about the Korean War that make the war memorable.

For readers whose grasp of the history of the Korean War is not firm, I have added a special introduction and two appendices to this book. The introduction is a summary of the war that I wrote for Robert Cowley and Geoffrey Parker, eds., *The Reader's Companion to Military History* (Boston: Houghton Mifflin, 1997), and it is reprinted here in altered form with the permission of the editor and publisher. The first appendix is a brief introduction to the general reading about the Korean War, most of it easily available in English. The bibliography is a composite of several booklists I worked on for various encyclopedia projects, and it is by no means comprehensive. I have assessed the research and writing on the Korean War in a series of journal articles over the past six years, with the most recent being "The Korean War: A 50-Year Critical Historiography," *Journal of Strategic Studies* 24 (March 2001), 188–224. An earlier version appeared in the *Journal of Military History* and may be found in revised form in Spencer Tucker et al., *The Encyclopedia of the Korean War,* 3 vols. (ABC-Clio, 2000). These reviews include a listing of other guides and bibliographies. The significant literature on the war should be neither forgotten nor misunderstood, but it requires a commitment to an intellectual and emotional journey whose rewards more than match its difficulty. The second appendix is a statistical summary, a related data sheet, and a chronology that I compiled for the use of my students in courses on the Korean War and American military history.

The issue of the romanization of the Korean alphabet, especially as reflected in this book, requires some explanation because I have chosen not to follow the new system (2000) of romanization designed by the National Academy of the Korean Language and officially adopted by the Ministry of Tourism and Culture, Republic of Korea. The Korean linguistic savants who designed the new system correctly analyzed the problem of romanization: The diacritical marks adopted in the McCune-Reischauer system, in use for almost a century, had almost completely disappeared in English usage, including the principal English-language newspapers published in Seoul, the *Korea Times* and the *Korea Herald.*

The Ministry of Culture and Tourism published a guide to the new system, *The Revised Romanization of Korean* (2000), which fails to explain that the essential difficulty is taking the Korean alphabet *(hangul)*—the triumph of King Sejong in 1446—and rendering it in English in ways that would capture the *sound* of aspirated consonants and compound vowels as well as the four consonants that not only could be aspirated or unaspirated (and thus having two different Korean letters) but also had two options in romanization, e.g., Busan or Pusan, Daegu or Taegu. The difficulty is that non-Korean speakers and readers have become accustomed to place and personal names (whether or not they are properly accented with diacritical marks) that are recognizable in one rendering and confusing in the new system—unless one is a student of the Korean language, not a large community outside of the Korean people themselves, and they know what the proper pronunciation is anyway. Does it make any real difference to a college student in Columbus, Ohio, whether the capital of North Korea is Pyongyang or P'yongyang when it is more important to know that Pyongyang is not Pyonggang?

I believe that the new system of romanization will only confuse Anglophone readers, for whom this book is primarily intended, so I have used what was informally known in Seoul as "the Herald romanization system," which was McCune-Reischauer without the diacritical marks. The National Academy of the Korean Language quite properly points out that P'anmunjom is less helpful to people who want to pronounce the Korean language *(hanguk mal)* than its preference, Panmunjeom, but the standard rendering of the second site of the armistice negotiations is normally spelled Panmunjom in English. The new system simply ignores—and does not solve—the problem of differentiating between aspirated and unaspirated consonants (and I can attest from personal experience that this is not easy for Westerners), and it simply compounds confusion by changing the letters *k, t, p,* and *ch* to *g, d, b,* and *j.* However pleasing the new system may be to linguists, it is simply another barrier to the Western understanding of Korean history, and I prefer not to be an accomplice to further confusion with the Korean language in the West.

ALLAN R. MILLETT
Columbus, Ohio
August 2001

# Introduction:
# The Korean War

A postcolonial conflict between Korean political factions that began in 1945, the Korean War became an international struggle in June 1950. The conventional phase of the war ended with a military armistice in July 1953, which froze the division of Korea. A Communist government under Kim Il-sung (1912–1994) ruled on one side of the Demilitarized Zone, and an authoritarian-capitalist regime under Syngman Rhee (1875–1965) ruled the other. The People's Republic of China and the Soviet Union remained active supporters of the Democratic People's Republic of Korea until the 1990s, and the United States forged a formal military alliance with the Republic of Korea and stationed air and ground units there throughout the rest of the century. A divided Korea remains a flashpoint for regional war.

Contributing to the global dimension of the Cold War, the war had many of the same revolutionary elements as contemporary struggles in French Indochina, Malaya, the Philippines, and Indonesia. The cost in lives made the war one of the worst since 1945: three million civilian and military deaths among thirty million Koreans; approximately one million total casualties among Chinese soldiers; and around 33,652 battlefield deaths for the Americans and 3,200 deaths among other non-Korean military personnel of United Nations Command. Probably about six million Koreans became refugees between the years of 1945 and 1953, most of them fleeing to South Korea. Oppressed by Japanese rule since 1905 and forced into participation in World War II, Korea struggled to survive its historic curse as the battleground of the great powers.

The Korean War began in the confused final months of 1945 when, by prior agreement, the United States and the Soviet Union rushed forces to Korea to keep order and disarm the Japanese army. Almost immediately, competing Korean political factions, some aided by the Japanese, tried to establish local governments and organize these local groups into some sort of national republican regime. Korean Communists, prominent members of the anti-Japanese resistance, emerged to organize People's Committees; they formed a popular front with non-Communist reformers to declare a Korean People's Republic. Above the 38th Parallel, the dividing line between the American and Russian occupying forces, the Communists received active Russian support, but at the cost of accepting a Soviet client, Kim Il-sung, as the dominant political leader. Kim had been a minor commander in the Northeast Anti-Japanese United Army, a force of guerrillas dominated by the Chinese Communists. Fleeing under Japanese military pressure in 1940 to the Russian Maritime Province, Kim joined a Korean special operations unit within the Red Army. He returned to his traditional family home of Pyongyang as a captain in the Soviet army. His nemesis in the south, Syngman Rhee, had an equally unique odyssey. Born in Hwanghae Province, also north of the 38th Parallel, of impoverished minor nobility, Rhee (Yi Sung-man) specialized in anti-Japanese agitation, which forced him into exile in 1905. He became a Christian, married a European wife, learned English, and earned three American college degrees. Always active in Korean nationalist politics, he served as president of a provisional government in exile under the patronage of the Nationalist Chinese. He returned to Korea in 1945 under American sponsorship.

Both the Soviet Union and the United States preferred a unified Korea, but not one dominated by protégés of their rival. Neither had difficulty identifying willing Korean politicians as collaborators. Russian sponsorship of Kim Il-sung showed more certitude than American sponsorship of Syngman Rhee, but the result was the same: the creation of two different, hostile, and armed regimes in 1948 that divided the Korean peninsula and people. Represented by Lieutenant General John R. Hodge, in futile negotiations with the Russians, 1946–1947, the United States passed the Korean problem to the United Nations in 1947. The South Koreans took to the streets to block any form of trusteeship. In the meantime, Rhee supporters took control of the national police, the police auxiliaries, paramilitary youth groups, communal militias, and the Korean National Constabulary, which became the Korean army in December 1948. Rhee loyalists or "professionals," which meant Koreans who had served in the Japanese colonial regime, dominated the police and army.

Similar appointments in his regime by Kim Il-sung gave preference to fellow Communists: Manchurian partisans, Koreans who had served in the Chinese People's Liberation Army, veterans of the Red Army, and a few authentic Korean guerrillas from south of the Yalu River, whose titular leader was Pak Hon-yong, chief of the Korean Communist party. Fleeing the south, Pak set up an organization of southern Communists to train guerrillas and organizers to subvert the Rhee regime. Other prominent leaders—Cho Man-sik, Kim Ku, and Yo Un-hyong—fell by the wayside.

The internal struggle for power in Korea involved violence from the start. From the autumn of 1945 until the spring of 1950, the Hodge military government (1945–1948) and then the Rhee regime (1948–1960) faced substantial protests, the first a series of strikes and riots over the distribution of rice and collection of taxes in 1946. The anti-Rhee forces, led by southern Communists, began a guerrilla war against the Republic of Korea (ROK) security forces on Cheju-do, a large island in the Straits of Tsushima, in April 1948. This vicious war, spurred by an army mutiny in Yosu, spread throughout the four southern mainland provinces of North and South Cholla and North and South Kyongsang. Assisted by American advisors, the ROK army and national police crushed the revolt, which may have claimed as many as thirty thousand lives. Many of the survivors fled to Japan, where they collaborated with the North Korean and Japanese Communists.

The guerrilla war also produced armed clashes along the Demilitarized Zone (DMZ) in 1949 and 1950. About half the Korean army (ROK army) of eight lightly armed divisions manned border positions while the other half fought the guerrillas. In the meantime, Kim Il-sung built his own forces with Soviet arms and advisors; the Korean People's Army (KPA) reached 190,000 in early 1950 with the return of two divisions of battle-hardened Koreans from China. Kim pressed Josef Stalin and Mao Zedong for military support for an invasion of South Korea and journeyed to Beijing and Moscow to cajole his patrons. Pak Hon-yong may have pushed Kim with promises of more rebellion in the south. On June 25, 1950, the KPA crossed the 38th Parallel with a combined arms army that badly outclassed the South Korean army (100,000) in tactical skill and heavy weapons.

Much to the surprise of the Communists, the administration of President Harry S. Truman sent air, naval, and ground force units to Korea to stop the KPA with the substantial assistance of the surviving half of the ROK army, which fought with the heroism of desperation. Although the U.S. saw no vital strategic purpose in defending Korea—and had announced so in early 1950— Truman saw many immediate reasons to fight, not run. His administration could hardly stand to lose another civil war in Asia after the debacle in China; he needed some sort of crisis to stir the nation to rearm and give military muscle to "containment"; he wanted to reassure the new allies of the North Atlantic Treaty Organization (NATO) that the United States believed in collective security; he wanted nothing to endanger the safe integration of Japan into the capitalist world, and he thought the United Nations should demonstrate its willingness to punish aggression. Truman, in fact, sought legitimization of his intervention in terms of United Nations' resolutions, not a declaration of war, a decision that would later cause him political problems. Irritated veterans wondered why a very hard war should be called "a police action."

The theater commander, General of the Army Douglas MacArthur, saw the war in different terms, for he found it an opportunity to reverse the Chinese Revolution, forge a great anti-Communist alliance system in Asia, stimulate the Japanese economy, and embarrass the Soviet Union. MacArthur's position had support from American "Asia Firsters," mostly Republicans, but found no sympathy in the United Nations and European capitals. MacArthur's public differences on the war's purposes and conduct eventually led to his relief in April 1951.

For almost a year the Korean War swept as far south as the Taegu-Pusan perimeter and as far north as the Yalu River, then settled into a geographic stalemate in the mountains north of the 38th Parallel. The initial KPA offensive conquered three-quarters of South Korea, destroyed much of the ROK army, and allowed invading and domestic Communists to capture and execute South Korean Christians, government officials, landlords and businessmen, and thousands of true innocents. American air strikes against the KPA ravaged refugee columns as well. The three American infantry divisions sent from the U.S. 8th Army in Japan fought poorly and fell back to the Pusan perimeter. Army and Marine reinforcements from the United States helped redress the balance, assisted by abundant air strikes from the U.S. 5th Air Force. By the end of August the KPA had stalled at the end of a tenuous supply line.

According to his own early plans, MacArthur directed a two-division amphibious landing deep behind the Communist army at the port of Inchon, and this force (X Corps) liberated Seoul in late September as the 8th Army broke out of the perimeter and struck north against the stunned KPA. The campaign of exploitation surged north across the 38th Parallel with United Nations approval in October with ROK forces in the vanguard. The bulk of the 8th Army pushed into the northwestern provinces, while X Corps moved by land and sea along the eastern coast. Six ROK divisions joined the two American forces, now reinforced with other U.N. contingents, the largest contribution (eventually a division) coming from the British Commonwealth. The victory proved short-lived and the unification of Korea impossible, for the Chinese now intervened with an expeditionary force that eventually reached six hundred thousand soldiers.

Mao Zedong and his advisors, who had considered intervention as early as July 1950, saw no alternative to a war with the United States, for they could not accept a unified, pro-Western Korea on China's border. They also believed that the United States would extend the war to mainland China, first by partisan war (already under way), then by an invasion by the reformed and rearmed Chinese Nationalist army. The U.S. 7th Fleet already stood in their way in the Formosan Straits. Finally winning Stalin's promise of massive air support, in the form of disguised Soviet air units operated from Manchurian bases, the Chinese first tested the 8th Army in a week's fighting in late October in which they found the Americans vulnerable to deep attacks and night actions.

In late November the Chinese People's Volunteers Force (CPVF) struck again and drove a demoralized 8th Army back across the 38th Parallel, through Seoul, and south almost as far as Taejon. The X Corps extracted itself with an amphibious withdrawal after an "attack in the other direction" by the 1st Marine Division. Punished by air strikes and suffering from logistical shortages as well as heavy casualties from the cold and combat, the CPVF halted south of Seoul in January 1951. In the meantime, General Matthew B. Ridgway replaced General Walton H. Walker, who had been killed in a traffic accident. Ridgway launched limited counterattacks in January through April 1951. For the fourth time in less than a year, Seoul was once again liberated. Chinese offensives in February, April, and May could not cope with a restored 8th Army, which had now reached a World War II level of competence. Ridgway's forces pushed the joint Chinese-North Korean armies back into North Korea, but Ridgway rejected proposals from several of his subordinates to mount an amphibious landing on the east coast, which would catch a substantial portion of the Communist armies. It was a lost opportunity.

Anxious to save their shattered armies, the Chinese and North Koreans asked for negotiations, but these talks by military representatives broke down in September as a result of mutual provocation, some accidental, some intended. Further United Nations offensive operations in September and October proved costly for both sides. The United Nations Command's (UNC's) air superiority did not appear to be effective enough to justify further ground advances. Ridgway, who had replaced MacArthur, ordered General James Van Fleet, his own replacement as 8th Army commander, to halt his attacks. Moving from Kaesong to Panmunjom, the truce meetings began again on October 25, 1951, and continued until the armistice of July 27, 1953. A superficial examination of the war's course over the intervening twenty-one months suggests that intransigence, ineptness, duplicity, and operational timidity doomed both sides to a "stalemated war," but such a view ignores how much both sides still had at stake.

The Korean War of 1952 to 1953 continued because both coalitions saw opportunities to exploit. One development affected the truce talks themselves: Both the Communists and United Nations Command held significant numbers of prisoners. The Communists found UNC prisoners of war (POWs) vulnerable to propaganda exploitation and intelligence gathering; American airmen may have been sent to camps in Russia, and they certainly went to China. The Communists wanted to tar the United States with germ warfare charges, "immoral" air operations, atrocities, and racist policies. The United Nations Command, on the other hand, found that many Communist POWs did not want to be repatriated; many Chinese and Koreans had been dragooned into the Communist armies. So afraid of this ideological embarrassment were the Communists that they planted agents in POW camps in the south to terrorize the dissidents and start camp uprisings, the most dramatic at Koje-do in May 1952.

The POW issue plagued the truce talks until both sides agreed to a system that would give the prisoners some choice about their futures. The Rhee regime made its position of noncooperation clear when it arranged the "escape" of twenty-seven thousand POWs in July 1953. Both sides had much to hide about their treatment of POWs, especially the Communists, who either murdered or did not attempt to save six thousand Americans and probably four times as many ROK soldiers. Of the POWs still held by the United Nations, eighty-two thousand returned to Communist control, but twenty-two thousand chose to settle elsewhere. The United Nations accepted back about fourteen thousand POWs of all nationalities, while 359 (including 335 Korean) captives chose to stay in Communist hands. Koreans on both sides, moreover, had executed thousands of "disloyal" civilians as the armies and partisans swept over their unhappy land.

As the truce talks continued, the Communists and United Nations Command sought advantages that might influence the course of the war or wound the surviving Korean regimes. Communist guerrillas still harassed military and civilian camps and villages in the south; in 1952 the Communist underground may have attempted to assassinate Rhee, and political plotting plagued the ROK government and army. Conventional Communist military attacks often tried to inflict embarrassing casualties on American units, but the principal target remained the ROK army, whose own competence waxed and waned in response to American training and Rhee-dictated expansion of the army and the placement of loyal generals. A Communist offensive in July 1953 cost the ROK army almost twenty-five thousand casualties.

United Nations Command air power appeared the most effective instrument of coercion. The U.S. Far East Air Forces pummeled not only Communist armies, but also economic targets and cities throughout North Korea. Although their efforts resulted in thousands of civilian deaths, the air attacks only drove the Communist elite and logistical system underground or across the Yalu. Special operations forces had even less success in infiltrating the North and starting a guerrilla war against the Communists. The effort to subvert the Kim regime was not without reason, for in 1952 his own government was torn by a coup attempt organized by Pak Hon-yong and his southern clique; Kim unmasked the plot and executed the plotters, including Pak. He also isolated North Koreans whose attachment to China or Russia seemed excessive, but he did not move against them until after the war. Nevertheless, the Rhee regime, which had no taste for an armistice, had some reason to hope for a collapse in Pyongyang. Rhee also knew that he had external support from American "Asia Firsters" and anti-Communist leaders in Asia, so negotiations did not enthrall him.

The armistice, however, reflected a more conservative appreciation of the war's costs and risks by the United States, the United Nations, Russia, and China. After Stalin's death in March 1953, Russia faced a succession crisis, troubled by unrest in Eastern Europe and a resurgent NATO. The American military build-up of 1950 to 1953 had shifted the "correlation of forces" in Europe. For China the survival of Kim Il Sung's regime seemed assured, and the Chinese government needed to focus on its domestic agenda and relations with Russia, whose nuclear might it wanted to share. In Washington, a new Republican administration under Dwight D. Eisenhower sought economic stability rather than a costly war. Moreover, even with Indo-China a lost cause, the security of Taiwan, the Philippines, and Japan looked promising. MacArthur's goal had been accomplished without MacArthur. Just whom Eisenhower scared by musing about the use of nuclear weapons in Asia is uncertain, but he certainly provided many participants with a special incentive to seek peace. With seven American divisions along the DMZ (eventually reduced to one, thirty years later), assisted by at least ten effective ROK divisions, the ground defense of South Korea looked assured, backed by the U.S. Air Force and U.S. Navy. The United States concluded a mutual defense and assistance treaty with South Korea in August 1953, which was ratified by Congress early in 1954 and backed by concurrent United Nations pledges to protect South Korea. Essentially, the United States accomplished its original war aims—to preserve the sovereignty of South Korea. It benefited by the international crisis, for the changed domestic political climate allowed a threefold increase in defense spending. The Chinese proved they had the will and enough military capacity to blunt a Western effort to reverse their revolution. Conversely, the Chinese Nationalists received a reprieve through a new defense pact with the United States. The Soviet Union, however, only awakened a sleeping American giant with its support of Kim Il-sung. The real loser was Korea, divided and ruined, which again had drawn in outside foreign powers to its own peril.

# Part 1
# THE KOREANS

# 1

# The Koreans

Fifty years after his death, Korean Christians still remember the story of Pastor Son Yang-won, a Southern Presbyterian and minister to a congregation in the southern port city of Yosu, Chollanam-do Province.

Pastor Son became a local hero in 1940 when he refused to order his parishioners to pay homage to the emperor at the Shinto shrine the Japanese placed at the entrance to every Korean Christian church. The Japanese political police sent Pastor Son to an island leprosarium to reconsider his rebelliousness. Three years later—unrepentant—Pastor Son returned home, since the Japanese had reason in 1943 to placate Korean nationalists, especially those who counseled nonviolence. Pastor Son's sons, Son Matthew Tong-in and Son John Tong-son, had been drafted into the Japanese service as war workers, so they were hostage to the pastor's good behavior.

With independence and liberation in August 1945, the Son family became reunited in Yosu and rose to prominence in the Christian community with their good works and stirring words. From his pulpit Pastor Son spoke against communal violence and for reconciliation. He had no easy task, since Chollanam-do had become a hotbed of political radicalism with the South Korean Labor Party (the Communists), the most vocal and active force in Yosu politics.

The Yosu-Sunchon revolt of October 1948 unleashed a communal fury that destroyed the Son family. The bloodbath started when the majority of the soldiers of the 14th Regiment, Korean Constabulary, mutinied rather than board transports for Cheju-do Island, the site of a vicious guerrilla war that had begun in April 1948. Like some of their comrades on Cheju-do, the lieutenants and senior noncommissioned officers who led the 14th Regiment rebels were dedicated Communists. Their long-range goal was to destroy the local civil officials and police authorities who represented the new government of the Republic of Korea in Seoul. Since Communists and other opponents of President Syngman Rhee had also joined the Constabulary, the Yosu rebels expected reinforcements. The timing of the Yosu revolt had more to do with the availability of weapons and ammunition (the regiment was exchanging its Japanese rifles for American M-1s) than the shipping order to Cheju. In any event, the Yosu rebels sent a party of soldiers and armed student radicals to Sunchon to raise the red flag and capture a crucial highway and railroad junction. As in Yosu, the rebels killed some Korean National policemen in battle, but most of the deaths occurred later when the rebels executed the policemen who surrendered. The police chief of Sunchon was stripped, wrapped in barbed wire, rolled through the streets, and then set afire. Later the city dogs ate him.

The rebel frenzy spread throughout Sunchon, and mobs of crazed youths roamed the city in search of worthy victims: police families, officials, and Christian notables of all ages. At the college where Matthew and John Son were students, a fellow student denounced the Son brothers as unspeakable reactionaries. Five rebels, including the informer, found the Sons at a Presbyterian deacon's home and dragged them into the street. Beaten and tortured by their captors, Matthew and John refused to renounce their faith or implicate others. The rebels tired of their fun and finally shot the Son brothers.

New troops of the Korean Constabulary came to Sunchon on October 22 to recapture the city for Syngman Rhee rather than to join the revolt. An assault force of two battalions, commanded by Major Paik In-yup, an ardent anti-Communist and lapsed Presbyterian as well as a valiant and skilled combat leader, drove off the disorganized and demoralized rebels. Throughout the city the loyalist troops found the bodies of massacre victims. They meted out the same sort of instant and final injustice to their own prisoners, but most of the postliberation suppression fell into the hands of civil judges and the Korean National Police. Among the suspects brought in by the police were the five youths who had murdered the Son brothers.

At the trial of his sons' killers, Pastor Son Yang-won gave his greatest sermon on the Christian themes of forgiveness, redemption, and rehabilitation. He saved the youths from a death sentence, and he even saved the informer from jail by offering to adopt him as a replacement son. Then new son of Son fulfilled all of the pastor's hopes. The youth became an ardent Christian, a better student, and a model citizen. As he promised, Pastor Son gave the repentant youth all the love and guidance he had provided to Matthew and John. The story of the Son family spread throughout Korea.

In August 1950 the 6th Division of the Korean People's Army, followed by the Communist political police, swept through Yosu in the advance on Pusan. Before the North Koreans retreated in defeat the next month, they executed their hostages, including Pastor Son Yong-won and his adopted son.

Just as the story of Pastor Son catches the tragic side of Korean life, the story of Professor Choi Hyun-pai represents a victory over adversity that is just as Korean. Professor Choi was a great scholar of languages and linguistics and a faculty member at Chosun Christian College, now Yonsei University. He was also a Korean patriot. For his outspoken opposition to the Japanese attempts to eliminate the Korean language from the nation's educational system, he was harassed, assaulted, and eventually imprisoned and tortured in 1942. He spent many years in solitary confinement. When he was released from prison in 1945, he immediately sought a position as an advisor to the Korean Department of Education with his fellow faculty member, Horace H. Underwood, who had just returned to Korea from exile in America. One of their collaborative projects was to change the textbooks (in Japanese and about Japanese subjects) in the primary and secondary schools of Korea. Getting rid of the old books was no problem. The Koreans burned them for spite and warmth.

Professor Choi decided that he also had an unparalleled opportunity to modernize the Korean language. In drawing up new dictionaries and gazetteers, he eliminated two thousand Chinese characters, replacing them with *hangul* equivalents. He also produced books in which Korean would be read horizontally top to bottom and left to right—and in books with a Western definition of "front" and "back." He argued that such a change would further democracy because it would allow the easier creation of Korean typewriters and typesetters and simplify the use of Western pens and pencils. Professor Choi and his small staff had their first books ready for distribution in November 1945.

The Department of Education had a distribution problem. The natural solution would have been to use the restored national railroad system to take the books to provincial capitals and then distribute them by truck to the larger outlying towns. Eventually the book-trickle-down plan would provide books for even the smallest schools. The first step proved to be the most difficult. The publishers could not ship on the railroads without special permits, which took money and time and efficiency beyond the Korean bureaucracy. To start the distribution process, Professor Choi organized one three-man team of two

Americans and one Korean (often himself) to drive a truck loaded with books around the country. Between January and March 1946, the book truck traveled five thousand miles and distributed a million books. In the meantime Professor Choi arranged speedier movement for the books by train. His last challenge was to ensure that the books were not stolen and used for fuel during that hard winter. The crisis passed that spring, and the Korean schools began a new era of learning.

# 2

# Mr. Lee

SEOUL, KOREA
December 1994

Lee Chang-sik and I are drinking coffee—too strong, he says—in the base-
ment apartment in the home of Dr. Horace G. Underwood, for whom "Yi
Si" has worked for thirty years. A survivor of the Korean War, Yi Si is seventy
years old and has raised two families in Seoul, his family's home for four generations. He has watched history and endured it. His heroes are Syngman Rhee,
Douglas MacArthur, and Park Chung-hee. Born in 1924, he grew to manhood in
Japanese Korea and remembers the exhilaration of independence in 1945.

My father had a small business in which he made and repaired tools as
well as worked with all sorts of metals. I went to a technical-vocational high
school that was sponsored by Western corporations to teach Koreans about
technology. We had no Korean words for many of our tools and machinery, so
we used English words until the Japanese insisted we use Japanese words for
things like a screwdriver. It was pretty silly and irritating. So was the military
drill we had to perform at school, pretending to stab people with sticks. I went
to work for the electric streetcar company toward the end of World War II and
escaped military duty in the Japanese army since I knew how to repair streetcar motors and electrical systems. We lived in downtown Seoul, then across
the Han at Yongdongpo near the shops. We welcomed the Americans in 1945

15

LEE CHANG-SIK

**Lee Chang-sik**

even though times were hard. I had known Americans since childhood, and I learned some English in the commercial school. My grandfather had become a Presbyterian, and the Reverend Horace H. Underwood baptized my mother. On the other hand, I didn't know any Communists, although there were certainly lots of agitators in Seoul after the war.

The war in 1950 came as a complete surprise.

The government told us on the radio that our army would defeat the Communists and that the United States would send planes and armies to help, but I wondered about who was winning when a South Korean armored car roared through Yongdongpo with the soldiers screaming that they couldn't stop North Korean tanks with their light cannon. Then the Han River highway bridge blew up. What an explosion! Luckily, my family and I were all south of the river when the bridge blew up. When the Communists reached Yongdongpo, they called all the men and boys to come to a local schoolyard or be jailed. They told us we would have to join the North Korean army or we and our families would starve. Some of us jumped over the wall and ran away, but the Communists had a second gathering after they had taken some people away, and I went. I was twenty-six, but I looked older, and I am small. I also pretended to be sick and frail, and I guess they believed me.

Yi Si laughs easily at this deception. He is indeed a small man, but he is anything but frail and even at seventy can still carry staggering loads on his *chige*. He rides a bicycle to work in Seoul traffic, off the main roads to be sure, but nevertheless an act of great courage and athletic skill. In 1950 he had no illusions that, as a skilled worker and Christian, he and his family could survive long in a Communist regime, but he counted on his "invisibility" and essential work for the streetcar company to buy him some time.

In September we heard that the Americans and South Koreans were winning the war, and we rejoiced when the United Nations army liberated the city. I got a job with a U.S. Army engineer battalion that built a temporary bridge over the Han, then went to work at the American airfield on Youi-do, which was designated as K-2. As an American employee, I had no choice but to leave the city when the Chinese defeated our armies. It was a terrible winter. I left my wife and two daughters in Seoul to live with relatives until I returned. I could not believe we would not win the war with MacArthur in command and more American soldiers coming.

Even though Seoul again was liberated by the United Nations forces, Mac-Arthur left Korea in 1951 and no new American divisions came to reinforce the 8th Army. Yi Si made his own adjustments.

I had an offer to go to the American airfield on Cheju-do, which was so far away that no one wanted to work there. I took the job as a maintenance man and eventually became the foreman of a group of Korean workers, male and female, that ran the laundry on the base and some other small operations. The Americans were easy to work for, and the pay—W,100,000 a month (over $100 in 1950)—was very good, much higher than Korean military pay. The Americans also fed us, gave us clothes, provided decent housing, and allowed us to buy American goods. The island, however, was a terrible place to work—too much rain and wind, too many ocean storms. It was also very crowded with refugees and with soldiers and civilian workers at the Chinese prisoner-of-war camps. Even after the armistice I continued to work on Cheju-do while my family remained in Seoul. I finally came home in 1959. I was disappointed to find Seoul still badly damaged by the war and jobs scarce, but I managed to survive until I went to work for the Underwoods. I was really lucky since no one in my immediate family died in the war.

Yi Si worries that his own children will not remember the ordeal of the Korean people in the 1950s, and he believes that the North Koreans are the same Communist criminals they have always been. He is glad South Korea has a strong army and national police force.

# 3

## A Korean in Ohio

**DAYTON, OHIO**
**October 13, 1996**

The office of Bryan Choi, whose real name is Choe Yong-wan, might be in Seoul instead of Dayton, Ohio. There is a picture of a Siberian tiger on the wall, a silk-screen print of Admiral Yi Sun-shin's "Turtle Boat," and a putter, golf balls, and practice hole. Bryan Choi, president of Architects Associates, has practiced his profession in America since he received an M.S. degree in architecture from the University of Minnesota in 1972. He came to Dayton in 1982 to work on the plans for the VA Medical Center Hospital. He formed his own company in 1987, and by 1993 the Dayton Chamber of Commerce arranged for him to receive a national award for his success as an entrepreneur. He is a serious golfer at the famous golf courses that surround Dayton. Early in his life, as a boy in Korea, he might have eaten a green, not putted on it.

Bryan Choi balances our conversation against phone calls and business matters. He switches to Korean to talk with his mother and brother, "quicker that way." He is now something of a local celebrity since his drive, professional skill, much of his time, and some of his money were instrumental in developing Dayton's Korean War Veterans Memorial, which honors Ohio's veterans of Korea and other wars. Located in Riverbend Park on the banks of the Great Miami River, the monument rivals its counterpart in Washington in size and surpasses it in artistic and educational value. It is Bryan's way of saying *kamsa hamnida* to his adopted land.

BRYAN CHOI

**Choe Yong-wan, 1946**

Born in Sunchon, Chollanam-do, in 1938, Choe Yong-wan went with his father, mother, older brother, and younger sister in 1942 to Harbin, Manchuria, where his father ran a department store. Grandfather Choe owned a large store in Sunchon, where he got along well with the Japanese and enjoyed the respect of his Korean neighbors. Although the Choe family were not Christians, they admired the American missionary-doctor Paul Crane at Alexandria Hospital, Sunchon, where Choe Yong-wan had been born. The Choe family was also large; Yong-wan's father had eleven brothers and sisters, all educated, ambitious, aggressive, and political but careful not to challenge the Japanese authorities. The family and business came first, last, and always.

In 1945 Mr. Choe's job disappeared with the Japanese defeat. The occupying Russians detained and questioned Mr. Choe, but released him for the time being. Mr. and Mrs. Choe, who had just had another baby daughter, decided they had better leave Manchuria quickly, and they sold all their family possessions and exchanged the money for gold in any portable form: rings, chains, coins, and jewelry. "My mother was the great organizer of our escape. She sewed all the gold into my brother's and my fur coats. They were heavy! She thought no police or railway officials would bother children. If they did, we were supposed to excuse ourselves to go to the toilet and drop the coats there, then go back for them later. Fortunately, we didn't have to test this trick."

The Choe family managed to get a train to the Yalu River in November 1945. The train ride south produced its own horrors. Yong-wan remembers the dangers posed by the tunnels and weather to the huddled passengers clinging to the car roof. At one point he saw blood seeping through the roof. At another point he heard a woman scream—and scream and scream. His father learned that the woman's baby had died and the other riders wanted her to throw the

BRYAN CHOI

**Bryan Y. W. Choi**

corpse off the train; she refused to do so until the train stopped and the baby could be buried.

It then took ten days to sneak across the river in a small boat. Groups of Russian soldiers, perhaps deserters, preyed on the refugees, killing and looting them. Korean families sheltered and fed the Choes without charge, although Mrs. Choe usually doled out a little gold to their hosts. Disease, murder, and starvation stalked the Yalu. Once back in northern Korea, the family caught a train to Pyongyang, then on to Kaesong, where the open railroad ended. Crowds of refugees gathered their scant possessions and walked toward the 38th Parallel, which was already closed. The Russians and North Korean military police and border guards did not have to work hard to discourage the refugees, for more bands of robbers roamed the roads, and the bodies of their victims lined the road south.

Much to Mother's unhappiness, Father went off to find a guide and a safe path into the southern zone. Mother did not want to wait anywhere, since she would be a helpless target with four young children. Before Father returned, Mother gathered us all up and walked south. My sister, whom she carried, was very sick. My brother and I staggered on in our heavy coats. A North Korean border guard stopped us, but Mother persuaded him to guide us to the border, bribing him with some goods. As he led us along, we found Father sitting at the side of the road. We crossed the border and found American and South Koreans at a roadblock. They bathed us with DDT, turning us all white, but we were too happy to care. They did not rob or search us.

The Choe family reached Sunchon in three days without incident, but Yongwan's baby sister died there of pneumonia. Mr. Choe found work through his family, but moved to Kwangju so that the boys could attend better schools. Kwangju, even its schools, was a political powder keg in 1947 to 1948.

There was great pressure to join one or another political club, to get into a gang. The gangs fought each other often. Teenagers organized the younger children for songs and chants. One youth mob stormed the government's

Youth Center for Liberty. Our family was divided. My uncle, who was a doctor, supported Dr. Rhee, and one of my aunts was a member of the South Korean Labor Party. She promised that North Korean tanks would liberate the south in nine hours. Uncle said the Americans would drop atomic bombs on Pyongyang. We were visiting Sunchon in October 1948 when the Communist uprising began. Aunt had told us there would be a revolt for two months, but she didn't know the exact date.

The Choe family managed to survive the rebel seizure and the Korean Constabulary's recapture of Sunchon, but Mrs. Choe was determined not to endure similar risks to her sons when war came in 1950. She packed up again and walked all day to a small, isolated village in the Chiri-san Mountains, where her aunt lived. Her relatives harbored the big city refugees while Father Choe remained in Kwangju to protect their home. However, Bosong village proved dangerous anyway.

The area was controlled by a guerrilla band of Korean National policemen and pro-ROK youths. Then the North Koreans came into the mountains to inventory all the food and confiscate it. The farmers were unhappy since they saw this as a new tax. The ROK guerrillas and North Koreans, which meant the SKLP [South Korean Labor Party] militia, too, fought each other. Mother feared we would be betrayed, but the cities were even more dangerous since they were being bombed by the U.S. Air Force. We could see railroads blow up, buildings in flames. I almost got hit from a shell casing from an aircraft cannon.

We were about to flee again when we heard about the Inchon landing. We knew Father was all right, so we returned to Kwangju, and soon U.S. and ROK soldiers arrived. The North Korean soldiers and SKLP leaders vanished overnight, but Communist guerrillas now roamed the hills. Mother became famous for setting up a relief operation in our schoolhouse, using U.S. rations and ROK-owned rice. Then the guerrillas attacked the schoolhouse and our home, but ROK soldiers drove them off. I saw the guerrillas shoot one soldier, but the Communists left. I saw bodies everywhere.

Peace was reestablished, but at a price since pro-ROK civilians hunted down SKLP members and killed them. The ROK soldiers shot anyone they thought was stealing rice for the guerrillas, but most of the killing was civilians of civilians. There must have been eight to ten such executions. I saw some of them, people digging their own graves, being shot and buried, then dug up by their families for proper burial. I was told that one of my uncles, a National Police supervisor, executed guerrillas in the Chiri-sans with his Japanese sword. Who knows who and how many died in those terrible times?

Choe Yong-wan remembers the rest of the war for its hunger, not its violence. Kwangju escaped battle damage, but not the shortage of good rice in

Chollanam-do. He ate rough grains, poor rice, and tofu. Even mold-ridden American cheese thrown out by the GIs fetched high prices in the black market.

Bryan Choi laughs, but that does not mean he finds any humor in his story. We are about to meet his wife, Jeannie, also a refugee from North Korea, and go to Dayton's NCR Country Club restaurant for dinner, a meal unimaginable in Kwangju in 1953. "I sometimes feel as if I will never have enough to eat," Bryan says as we leave his office.

# 4

# The President
# as Refugee

**CENTRAL ADMINISTRATION BUILDING**
**EWHA WOMEN'S UNIVERSITY**
**SEOUL, KOREA**
**August 1998**

I arrive at the office of Dr. Chang Sang (Ph.D., Princeton University, 1977) late for my appointment and more than a little wet from climbing up a hill to Ewha Women's University, the world's largest women's university and one of the best. Dr. Chang, the first married president of Ewha, had talked to a reporter from *arirang,* an English-language magazine for the foreign women's community in Korea, and I had been intrigued by President Chang's brief account of her life during the Korean War. I thought there was probably more to the story—and there was. Horace G. Underwood had helped me arrange the interview. As I fussed with my damp shirt and notebook, the secretaries in the outer office plied me with cold fruit juice. Then the president came out to greet me and graciously guided me to the traditional Korean office, furnished with couches and tables decorated with tasteful artwork and miniature orchids, designed for conversation and more fruit juice.

President Chang is everything I had read and heard: poised, attractive in an academic-matronly style, personable, and very impressive. Perhaps the best way to describe her is a steel *mugunghwa*. Considering the struggles of her childhood, her optimism and energy are extraordinary. President Chang responds to my first questions about her early childhood in North Korea with a matter-of-factness that belies the hardships of the times.

We lived near the Yalu in a small town, just my mother and me. My father had died when I was still a baby, and my one older sister had gone to Seoul for schooling. We owned some property and lived quietly with our fellow Christians, but when the Communists began to arrest people in 1947, my mother and I took what we could and fled to Seoul to join my sister. We could take almost nothing with us, so we were now poor, but we brought our Bible and hymnbook. We reached the 38th Parallel, but there Communist border guards stopped us. Many other refugees were robbed, beaten, imprisoned, and murdered, but our guards turned us loose when a local village woman promised to give them extra food if they released us. I had been praying to God for deliverance during a trip to a filthy privy when this woman arrived with the soldiers' food. It was a moment I will never forget. After some debate, the guards showed us to the border, and we crossed the 38th Parallel and into a new life. We later learned that some of our relatives in the north had been jailed and murdered.

Life in Seoul was not easy since none of us had any money. We lived with other refugees and my sister in a hovel near Seoul Station. My mother did odd jobs and tried to teach me since I should have been in school. For some time we went to a food kitchen run by American missionaries for our one real meal a day. I tasted coffee for the first time. On one of these trips a missionary gentleman asked me why a big girl like me wasn't in school, and I told him I didn't have any money to go to school. He said he could arrange for me to go to a church school, which I did.

Our biggest problem during the winter of 1947 to 1948 was staying warm, so I roamed from construction site to site collecting scraps of wood for a fire. The wood, however, was very wet from being outside and smoked badly. My mother said we needed paper to start a fire and dry the wood, but paper—even newspapers—was very hard to find. Then I got a good idea, which was to compete with the neighborhood boys in playing *takk gi chi gi*. You know the game? You use folded pieces of paper that you throw to hit your opponent's *takk gi*. If you turn over your target, you get your opponent's *takk gi*. The boys made fancy paper forms, but I made mine completely functional, even if they looked bad. I won all the time, and that's how I collected scrap paper for our fire.

The next year, the Chang family moved from Seoul to a village north of the city, where Chang Sang's sister had a teaching job in a small school. When her sister, who was often sick, got a better job in Seoul, Chang Sang's mother moved to Seoul, too, to take care of her. At the age of nine Chang Sang lived alone in a small room in a friend's house so that she could continue her schooling. A very good student, she tutored her classmates, who paid her with vegetables and fruits, but no one had much rice to share. One day she visited an aunt and uncle who lived near the East Gate of Seoul to ask for help. She walked the entire distance to the city, where she stayed. In the spring of 1950 Chang Sang, now age eleven, had created a small life for herself that centered on her family, her schooling, and her religious faith.

YONSEI UNIVERSITY

**Dr. Chang Sang**

I remember how surprised we all were when the war started in June. As refugees from North Korea, we felt especially vulnerable—and of course we were Christians, too—because the local people might turn us in to the Communist authorities for favors and food, and certainly we could expect no help. Some of my relatives fled south, but I returned to the village, where we felt safer.

I remember people talking about how General MacArthur would come and save us. The only thing that happened was that U.S. Air Force planes bombed our village, and I saw my first people killed in war. They looked horrible. Every day we prayed for the arrival of American soldiers. We took what food we had and divided it into thirty days of rations as we waited to be liberated. Then one day we saw North Korean soldiers fleeing up the road, heading for safety. They were very young and very frightened. Two of them stopped at our door and begged for food, and we learned that they came from the same part of North Korea as we did, so we fed them. The villagers were very angry with us and again questioned our loyalty to the Republic, but we convinced them that it was our Christian duty to help the unfortunate, even Communist soldiers.

As the weather turned bitterly cold in December, Chang Sang learned that the United Nations forces had been defeated by the Chinese in North Korea and that the war had turned against the South Koreans. Her family packed for more flight, bought places in an open truck, and fled to Taegu, flooded again with refugees. The three women lived in a small room, and Chang Sang attended an outdoor school in a tent all through that winter. As the war moved north again, she and her family returned to Seoul even though the city was now badly damaged.

After attending five different primary schools in six years, Chang Sang and her mother were determined that she would have a better middle school experience.

> I actually started middle school in Taejon, where we had moved in my last year of primary school. I continued to be a top student. My mother and I just assumed I would keep going to school, but a neighbor told us we were too poor to pay the tuition. My mother felt crushed by this cruel comment, but I told her we would manage somehow with God's help. We didn't feel broken, and everybody else was poor, too. I became determined to win more scholarships, which I did, but I didn't ignore other school activities. In fact, I remember being a student group leader when we protested the Armistice of 1953. We thought the Americans had betrayed us again. I had a loud voice and a strong physical presence, so I made speeches against the armistice and led group chants and songs. It was all very exciting. Anyone who wanted to compromise was called a *to-gang* person. *To-gang,* which means literally "crossing the river," became popular after the destruction of the Han River Bridge at Seoul in 1950, which trapped so many people north of the river. After the war, many people refused to live in old Seoul, but found homes south of the river so they would never be trapped again, so they were called *to-gang* people.

President Chang and I share some amusement at the thought of the present *to-gang* people trapped in their Hyundai and Daewoo sedans every day on Seoul's many bridges, struggling to reach their homes "across the river." President Chang Sang, hardened and softened by war, would never be a *to-gang* person.

# 5

## The Rescuers

In the files of the 8th Army history office rests a story that goes to the heart of the Korean War. Park Yong-dae, former village elder, had written to the Ministry of National Defense in February 1989 about an injustice. He had written before in 1983 and received no response. His sense of outrage grew. In 1964, he charged, the U.S. Air Force and Korean government had given medals to Kong Sung-tae and Kong Kwan-gik for rescuing American airmen from the waters south of Kanghwa-do, the large island just south of the Han River estuary. Everyone on little Joomun-do knew the Kongs did not deserve medals. They were Communists now, and they had been Communists on July 12, 1950, when the islanders had rescued ten American airmen. Thirty-two years old at the time, Park Yong-dae remembered the risks, the fear, and then the thrill of eventual liberation: "I was moved to tears as if it were rain in my gratitude to the American soldiers. At that time I looked to the mountains and streams. It was such a sad time then . . . nature was crying. At that time fire started in my eyes . . ." It seemed like only yesterday when the great silver plane had plunged into the lives of the Joomun-do fishermen.

The twelve B-29s of the 19th Bombardment Group dropped to nine thousand feet to unload their bombs on the Han River railroad bridge. With all bombs away by 1516 hours, the raiders turned west on a heading of 250 degrees and started the outward-bound flight to Okinawa. Despite scattered clouds at twenty thousand feet, visibility was at least ten miles. So far the first B-29 raid of the war had gone well, but at 1530 two Yak-9 North Korean fighters made one surprise pass at eight thousand feet and riddled B-29 No. 44-69866, which had lagged behind to take photographs. The plane's number three engine burst into flames, and a ruptured fuel tank sprayed flames along the fuselage. The pilot, Captain Paul W. Ridenour, and copilot, First Lieutenant Horace G. Codling, feathered the engine. They were about to become the only B-29 crew shot down in the war's first three months.

There were twelve men aboard, a regular crew of eleven and an Air Force photographer. Enveloped by smoke and flame, the crew did not meet the crisis with calm. Ridenour blurted, "Let's get out of here" over the intercom, meaning, he asserted, that he would fly the plane as far as he could if the fire could be extinguished. The bombardier thought he meant "bail out" and punched out of the nose and disappeared forever. The copilot turned on the warning bell when the radio operator reported that a shallow dive had not extinguished the fire. The aircrew went for the hatches except for one gunner, who also disappeared. Five enlisted airmen and the photographer went into the water, spread over several miles. Jumping later, the pilot, copilot, navigator, and flight engineer landed over a broad expanse of the island-dotted West Sea, but by 1900 they had been reunited on Chongbong-do by Korean fishermen, who had pulled them from the sea. The plane crashed in a shallow bay and sank. When an American search airplane cruised over the area for thirty minutes, its pilot saw no sign of the B-29 or its crew.

The villagers greeted the Americans with a torrent of Korean questions and asserted that the Communists were nearby and would surely investigate. The Americans must leave quickly. One teenage boy knew enough English to translate, so the Americans knew that one question came up again and again: "Are you Christians?" The puzzled Americans said *yes,* wondering what difference it made. They thought it was more important to give the Koreans the U.S. dollars in their survival kits. Everyone agreed that they should get out to sea quickly, hidden in the morning rush of fishing boats, so they could start sending distress signals on their survival radio.

Accompanied by the English-speaking boy—a refugee from Seoul, they thought—the four Americans sailed south for four days, changing boats, until a South Korean navy patrol boat found them on July 16. Their boats were part of a sea-borne exodus, fleets of small boats carrying Koreans south. The Americans met many refugees who knew about the United Nations intervention and urged the airmen to use nuclear weapons on Pyongyang. They arrived safely in Pusan

U.S. AIR FORCE

**B-29s bomb targets in Korea**

and arranged a flight to Japan, but they had to tell their sobbing boy-guide that he had to stay in Korea. They got him a job with the Air Force Office of Special Investigations and persuaded the vice consul to help him. Then they left.

The six enlisted men who had tumbled out of No. 44-69866 faster than the cockpit crew either plopped down at sea or landed on several small islands. More Korean fishermen pulled them from the water or rescued them from the shoreline. The central figure in the rescue was the "headman" of Joomun-do, Park Joo-won, aided by Park Yong-dae (his nephew), Park Hyong-won (his son), and Lee Hong-suk. Although extremely nervous and, according to Park Yong-dae, not entirely stable, Park Joo-won spoke enough English to communicate with the Americans. He asked if they were Christians and asserted that his villagers worshiped God through Jesus Christ and not Karl Marx through Kim Il-sung. Park Joo-won warned the Americans that the Kong family on another island were ardent Communists and surely would come looking for the aircrew survivors. He also convinced the Americans they were among friends and must leave on the morning tide. Through the night of July 12–13, around twenty-five Koreans fed, bandaged, and dried the Americans. One was a lone ROK army lieutenant with an M-1 rifle, who identified himself as a guerrilla organizer.

When their fishing boat departed Joomun-do at 0700 on July 13, Park Joo-won, a guide named Kim Tae-hung, and another young refugee joined the regular crew of three and the six airmen. The overloaded boat wallowed out to sea and joined a convoy of refugee boats headed south. After one night at sea, the boat reached another Christian village. The Americans ate and rested, reassured by pictures of Truman and MacArthur on the walls of their safe haven, a school-house. Then they found a pamphlet in Korean graced by Stalin's portrait, and their anxiety returned. The airmen could not get Park Joo-won's name straight, but they all later testified that "the old man" had kept the rescue operation alive. The next day, a larger powerboat appeared, carrying six ROK soldiers and "men with briefcases," whom the Americans assumed were public officials or intelligence agents. The Koreans immediately began haggling over who had priority on the boat, but Park Joo-won won the day by presumably arguing that only he could guide them south and that he wanted the Americans rescued. In any event, he, Kim, the boy, four soldiers, one "briefcase man," and the crew continued their voyage south. After two more days of uncomfortable and anxious travel, the Korean *Pequot* found a great white British destroyer, HMS *Alacrity,* which took the airmen directly to Japan. They never knew the names or fates of their rescuers.

As Park Joo-won predicted, the Communists came to Joomun-do, terrorized the villagers into admitting their crimes against Socialism, and executed four "traitors," including Lee Hong-suk and the would-be guerrilla leader. The two Park boys and their families hid with other Christian resistors. They identified the notorious Kong Il-bong as the leader of the Communist irregulars who invaded and looted Joomun-do and murdered the four loyalists. In September 1950, when the South Koreans returned to the offshore islands, the Park boys led a group of ROK Marines, national combat police, and Christian guerrillas to the Kong's island. The raiders arrested four leading Communists. They executed Kong Il-bong.

Yet in 1964 when the Allies finally recognized the Joomun-do heroes, they decorated cousin Park Hyong-won and the martyred Lee Hong-suk as well as the two Kongs. Park Yong-dae did not plead in 1983 or 1989 for his own worthiness, only that the ROK government strip Kong Sung-tae and Kong Kwan-gik of their citations since they, the father and uncle of the infamous Kong Il-bong, had been the hated enemy, not local heroes. He especially wondered why his own uncle, Park Joo-won, nearly crazed by fear and fully aware of the likely fate of his family, had never been honored for the rescue of six American airmen.

# 6

# In Search of
# Lost Honor

SEOUL, KOREA, 2000, to
COLUMBUS, OHIO, 2002

Seventy-year-old John Y. Hong, once known as Hong Yoon-hee, a resident of San Mateo, California, faced a skeptical audience at the Press Center in downtown Seoul. Hong had returned to his native land to enlist public opinion—through the Korean media—in his crusade to reverse his court-martial conviction for treason, desertion, and espionage in September 1950. Mr. Hong passed out a thick précis of arguments and documents, "The Hong's Tragedy Records in the Korean War," to show that his conviction was unjust. Moreover, he said, he was really the unsung hero of the last great battle of the Pusan Perimeter, the defeat of the North Korean army in the Second Battle of the Naktong River. Instead of a medal, Hong received a jail sentence and lifelong dishonor. "I am living with grudges in whole life."

Like many of his countrymen, Hong's nightmare began on June 25, 1950, in Seoul. Two years before, he had left his home, the village of Mokok-ri, Munkyong-gun, Masung-myon, Kyongsangbuk-do in the mountains north of Taegu. A middle school dropout for political reasons, he found little work in postliberation Korea; so, being bright and physically fit, he joined the Korean Constabulary on March 27, 1948, at age seventeen after further private schooling in Seoul. He must have impressed someone because he became an investigator for the General Inspectorate, Headquarters, ROK army, Seoul, whose mission was to ferret out disloyal soldiers. By June 1950 Mr. Hong was Sergeant Hong, and he had orders to attend the next class at the ROK Military Academy. At his request, however, his orders reassigned him to a shorter (and academically less demanding) precommissioning course, the Infantry Officer Candidate School at Sihung, just south of Seoul. He reported in on June 24 but learned that his class did not begin until July 10. An amiable Captain Kim invited Hong to stay with his family in Kim's home north of the Han River. Kim told Hong he wanted someone to watch over his wife and young children while Kim ran some errands. Hong did not know Kim's business, captains not confiding in sergeants, but Hong found himself with the Kim family when he heard on the radio that the North Koreans had come across the border and were headed for Seoul.

Hong's story about his actions and whereabouts between June 25 and 28 is vague. He probably panicked. The Kim family disappears from his narrative. He makes no claim that he looked for an army unit to join. He recalls learning that he was trapped north of the Han when ROK engineers prematurely blew up the main rail and road bridges. He could not find a boat to cross the river. In desperation—like many other Seoul citizens—he sought refuge in the back-street apartment of a hometown friend, Park Chul-sun. (In 1999 Park verified this part of Hong's tale.) Park told Hong, however, that Park's friends and family were really Communists, or at least opponents of the Rhee regime and would turn in Park and Hong to curry favor with the invaders. Hong thought Park himself had been a Communist since 1945 and had wanted Hong to spy for the Communists when they first met in 1949. Park had a solution for Hong's desire to leave Seoul and head south: Hong should join the People's Army, march south as a Communist soldier, and then defect to his own army. Fearing betrayal, Hong leaped at the idea.

On July 11, Hong Yoon-hee joined the People's Volunteer Army, a corps of young people enlisting to serve in some capacity in the Korean People's Army. Hong gave his name as Hong Kwan-hee, a student at Seoul National University and an ardent radical. For a middle-school dropout to pretend to be a Seoul National student was itself an act of faith. Hong joined a group of teenage boys and girls—the Kyongnam Group—and on July 14 marched south without arms, uniforms, or training. With no idea where they were going or what they would do, the Kyongnams wandered around central Korea, doing housekeeping chores for the North Korean army. When the group entered Kyongsangbuk-do, Hong's anxiety soared for fear someone would identify him as an ROK army soldier. He felt a strange relief when he finally (August 25) was assigned as an unarmed orderly in a field hospital and sanitation unit of the KPA 1st Division, in reserve for reconstitution in the Palkong-san area northeast of Taegu. Hong learned that the division was preparing for a great offensive on September 1 that would take the People's Army to Pusan in ten days and win the war. "I was astonished and worried about the fate of the Nation."

Despite heavy security patrols around all the division camps, hidden from American air strikes in wooded mountain draws and ravines, Hong managed to slip away around 11 P.M. on September 1. The security patrols were not well organized since a one-day's postponement of the division attack had created some confusion and unit countermarching. After three hours of walking, Hong became lost. Probably

JOHN HONG

**Hong Yoon-hee**

confused by dehydration and fear, he hid in a Confucian shrine and immediately fell asleep. He dreamed that his mother came to him and told him he would escape. Waking at dawn, Hong stumbled into the woods and immediately ran into a patrol from the ROK 1st Division. Equally surprised, the ROK soldiers at least did not shoot Hong before he was able to convince them he was a defector. Wisely, he had already thrown away a rifle he had stolen. Overcome by relief and joy, Hong hurried off with the patrol to tell his big news about the day's attack.

Sergeant Hong Yoon-hee spent the next nine days—while the fighting raged along the Naktong front—telling his story over and over to South Korean and American intelligence officers and interrogation teams of the Allied Translator and Intelligence Service (ATIS), Far East Command. Hong remembers his interrogators as friendly and impressed with his truthfulness and patriotism. Someone told him he had a natural talent for future intelligence work behind enemy lines. Hong rejoined his home unit, which had moved from Taegu to Pusan. He again received orders to Officers Candidate School. He believed his information about the North Korean attack had contributed to the United Nations Command's victory in the Second Battle of the Naktong River. He had no way of knowing (and his interrogators probably did not know) that American signals intelligence units had already alerted Lieutenant General Walton H. Walker, 8th Army commander, of the North Korean attack and warnings from three KPA defectors had only confirmed the information Walker already had.

On September 11 Sergeant Hong's world collapsed forever. Three very tough Korean military policemen marched into his office and arrested him for treason and espionage. Hauled off in protest, Hong found himself in the rough hands of Korean Military Police (MP) interrogators who had learned their torturing skills from the Japanese. They treated Hong to a sample of nonfatal electrocution, beatings, burning, body contortions, and simulated drowning, the old standby "water cure." Hong recalls that he stuck with his story and claimed his innocence. He may have confessed, and he may not have. It made no difference since the MPs said he did. On September 15 Hong got his fifteen minutes with a military tribunal, was found guilty of espionage and treason, and was sentenced to death. Upon review, his sentence was reduced to life imprisonment, then ten years, and then (finally, in February 1951) to five years at hard labor. All his appeals for a retrial went unanswered. With no prospects for employment and too ashamed to return to his family, Hong left prison in 1955 for a life of wandering.

▬▬▬▬

Hong did not provide much information about how he managed to reach the United States in 1973 or how he made a living. He certainly remained troubled by his disgrace and his nation's failure to reward his heroism. He read everything he could find about the first months of the Korean War. He made four trips to Washington to search for documents in the 8th Army records. He searched the interrogation reports of the ATIS, but he could not find his own. Instead he became obsessed with the case of Major (KPA) Kim Sung-jun, the operations officer and acting commander of the 19th Regiment, KPA 13th Division, who defected to the 8th Army on September 1, 1950, with plans of the North Korean attack. Hong felt Kim had stolen his fame for revealing the KPA's plans. Kim was no hero. He had been arrested for poor leadership in the failed offensive of August 19–21, an attack that reduced the 19th Regiment from eight hundred to sixty effectives by American air and artillery strikes. Kim thus had plenty of reason to defect. "Hong's return saved Korea, assisted the strategies of the U.N. forces, and saved hundreds of thousands [of] lives."

Hong concluded if he could recapture his status as hero, he could win a retrial, but he would have to discredit the mysterious Major Kim. He found Kim's ATIS interrogation report—in fact, several of them—and read that Kim really

had not said much of value about the
September 2 attack. Hong did not
care that Kim's reports provided little valuable information about the
North Korean army. Kim had not
given details about the offensive, and
the Korean and American historians
had lied about Kim's role in the allied
victory, which infuriated Hong. (In
fact, the Kim story nicely masked
the SIGINT radio intelligence operation, a common ploy that at least
fooled the historians.) Hong pursued
Major Kim like Ahab's quest for
Moby Dick, assuming Kim had refused repatriation and lived (or had
lived) in South Korea or the United
States.

**Mr. John Hong**

Hong found two other NKPA 13th
Division nonrepatriates, former Col-
onel Chung Bong-uk and former Lieutenant Ahn Jong-il. The division artillery
commander, Chung had defected on August 22, one suspects also under a cloud
for the failed attacks, but perhaps also as a South Korean spy. Ahn had been
captured on September 16. Hong studied their ATIS reports and found no
mention of Major Kim. When Hong contacted Chung, now a retired major general in the South Korean army, and Ahn, neither said he knew Major Kim during the war or since. Hong's quest continued.

In January 2000 Hong met Professor Pang Son-ju, a retired Korean American academic who does Korean War research and copies records in the United
States for the archives of the Korean Institute of Military History, Seoul. They
discussed Major Kim. Professor Pang casually remarked that a search for Kim
would produce little since Kim had been repatriated to North Korea on August
7, 1953. Hong could not believe this news, but Professor Pang verified the claim
from a list of exchanged North Korean officers. Why would a traitor—whose
treason had become a staple item of the Korean War's history—go back to certain death? Hong now believed Major Kim was a special agent, loyal to Pyongyang, a fake defector whose intelligence mission was to confuse the Americans
with false information that would discredit Colonel Chung. This revelation
brought Hong's "grudges" to a new boiling point. He even pursued information

about Kim and his own bogus KPA identity as Hong Kwan-hee through the North Korean mission to the United Nations. He heard nothing but a polite disclaimer of knowledge and lack of records. Kim was gone without a trace.

Hong achieved greater success in finding his own records. In June 1999 he finally located his court-martial records and accompanying documents in the South Korean army's personnel archives in Pusan. With shouts and tears, he waved his file for all to see, and the soldier clerks around him broke into cheers and clapping. Their true friendship diminished his own fear that the governments of both Koreas wanted him dead, although he could not say exactly what threat he represented to them.

After telling his story, Hong again disappeared from Seoul. Only his press handout remained. He continued his hunt for Major Kim and his own lost honor. In the summer of 2001 Hong appeared in the Washington office of Dr. Richard Gorell, a senior Army historian and former command historian of the United States Forces in Korea. Hong vowed that his search for evidence on the mysterious Major Kim and of his own innocence would continue until he died. In January 2002 he called me to insist that his quest for vindication would continue.

# 7

# A Korean University
# Professor and General

CHEVY CHASE, MARYLAND
May 7, 2000

The neat, small, elderly Korean gentleman sitting across the table from me in a chic restaurant just off Chevy Chase Circle looks exactly like what he is: a distinguished retired professor of economics from The Catholic University of America. No American would ever think he was also a retired major general, Army of the Republic of Korea, and a wartime division commander. His name is Kim Ung-soo, and his story is not just one of survival, but of accomplishment as well. He tells me about his life as we make our selections from the menu— two salads for geriatric good health—and sip iced tea.

General Kim talks about his childhood and the forced internationalism of the Koreans in the 1920s and 1930s:

> I was born in Nosan, near Taejon, in 1923, but my grandfather took my family from Korea to Harbin, Manchuria, to escape Japanese political and cultural oppression. We joined a community of Korean nationalists. My grandfather wanted to keep my father, an extreme nationalist, out of Japanese hands and in a Korean school. My father became an office worker for the Trans-Siberian Railroad, and we lived in a White Russian area, but the Japanese police still kept us under surveillance as they did all known Korean national-

37

ists. I went to an "independence school" for Koreans, and there I learned about politics, mostly watching playground fights between ultranationalists and Communist children. All of us lived in fear of the Japanese political police, who periodically raided our village to confiscate political books, including one of my favorites about George Washington and his father's cherry tree, also Father's favorite story. The Chinese soldiers were worse because they took our rice and stole other things. Often we had to eat rough grain instead of rice, which we hated. Actually I started my student days in a Chinese school. I liked all the mathematics, but I didn't know enough Chinese to continue. The Korean school was taught in Japanese, which I learned to read and speak. I must have learned everything pretty well, because I eventually won a scholarship to an elite Japanese preparatory school. I was one of five winners of the thousands who applied. I actually wanted to go to a Chinese school.

We all took military training since it was required by Japanese law. I had no special aptitude for soldiering, but I ended up as a common soldier in the Kwangtung Army facing the Chinese Communist 8th Route Army in 1944. In 1945 I learned that I had been admitted to Kyoto University, but first I had to pass the officer candidate training course, which I did, and became a warrant officer in May 1945. Then I left for the university. So I was in Japan when the surrender came. I actually received my commission in the Japanese army after the war ended. I went to Seoul in November 1945. I saw no future in Russian-occupied and Chinese Communist-dominated Manchuria.

I became one of the first 110 officers commissioned in the Korean Constabulary, but I joined later than most of my peers, in May 1946. My academic record got me into the Constabulary, and I also had been admitted to study law at Seoul National University, but the university was in turmoil. To tell you the truth, I thought the Americans let anyone in the Constabulary, even known leftists. Anyway, my staff skills made me an assistant to Colonel Yi Ung-jun, who was the inspector general. I then went to other administrative posts in the Seoul area, including the 1st Regiment. As a captain I commanded a supply company in Yongdongpo, which was really a dumping ground for soldiers suspected of political activism. That was a challenging job. Colonel Yi rescued me by having me assigned to his staff with the 1st Brigade in 1947. I kept attending law classes, which I thought were easy. As my military duties became more time-consuming, I dropped out of law school. Colonel Yi was a fine soldier, a good example for a young officer. Although he had graduated from the Imperial Military Academy, he was a "hands on" commander, inspecting everything, asking many questions. He was also a hard worker, unlike Japanese senior officers. He wasn't very nationalistic or political. He just wanted to be a good military officer. I liked him very much.

I became involved with the Cheju-do Rebellion during 1948 as a judge advocate and aide to Yi Pom-suk, who commanded the paramilitary National Youth Corps and became Korea's first prime minister. I was the defense

KIM UNG-SOO

**General Paik Sun-yup, Chief of Staff, ROK Army, and Brig. Gen. Kim Ung-soo, 1953**

counsel for the court-martial of Lieutenant Mun Sang-gil, the mastermind of the murder of Colonel Park Chin-gyong. Actually I was much more impressed with the two corporals who did the shooting. They were courageous and dedicated Communists, not a treacherous opportunist like Lieutenant Mun. I also learned a great deal about Kim Tal-sam, the rebel leader, and he must have been a very forceful and effective leader. The Communists wanted to capture Cheju-do and to turn it into a Communist base area like Yenan Province. After this assignment I went to a logistics post and immediately developed an ulcer, which is an indication of how little I liked the work. My last assignment before June 25 was as chief of staff of the Capital Division. I was a colonel and twenty-seven years old when the Communists invaded.

As we eat and General Kim talks, we occasionally chat about contemporary Korean politics, which the general follows closely. He finds President Kim Dae-jung's "sunshine policy" toward North Korea much too optimistic. Neither of us could anticipate the president's trip to Pyongyang the next month, the very anniversary of the beginning of the Korean War. We talk about the fiftieth anniversary plans in Korea and the United States and decide that the events will not be very memorable, certainly not as exciting as the North Korean invasion.

Our division headquarters was south of the Han River, and we didn't send too many troops north to defend the city since our regiments were already widely scattered. We pulled our forces together to defend the line south of the Han River, commanded by Major General Kim Hong-il. I was his G-1, which meant finding troops. General Kim was an excellent soldier, tough, honest, very knowledgeable in military operations, very firm. He had been a general in the Chinese army. He was also tall and carried himself well. He hair was unusually gray for a Korean man, but he looked very impressive, totally in control. Well, we couldn't hold because we had too little ammunition and no effective antitank weapons, so we fell back to the south and hoped that the Americans would come with more ammunition, lots of artillery, and some weapon that could destroy a T-34. Of course, we finally held at the Pusan Perimeter. In the meantime, I went to command the student regiment, Combined Arms School, Pusan. Incidentally, I never saw an order from ROK army headquarters to shoot political prisoners, although I'm sure some suspected Communists were killed in the summer of 1950.

In 1952 I became the personal assistant to Lieutenant General Lee Chong-chan, chief of staff of the army. General Lee had a keen sense of justice and sympathy for the common people. He was a populist, I'd say, and he thought President Rhee was too autocratic and unwilling to give up power. That is why General Lee refused to release troops to support Rhee's martial law regime in Pusan in 1952, which cost General Lee his position. Lee was not especially pro-American, and I don't think he would have participated in a coup. He felt like an outsider, especially since his wife had been a *kaesing* woman, which was socially unacceptable. General Lee was a very good officer, one of the best I observed. Yi Hyong-kun was too arrogant, too much like the Japanese, too inflexible. Min Ki-shik, on the other hand, was brilliant but erratic. He had tremendous energy and courage, but he was unpredictable, too emotional, almost too energetic. I also knew Kim Chong-o well. He was a solid professional soldier, honest, not too complicated or learned. He had been a Japanese student volunteer or *hakpyong*. He was comparatively mild-mannered, but firm. His 9th Division was a good one, the victors of the Battle of White Horse Mountain.

In 1953 I became the commanding general of the 2nd Division, which was then stationed in the Chorwon area. We took over the White Horse Mountain sector, which was still active even after the beating the 9th Division had given the Chinese. I was really nervous about being a division commander since I had so little time with troops, and I was small and looked even younger than thirty years old. I decided I would have to be unusually active, so I did three things. I visited my troops constantly, mostly at night, and I learned a great deal about my division, more than anyone else, so I commanded through greater knowledge. For example, we had a problem with an artillery battery firing wild rounds, so I gave it a surprise inspection and found that the cannoneers were asleep. The porters of the Korean Service Corps were firing the howitzers, just blazing away, happy as can be, but they didn't know how to make the corrections in elevation and deflection sent down to the guns from the fire direction center, so they never adjusted their fire. Well, I got that problem fixed. Another thing I did was attack corruption in our mess halls. Some officers and NCOs [noncommissioned officers] were stealing food and selling it on the black market. I put a stop to that crime against my soldiers, and we improved the mess hall food. That was a good morale booster. The last practice was to visit my hospital often and unannounced to make sure my wounded soldiers were being well treated with the best medical care we could provide, which was certainly not very good. I think my sincere interest in the wounded also helped morale. My advisors and I thought we had a good division when the war ended.

**Professor Kim Ung-soo, 2000**

After the war, General Kim continued to serve in responsible staff jobs and commands until his forced retirement by President Park Chung-hee in 1961. He served as ROK Army Deputy Chief of Staff for Logistics and Operations and Training as well as an army chief of staff and a corps commander. He received three Korean decorations for his wartime service and four Legions of Merit from the U.S. Army. None of his honors and talents would protect him from Park's purge of generals from North Korea, especially a devout Methodist as General Kim had become. As an expatriate retiree at the age of thirty-eight in the United States, Kim Ung-soo earned three degrees in economics at the University of Washington and The Catholic University in eight years, and two years later he became a faculty member at his last alma mater. He became active as an elder in the Korean United Methodist Church of Greater Washington and a leader in the Korean American associations that support the YMCA and scholarships for Korean American students. He returned to Korea in 1982 and 1990 to teach at Korean universities. He is pleased that Korea now has the freedom he and his comrades fought for from 1948 to 1953.

# 8

## Soldiers of the Korean People's Army

The Korean People's Army crossed the 38th Parallel with revolutionary ferocity. Well armed and well trained, the North Korean soldiers believed they were invincible. The nine divisions of infantry and one tank division (attached by brigades to the two principal task forces) that invaded the Republic of Korea were reasonable copies of the World War II Soviet motorized rifle divisions, complete with both self-propelled and towed artillery. The Korean People's Army had three divisions of veterans of the Chinese civil war as well as thousands of other former guerrillas and members of the Soviet ground forces. The original ninety-seven thousand soldiers of the KPA "army of Korean liberation" were probably equal to any army in Asia (including the U.S. 8th Army) and comparable to the best of the Imperial Japanese Army at its peak. The weakness of the KPA was that it had few ready reserves. Its field medical system and logistical structure could not sustain a long war, especially under the constant threat of air attack. Its morale also proved brittle under the strain of continuous combat and accumulated losses, physical deterioration, and the return of realism when the "puppet troops" of South Korea did not surrender or flee.

The experience of Major Kim Kyong-hun, a medical doctor on the staff of the KPA's 40th Field Hospital at the age of thirty-seven, illustrates the perils of rev-

**North Korean soldiers meet their Chinese comrades**

olutionary equity and North Korean desperation in 1950. Major Kim came from Haeju, Hwanghae Province, a hotbed of socialist enthusiasm as well as Christian resistance. After six years of primary school, Kim abandoned formal schooling to serve as an apprentice herbalist and purveyor of Chinese cures. His ultimate goal was to pass the national medical examination of the Democratic People's Republic so that he could start an independent practice. He finally passed the medical examination in 1950. The examination was a series of short tests, all in essay form, in which he wrote about how he would diagnose and treat a series of hypothetical patients. During the test he examined two patients, but treated neither one. His examination in obstetrics was oral. The system assumed he would train himself on the job with patients after he received a license.

Doctor Kim entered the KPA by conscription on June 15, 1950, and joined the 40th Field Hospital four days later as its chief surgeon. Six of Kim's staff of twelve officers had attended medical school; none could perform more than the most primitive type of surgery. The fifty nurses were far more competent than the doctors, Kim thought. Having formed in Pyongyang, the 40th Field Hospital went into liberated South Korea with the first invasion forces and started treating patients during the first (and unsuccessful) attack on Chunchon. The hospital moved south behind the combatant troops, moving through Chunchon, Hwachon, Hoengsong, Wonju, and Chongju before it reached the battlefields of the Pusan Perimeter. Doctor Kim estimated that by August 2 his staff treated five thousand wounded from the KPA 5th and 12th Divisions. It processed another two thousand wounded by September 15. The first respite came on September 24. After a week of bloody ruin for the KPA, no patients came to the hospital, but only because the KPA 2nd, 4th, and 9th Divisions had withdrawn without any notice to the hospital. When no orders came for three days, the commanding officer, political officer, head nurse, and some favored party cadres took the one remaining truck, loaded it with food and weapons, and fled north. Kim and the rest of the staff loaded their personal effects into packs and walked north to Chongju, where they were captured on September 27. They left the wounded behind.

After completing his POW interrogation, Kim disappeared among the almost 120,000 North Korean POWs held on Koje-do Island. His fate after his surrender is unknown, but one supposes he had ample opportunity to hone his medical skills as a prisoner of war.

The military career of KPA Sergeant "Park" (real name unknown because the interrogation report does not identify the sergeant by name) began with Park's induction into the KPA in July 1950 and ended with his capture on March 19, 1951. At the age of seventeen and after three months of training, Park joined the mortar platoon of the 3rd Battalion, 1st Regiment, KPA 7th Division, originally formed around a cadre of Sino-Korean veterans of the Chinese civil war in May 1950. His division had retreated north from South Korea, where Park joined it in the cold autumn of defeat in 1950.

When his division returned to the war in early 1951, it did not last long in the face of the 8th Army's firepower. By March the 3rd Battalion numbered only six officers and 150 men, armed with one 82-millimeter mortar; two American .50-caliber heavy machine guns, with five boxes of ammunition; fifteen Russian light machine guns; fifteen PPSh submachine guns, with five hundred rounds each; seventy Russian rifles; and four hand grenades for each man. Even with replacements from two other divisions, the battalion could not replace its losses.

On March 5 the 3rd Battalion occupied a hill about ten miles north of Hongchon and prepared to contest another advance by the U.S. 2nd Infantry Division. The battalion political officer, a captain, continued to spread the story that the North Korean army would soon be reinforced by three thousand especially trained comrades who had been training in Russia to fly planes and drive tanks. Few soldiers believed his promises, made too often with no fulfillment. The commanding officer and political officer made more compelling promises: They would shoot any soldier caught with a United Nations safe conduct pass and surrender leaflet. They were as good as their word about shooting their own soldiers. When the Americans attacked, about one-third of the 3rd Battalion, including Sergeant Park, broke for the rear. The battalion commander opened fire with his pistol and hit Park in the shoulder. When Park regained consciousness, all of the battalion had disappeared, as had the Americans. Park struggled north toward home for two days, begging food from villagers, until he was found by a South Korean guerrilla unit, which, much to his amazement, treated him like a proper prisoner of war. The political officer said that the Americans shot prisoners, robbed Koreans, expected to make Korea a Japanese colony, and that most of the United States Army had come to Korea since the "puppet troops" would not fight. Park now believed that these bits of information had all been lies, and he was pleased that for him, the war was over.

▓▓▓▓

Ju Young-bok, engineer, welcomed the liberation of northern Korea from Japan, but he had some reservations about having Russians in positions of influence. Nevertheless, he believed that socialism would be the path of revolution Korea should take. He watched the nationalization of industry and the beggaring of the affluent with some disquiet, but not much. A good deal of the repression in northern Korea made no economic sense and insulted Ju's scientific sense of correctness, but he watched these developments safely from inside the Korean People's Army. In the autumn of 1946 he became an interpreter for the Russians. By 1949 Ju had become a major in the engineering department of the KPA's headquarters in Pyongyang. Among his duties was to receive and inspect shipments of tanks and other vehicles pouring into Wonsan Harbor. He learned that the haste was linked to the news that South Korea would invade the north in June. The Korean People's Army must strike first. Major Ju distributed copies of the basic operations order before he departed for his wartime billet in the headquarters of the KPA II Corps, concentrated opposite Chunchon in the west-central sector. He saw Russian advisors everywhere, many of them in civilian clothes. He crossed the border at Chunchon and found to his amazement that there were no signs that the South Korean army had made preparations to invade the Democratic People's Republic of Korea. Ju had been told that the Special Envoy to Japan, the Honorable John Foster Dulles, and the U.S. Ambassador to Korea, John J. Muccio, had demanded a "march north."

Surprise after surprise chewed away at Major Ju's faith after June 25. The puppet troops fought well despite their inferior weapons. The Americans sent planes to bomb and strafe the Korean People's Army columns. Many of the southern Koreans did not greet their liberators. The war did not end in two weeks as had been promised by General Kang Kon, the KPA's great field commander. All the promises of support made by the Russian advisors turned out to be false promises. When Major Ju went to Seoul to help organize the city's defenses, he saw thousands of conscripted young men and women sent off to the battlefield in the south to meet certain death. When the Korean People's Army began to disintegrate in September and October, a completely disillusioned Major Ju took the first opportunity to surrender to the United Nations forces, but only to the Americans, not the South Koreans, who would not take kindly to a North Korean officer who had been an enthusiastic invader.

After three years of terror-stricken captivity, Major Ju refused both repatriation to North Korea and political asylum in South Korea. The odds of his survival in either country would have been slight, his chance for a normal life virtually impossible since no one would trust him enough to give him a job. Turning his back on his homeland and his family, Ju Young-bok emigrated to Brazil, a member of another Korean diaspora.

# 9

## Founders of an Industrial Empire

When my family and I arrived in Seoul in March 1991 for a four-month Fulbright professorship, we came armed with the names of two people we were supposed to meet: Dr. Horace G. Underwood of Yonsei University and Chung Se-yung, chairman of Hyundai Motors. We knew little about either man. Horace was a longtime friend of Mrs. Betsy Fletcher, wife of a retired Ohio State professor and a "missionary kid" from Pyongyang; we had just met her at a current affairs seminar she had organized for Wesley Glen, a retirement home. Martha and I had never set eyes on Chung Se-jung, although we recognized a Hyundai when we saw one. We knew Chairman Chung had attended Miami University in Oxford, Ohio (M.A., 1957), when my father had been its president (1953–1964). According to Korean custom, Chairman Chung sent my parents annual Christmas gifts. One package contained two Korean wedding ducks, which looked to me like well-painted nonbuoyant decoys rather than symbols of lasting marital fidelity. At our briefing in Seoul we met another Korean Miami graduate, Professor Cho Sung-kyu, head of Yonsei's English department. Professor Cho spoke with Chairman Chung and, lo and behold, the Miami alumni of Korea came to meet us at a five-star hotel luncheon paid for by Chairman Chung. The Korean equivalent of Henry Ford chaired the lunch and held forth in rapid-fire Hanglish (a mixture of Korean and English). It was memorable. I knew nothing about how the Hyundai industrial empire had flowered in the wreckage of the Korean War.

Someone always makes money in the middle of a war, even on a battlefield. The campaigns of 1950 and early 1951 ruined most of the Republic of Korea. In almost every infrastructure category—public buildings, homes, factories, port facilities, roads, bridges, railroads, schools—South Korea lost more than half of its economic base. American economic experts estimated in 1953 that $1 billion over three years would be necessary to rebuild Korea to prewar conditions. The only builders in South Korea in 1950 to 1953 were the U.S. Army and U.S. Air Force, with the U.S. Army Corps of Engineers and the U.S. Army Quartermaster Corps the principal contractors. An American air-ground expeditionary force of half a million and a Korean national army growing toward the same size required buildings beyond imagination—and quickly. Some of the construction materials and almost all of the labor would have to come from within Korea. The work also demanded local entrepreneurs who could join the labor and the materials. One of these men was Chung Ju-yung, the head of a family of five brothers (including Chung Se-yung) and a sister who became the first generation leaders of the Hyundai *chaebol*, one of the largest conglomerates in Korea by the 1990s. In 1950, however, the war had ruined the first Hyundai enterprise, an automobile parts and repair business in Seoul. At age thirty-five, Chung Ju-yung would have to start over, and only the American army had capital and materials for his latest dream—forming a Hyundai construction company.

As the eldest son and dominant personality, Chung Ju-yung (born 1915) had determined the family's collective goal: to become so wealthy and powerful that the Chungs would rule the new postcolonial economy. Ju-yung already had broken with the past and rejected his inheritance, a family farm near Asan, Kangwon Province, now north of the Demilitarized Zone. He ran away from the farm at fourteen and found a construction job at Wonsan. His father brought him home, where he returned to a Confucian school run by his autocratic grandfather. In 1934 Chung Ju-yung ran away to Seoul and worked as a construction laborer, as a longshoreman, and then as a rice delivery boy. At twenty-one, his energy and ambition, creative bookkeeping, and bargaining skills put Ju-yung in charge of the rice company. But he did not own it. Japanese rice controls then destroyed the business, and Ju-yung returned to Asan temporarily. It was 1940. He now, however, had financial backers (still of mysterious identity, thus probably Japanese), and he returned to Seoul and started an auto repair business, specializing in making replacement parts for American cars. Chung Ju-yung knew nothing of automobile mechanics; he could not read English; he had no religion and no real principles except profit. Like John D. Rockefeller, he saw war as an arena for enterprise. His admitted key to success was deception—his workers cleaned parts but did not replace them. Often that was enough to return cars to service; in other cases his mechanics cannibalized other cars. By

1945 the business was thriving, largely through Japanese patronage. The Japanese regarded the Chungs as unusually trustworthy, for Koreans. Ju-yung had no politics. "I am merely a man who became rich from his toils . . . there is nothing better than earning extra money . . ." His first mission upon liberation was to gather his family in Seoul and out of Communist hands and put them to work in a new, enlarged company, the Hyundai Auto Repair Company. Now he had a new problem: how to work with the American military government, the people with money.

Chung Ju-yung turned to a younger brother, Chung In-yung, born in 1920, who was determined to be his brother's equal. Advanced education, including learning English, would be his leverage, and he had ducked military service or forced labor by attending an exclusive Japanese private college. Ju-yung wanted some return for his investment. His brother did some minor interpreting work for the military government, while Ju-yung cultivated the new political elite, including Syngman Rhee. The two oldest Chung brothers fled all the way to Pusan in the summer of 1950, not just fleeing the Communists, but also chasing Army contractors.

While the war raged on, the Chung brothers wheeled and dealt. They formed the Hyundai Construction Company and the Hyundai Commercial Transportation Company. They started with a small workforce and made wooden floors for tents and erected Quonset huts. In three years the Chungs were building warehouses, port facilities, air runways, headquarters buildings, and barracks. The company did projects on three hundred Army posts. Chung Ju-yung relished the company's profits, which often ran as high as four times the actual project costs. Hyundai builders cut corners on materials and squeezed more work out of an unskilled work force, but Chung Ju-yung rewarded workers who learned technical skills from the Americans. No firm figures can be attached to Chung enterprises, but the U.S. Army spent at least $2 billion on local construction in Korea, and the Chungs got their share, certainly in the tens of millions of dollars in a country with a per capita income of sixty dollars a year. Chung Ju-yung saw concrete as the staff of life.

The Americans who dealt with Hyundai Construction knew that the Chungs practiced all sorts of kickbacks, contract padding, unfair labor practices, corruption, noncompetitive sweetheart deals among supposedly competitive Korean companies, and all sorts of risk-reducing, profit-enhancing practices. Yet if the Americans knew what they wanted and demanded that their standards be met, the Korean contractors would eventually get the job right. Hyundai Construction's record was as good as any and better than most.

The armistice brought an end to most of Hyundai's military contracting, but the Chung brothers were prepared for another brave new world. They had learned how to build bridges on a very unprofitable bridge project at Taegu. They won the contract from Syngman Rhee to rebuild a national monument, Han River Bridge One. Within months the Chungs had new contracts worth $5 million for U.S. military projects in Seoul and Inchon. They never looked back.

In 1993 the Korean Office of National Tax Administration announced that Chung Ju-yung had the highest annual income in Korea, roughly $150 million. By the time of his death in March 2001, at the age of eighty-six, Chung Ju-yung had brought the Olympic games to Seoul in 1988, been a third-party candidate for president, created a luxury resort in North Korea, sent dairy and beef cows to the starving North Koreans, and promised to turn Kaesong into an advanced technological center and site for car making. *The Economist* (Great Britain) estimated that the five Hyundai *chaebols* among Korea's thirty largest corporations had a combined value of over $100 billion. The Chung empire started with tent floors.

# 10

## The Teenage Guerrilla

SEOUL, KOREA
December 1994

L ike most retired Marine lieutenant colonels of his generation, Mark C. Monahan, fifty-nine, is a Vietnam War veteran. That he is also a veteran of the
Korean War does not make him one-of-a-kind. But Mark Monahan, with
a Ph.D. in Chinese language and literature, is a professor in the international
education division of Yonsei University and the University of Maryland-Asia,
which is exceptional for a former officer in the Korean army's special forces and
an active participant in the military revolution of 1961. Before he was adopted
by an American family at twenty-five, Mark C. Monahan was Chang Kil-yong,
and he fought the Korean War as a teenage guerrilla. He recalls his lost youth
with considerable *han*.

My family had lived for generations on the west coast of Hwanghae Province about ten miles from the town of Songhwa. The nearest big town was
Changyon, another ten miles away. My father and grandfather were well-to-
do farmers and landholders, real *yangban*, except that they had modern ideas.
My grandfather was a Presbyterian elder, and my father always supported the
local church by providing housing for the pastor who visited our village once a
month. We lived a self-sufficient life on our farm, and we made some money

from the rent and crops of our tenant farmers. In 1945 my father sent my older brother to school in Seoul. Soon after independence, however, Korean Communist officials, led by one of our tenant farmers named Lee, came to our home and arrested my father, who was then sentenced to five years in prison for being an "enemy of the people." That left my mother, a very determined woman, and me to run the family farm and business. Even under Communism we did all right while we waited for my father's release from prison.

The night before the Korean War began we had a heavy rain—thunder, lightning, the whole works. The next morning the air smelled as clean and fragrant as I've ever smelled it. The trees and flowers looked wonderful, suffused in light by the sun. But my mother and I heard this rumbling noise to the south. She said it must be the storm, but I could see no clouds and I didn't think she was right. Of course, what we heard was the tremendous artillery fire along the 38th Parallel. At first the war meant nothing to us. Then Communist recruiting parties came to our village to find more soldiers. I thought I would not be taken since I was only fifteen, but by October you could tell that the Communists were desperate. We heard a rumor that the Communists were losing the war, and soon all political cadres left our *myon*. We heard that the U.S. Army and the South Koreans would liberate us, so we held a great festival with the best food we had, and we went to church without any fear. We never saw a North Korean soldier or United Nations soldier in our village.

After the joy of liberation, the news that the Chinese had entered the war and that the Communists would soon return came as a great shock. Of course, the weather turned cold, and we had more snow than I had ever seen before. One day we heard the Communist soldiers were only five miles away, and I could see long lines of people struggling through the snow into the mountains along the coast. Someone had said that a South Korean ship was taking away anyone who wanted to flee the Communists. We also thought about fleeing south into South Korea. Mother gathered warm clothes, food, and blankets that we could carry, but she wanted to go into the mountains to wait for the return of the United Nations soldiers. I thought we'd better get the hell out while we had a chance, and that meant going to the coast or heading south. I knew that if I stayed I would be either shot as a "capitalist" or, more likely, drafted into the North Korean army. Mother refused to leave. She said she would wait for Father to be released from prison. I thought he would already have returned home if he was alive, and I wanted to get out.

I left her standing by our home and joined the stream of refugees trudging toward the coast. I don't know how many people I saw struggling through the snow, but it must have been thousands. When I finally reached the coast, I could see a South Korean ship, probably some sort of amphibious vessel, lying offshore just out of mortar range—and the Communists were trying to hit her. Small boats of all kinds, including fishing boats, were picking people up at the cliffs and taking them through the shellfire to the ship. I was amazed that the people remained so quiet except for calling out names to one another, but then someone said that the last boat had arrived. The crowd moaned. I just jumped from the cliff right on top of some guy, and we both tumbled on the deck. I had no intention of being stranded on the cliffs with the other people.

The ship, of course, was a madhouse, packed with people and their pitiful belongings. There was very little food and water and too much crap. I have no idea how many people were aboard, but it had to be more than a thousand. After the ship got under way, some ROK marines divided the refugees. All the old people, women, and children stayed aboard for the trip south to Pusan, while the young men, maybe five hundred of us, transferred to another ship. There we learned we had just joined the South Korean army and that we

**Lt. Chang Kil-yong, ROK Army**

MARK C. MONAHAN

would go to Cho-do Island for basic training. We would remain at military bases on the islands off the west coast of North Korea. After two or three weeks under the most primitive conditions we began military training, including shooting American weapons. We slept packed in an old schoolhouse and washed outside in the snow and cold. Then we went south to a bigger island, probably Paengnyong-do, to a larger military camp, where we organized companies according to where we came from in Hwanghae Province. I became a member of the White Tiger Unit of the 1st Partisan Infantry Regiment. Of course, we had no idea that we had become members of Army Unit 8240, the United Nations Partisan Forces, Korea, a guerrilla force modeled after the OSS [Office of Strategic Services] units of World War II. Our teams were code-named "Donkey," and then numbered. I think we were "Donkey Six." We did see our first U.S. soldiers at "Leopard Base," one of whom was black. The U.S. cadre at "Leopard" numbered around twenty-five. I had never seen a black man before, so I found his appearance amazing. We received uniforms—mostly U.S. Army castoffs—and weapons. I became a radioman on an AN/GRC-9, a radio we used to communicate with planes and ships, and I carried an M-2 carbine. I really didn't work the radio, just pumped away at the hand-driven generator. I did what I was told. We had some very tough NCOs, most of them from the Korean Marine Corps, so we didn't want to make them mad or they'd beat the crap out of us.

I never did learn exactly what our mission was, but we made ten-day patrols into Hwanghae Province to learn what the Communists were doing. Some units raided enemy coastal outposts, but mine did reconnaissance work, which meant that we avoided all contact. At first we took food from the peasants, but they said that the Communists would kill them if they helped us, so my team leader said we would eat only what we could carry. Our food supply thus limited our area of operations. Basically, we tried to observe Communist troop movements and report them, so that U.N. aircraft or ships could attack targets along the roads south. Our leader was very cautious; we thought he was great. We never had a firefight, although other units did. I remember a friend of mine being all shot up with a burp gun. Some units just disappeared. My strongest memory is the smell of American C-rations cooking over a small fire. I never smelled food so good, and I ate all I could get my hands on. I had no idea I would eat so many Cs all over the world as an American Marine!

We stayed on our island bases until the armistice, when we finally went to South Korea. I took a discharge from the Army in 1954 as a sergeant because I wanted to go to school. I remember seeing the schoolboys in Seoul after the war, carrying books and wearing school uniforms, running to their classes. They were not much younger than I, but the war had cost me my teenage years and my education. After a try at attending a Presbyterian seminary for about a year, I went back to the Army. I didn't know anything except how to be a soldier. I never learned what happened to my mother, but my father escaped and came to Seoul. And I ended up in America.

One moist summer day in 2000, Mark walks over from his apartment and announces that I am going with him to visit Paengnyong-do Island, or Py-do in local usage. We are going to take the subway to Inchon and then catch the hydrofoil ferry to the island, which at 37 degrees and some minutes, is South Korea's northern-most presence in the West Sea. North Korea is about seven miles away, and Mark says we will be able to see Changsan-got, the most famous point of land in Hwanghae Province. We will be the guests of the Black Dragon Brigade of the Hae Pyong Dae, or South Korean Marine Corps, which administers the island and provides security for the multiple agencies that do their business with long antennas and big radar dishes. For all its military activity, Py-do still entertains tourists and provides a home for a colony of fishermen and truck garden and rice farmers. Mark says most of the islanders are Christian refugees from North Korea. There do seem to be an unusual number of attractive churches in every hamlet. The real attraction, however, is to accompany Mark on a voyage of memory. When his guerrilla unit was not raiding from Cho-do, it trained and got R&R on Py-do. Py-do also has an unusual beach. It is so flat and firm that in low tide it can serve as a landing strip, and even today it holds up well under the pounding of local speedsters who cannot quite get their Hyundais and Daewoos airborne.

Despite a springtime naval battle between the coastal patrol boats of the two Koreas, the Py-do area is now quiet, in fact too quiet for the ROK Marines. According to an agreement between Kim Dae-jung and Kim Jong-il, electronic warfare and infiltrations have come to a halt between Py-do and Changsan-got. The "sunshine policy" shines on Py-do: more tourists, more development—maybe. The Black Dragons, however, stay on the alert. We spend one night on mats on the floor of transients' military billet after a restrained communal Korean meal. Even without excess *maekju, soju,* and *makoli,* we do not sleep well. It is hot and the "beds" are flat—and our bodies are definitely not flat. Mark drags him-

THE AUTHOR

**Lt. Col. Mark C. Monahan USMC (Ret.), Paengnyong-do, 2000**

self to the head: "I am not an old Marine now, just old." I feel much the same way, so we agree to cut the visit short by one night and get back to our more comfortable mattresses in Seoul. We make the most of the day.

Mark finds the site of one of the guerrilla camps, where one rusting Quonset hut remains as a memorial to the expatriate partisans of Donkey Force. Mark enjoys seeing the old photographs inside the hut. He recalls that the huts were warm and comfortable and that the morale of his unit was always high on Py-do, which seemed much safer from invasion than did Cho-do. With all the mysterious units and people who worked out of Py-do in the 1950s, the place was never boring. Compared with life in the ROK army on the mainland, the lot of the partisan was a happy one, except for the family separations.

On the way back to Inchon that afternoon, we watch the arrival of the North Korean families who have come to Seoul for some very well publicized and carefully arranged reunions. Loaded with fresh seafood or beer, the tourists on the ferry watch the television in fascination for some very unscripted events of substantial symbolism. Some of the oldsters are too feeble to communicate, no matter how loudly their children yell. Several medical emergencies arise. An appalling argument takes place in one family about who deserted whom. There is no question that our small sample of Korean public opinion favors the family exchanges. Mark has applied for permission to visit Hwanghae Province to search for his relatives, but he estimates that, given his military history, Pyong-yang will not allow him to visit. That he is now an American citizen may also push him down the list, which numbers in the tens of thousands. As the ferry bounces along toward Inchon, we watch the dying sun bring a thousand points of light to the gentle waves, and we both sleep like old men.

# 11

# The MiG Pilot

**HONOLULU, HAWAII**
**June 2001**

The panel of aging airmen is enjoying the chance to relive their glory days of aerial combat in the session "The Air-to-Air War: Stories from MiG Alley." It is a panel at the Commander Pacific Air Forces "Korean War Air Power Symposium" that has empty seats in the ready room; two American aces cannot attend, and the Russian and Chinese aces do not arrive either. The stories flow on ". . . there I was at Angels 28 . . ." Down the table a middle-aged Korean man, casually dressed and relaxed, smiles at the conversation. His name is Kenneth Rowe, and he is a former defense contractor and retired professor of aviation at Emory-Riddle Aeronautical University. He is also a survivor of the Korean War aerial duel in MiG Alley. He is former lieutenant No Kum-sok, pilot of the Korean People's Air Force. In September 1953 he flew his MiG-15 bis (improved) into South Korea and claimed political asylum. His aircraft—now exhibited at the U.S. Air Force Museum in Dayton, Ohio—was the first intact MiG to fall into the hands of Air Force intelligence. Ken Rowe, now sixty-nine but able to pass for fifty, smiles broadly as he begins his remarks. "Thanks for not shooting me down!"

No Kum-sok has told his story to many audiences since 1953, and he tells it well, consistent in the facts, clear about his state of mind, and unapologetic about his treason. He clearly regrets that his defection cost the lives of at least five people implicated by their association with him. One of them was his best friend, Lieutenant Kun Soo-sung, who knew his plan to defect and did not inform on him. Another may have been his uncle, You Ki-un, an officer who once vouched for No's dedication to Communism. Another was a battalion (aviation) vice commander who had also vouched for his loyalty. The others were in No's chain of command, and No regards their execution as a normal risk in Communist military forces. No Kum-sok also is clear that he did not defect for money. He claims he did not know of General Mark W. Clark's Operation Moolah, an offer of $100,000 to any MiG pilot who would fly his aircraft into United Nations Command's eager hands. The pamphlets did not reach his airbase in Manchuria, and no one had a radio that picked up transmissions unapproved by Kim Il-sung. He won himself and his future wife—as well as his three children and his mother—a good life in America without expectation of reward. It is clear that he believes his own countrymen would have executed him for political dissent had he not escaped.

No Kum-sok's journey to the cockpit of a first-line Soviet fighter interceptor, the vaunted Mikoyan-Gurevich 15, had the twists and turns of a jet in a dog-

U.S. AIR FORCE

**Lt. No Kum-sok, KPAF, 1953**

fight. Caught on the wrong side of the 38th Parallel in 1945, No had few options but to "break left" politically to survive and to enter the North Korean armed forces. The son of a middle manager and technician of a Japanese power company, No grew up in several company towns on northern Korea's eastern coast or along the Yalu River. His father, who specialized in railroad operations, advanced on his energy, technical expertise, athletic ability, penmanship, and fluency in Japanese. Mr. No was a Canadian Presbyterian, Mrs. No was a Catholic, but neither made their faith a matter of politics in the colonial Korea of the 1930s and 1940s. Young Kum-sok sometimes attended Protestant services and was always enrolled in good schools. He visited relatives in Hamhung and Sinhung, his parents' homes. He was an only child, and until 1945 his life was privileged. His father traveled extensively, even out of Korea, as part of the desperate effort to squeeze more efficiency out of the Japanese empire of the 1940s. The Japanese surrender shattered No Kum-sok's world.

The No family avoided the worst horrors of the initial Soviet occupation, which they saw in the mining-industrial city of Kanggye, but Mr. No could not adjust to the New Order. He went to Seoul across the Russian-patrolled 38th Parallel to collect his back wages of months and found the company office closed. He returned with a book about Abraham Lincoln for his son, as young No Kum-sok liked American history. His teachers tended to believe in America's goodness, the reconstruction of cooperative Japanese-American relations, and the essential evil of Communism. They soon lost their positions. Young No, however, found the Communist critique of Christianity attractive: It was based on silly Western notions, extolled pacifism, and stood in the way of progressive scientific materialism. Life turned hard even though the No family moved to Hamhung, living on savings, the sale of their household goods, and the generosity of relatives. No's uncle You, a fervent Communist, got young No into a good technical high school. Mr. No, a notorious anti-Communist, died of cancer in 1949, but his death did not remove the reactionary stigma from the No family. Kum-sok could not go to college, however fine his grades. In desperation he applied to the People's Naval Academy. First rejected because he admitted that his father worked for a Japanese company, No lied his way past the screening board on a second attempt by calling his father "an industrial worker." In July 1949 No Kum-sok left his widowed mother, who sold kitchen supplies, for the Naval Academy at Najin, a former Japanese naval base near the Russian border.

The Korean War caught No Kum-sok at the end of a difficult first year as a midshipman. The unrelenting oppression and chasm between what the cadre said was true Socialist behavior and the real system of exploitation and duplicity convinced Kum-sok that somehow he had to escape this Korea. After the war began, the academy moved to Chongjin so that classes could be held in bomb-proof railroad tunnels and obscure barracks. The curriculum was a mix of college physics and math, chemistry, meteorology, Communist indoctrination, Russian history, and infantry training. Kum-sok learned to get Bs on all subjects academic, ideological, and military. It was a "kind of living hell." Conditions worsened as North Korea imploded in defeat. Sometime in late September 1950, two-thirds of No's class were suddenly subjected to a battery of mysterious physical and mental tests. No Kum-sok was not part of the group, but he

**Mr. Kenneth Rowe, 2001**

talked his way into it, took the tests, and passed with ease. He had concluded that his class was about to furnish "volunteers" to reconstruct the North Korean air force, which, like the navy, had been largely destroyed in 1950. He guessed correctly and left for flight training in Manchuria. The Chinese were now in the war, but Kum-sok still thought the war would end before he qualified for combat flying.

No Kum-sok thought his pilot training would last a year, but in ten months his Russian instructors said he was ready to fly the MiG-15 against the American F-86s patrolling the Yalu air space. Lieutenant No doubted it, but being a first-line jet pilot had real advantages—if one could stay alive. The flight training was grueling, as predictable, but the food and quarters improved dramatically. Kum-sok thought the Russian instructors were competent but seemed mostly concerned about their vodka supply and going home. The Korean officers were, in his estimation, incompetent blowhards who thought party loyalty came before competence. The one overriding impression Kum-sok received throughout his flight training was that American pilots flying F-86s—even though outnumbered—ruled the skies. Even the MiG-15s with some flight advantages and heavy cannon could not drive off the F-86s, although the MiGs could make any daytime mission miserable for other United Nations aircraft. The Russian and Korean instructors pushed No's class hard. The class lost members because of poor performance and lack of political correctness. Of one hundred pilot candidates, seventy eventually qualified to fly. The MiG-15 pilots were required to complete one hundred solo hours (fifty in jets) before going to an operational squadron (Russian) stationed at one of the several bases near Andung on the Yalu. Even with a numerical inferiority of one to six, the American F-86s were keeping the MiGs at bay while other UNC aircraft attacked North Korean towns, railroads, and truck convoys.

When Lieutenant No Kum-sok reported to the Soviet 324th Fighter Air Division at Andung, the air war had taken its basic shape. The Russians and Chinese were not going to leave their base sanctuaries to undertake offensive air operations. They would fly to forty thousand feet inside Manchuria and dive as fast and far as their fuel allowed to attack American B-29 bombers, their principal targets. Any other tactical aircraft were, of course, fair game, but the Russians and Chinese first had to break through the combat air patrols mounted by the two U.S. Air Force wings of F-86 jet interceptors. The Soviet air expeditionary headquarters, the 64th Fighter Aviation Corps, had already mounted a major air defense campaign, deploying three fighter divisions (around 150 MiG-15s) and two more mixed divisions of support personnel, night fighters, naval aviation, and searchlight units. The MiG-15 pilots came from the Soviet Air Defense Force (PVO), not Frontal Aviation, and rotated to and from the Moscow air defense district. By war's end twelve MiG-15 divisions had rotated to and from Korea. The People's Liberation Army Air Force eventually deployed ten fighter divisions and two bomber divisions of an estimated eight hundred pilots and sixty thousand support personnel, all deployed in Manchuria. The Chinese might have moved aircraft into North Korea, but only after the reborn North Korean air force had moved south first to test American reaction. The first experiment in October to November 1951 showed early promise when the MiGs shot down four B-29s and damaged others after the Americans tried to bomb three new airfields in North Korea. The bombers returned to night operations and destroyed the fields. The North Korean air force sent a new MiG regiment to Uiju Air Base near Andung, where the Russians had placed some antiaircraft batteries. No Kum-sok was among the pilots chosen to break the American will to enter MiG Alley. He was nineteen years old.

For the next twenty months, Kum-sok flew more than a hundred combat missions as part of the standard twenty-four-aircraft formation employed by the North Koreans. He wrenched his MiG around the sky, occasionally blasting away at a distant target with his three cannon. He doubted that he ever hit an F-86, but he claimed kills, however fanciful, because every surviving MiG pilot did so. No experienced every limitation of the MiG-15: no radar, heavy stick, primitive avionics, substandard workmanship, high fuel consumption, a horizontal stabilizer on the tail that blocked his rear vision, no G-suit, and poor gun sights. His comrades perished all around him: killed in combat or air accidents, suicides, and even three executions for bad attitudes. No used his plane's high ceiling (fifty thousand feet) and ability to climb and turn to elude the F-86s. His anxiety rose in April 1952, when the Americans began to enter Manchurian air space in low-level attacks in order to pick off MiGs as they took off and landed. All the Communist air forces sought more aggressive engagements, but their own losses soared and never reduced the seven-to-one loss ratio produced by the

F-86s in aerial combat. On the ground No was a star party loyalist, leading self-criticism sessions and denouncing most of his senior officers for incompetence.

Behind his facade of ardent Communism, No Kum-sok thought about flying his MiG to South Korea. He knew that another pilot had flown south to freedom in May 1950, in an IL-10. So did No's superiors, who used a system of informers to ferret out any signs of disaffection. If No was to escape, he would need silence and patience. The futile conduct of the Communist air war fueled his determination; in a desperate effort to hurt the U.S. 5th Air Force in 1953, the Communist air commanders (only the Russian was a pilot) threw inexperienced pilots at the F-86s, which sent American "kills" soaring. In desperation, General Wang Dae-yong, the senior North Korean combat air commander, formed a special air regiment to train for low-level raids on American air bases around Seoul. As one flight leader, No Kum-sok studied his target with great care, Kimpo airfield. General Wang wanted to fly the mission, but the Russians vetoed the operation and had Wang relieved. Although the tempo of operations did not slow with an armistice in July 1953, No Kum-sok thought his chances of escape were improved, for his unit left Manchuria for an airfield just north of Pyongyang. His determination increased when he learned that his loyalty was again under review.

On September 21, 1953, Senior Lieutenant No Kum-sok turned a routine patrol into a dash for freedom. His crucial ploy was to convince his wingman to take off first and not fly in tight formation. When the wingman turned back to the north, No dropped to twenty-three thousand feet and went to maximum power. He landed at Kimpo against the flight pattern, much to the amazement of the American pilots taking off and landing. American radar did not pick up MiG-15 No. 2057. Avoiding a collision, No taxied to a halt, pulled back his canopy, and surrendered to about fifty excited American pilots and ground crewmen, all of them eager to shake hands. He handed his pistol to Captain Cipriano Guerra, USAF, and began a new odyssey to freedom and a life in America as Kenneth Rowe, intelligence expert on the North Korean air force, anti-Communist spokesman, media celebrity, and aviation consultant. He also suffered from anxiety and depression for more than twenty years. Now known as Ken Rowe, his best friends are the American pilots he flew against in the thin, cold air of MiG Alley.

# 12

## The Student Becomes
## a Soldier and a Scholar

**SEOUL, KOREA**
**July–August 2000**

Someone at the Korean War conference at Yonsei University asks me if I am still interviewing veterans of the war, and I reply that I am. My acquaintance points to a short, comfortably padded gentleman who is clearly friends with almost everyone in the conference room, a man who laughs easily and carries on three or four conversations at once in both English and Korean. "That's General Lee Tong-hui. He used to be the academic dean at the Korean Military Academy. He was a student volunteer in the war. He has many stories." Later I introduce myself to Brigadier General Lee Tong-hui and get his business card, and he agrees to an interview. About four weeks later we meet during a rainstorm in the coffee shop of the Seoul Plaza Hotel. We watch the traffic crawl by Duk-soo Palace and split onto the two boulevards divided by City Hall. General Lee and I start by talking about my Korean army graduate students whom he sent to Ohio State almost twenty years ago, and we agree that he had made good choices. One of them, Colonel Huh Nam-sung, is the dean of the faculty of the National Defense University and the other, Kim Kook-hoon, is a brigadier general and a leading Ministry of National Defense expert on arms control and international negotiations. He has just been to Pyongyang with President Kim Dae-jung.

General Lee recalls his early years and how he became involved in the army:

Who said I was a student volunteer? Well, I was a student, but I certainly didn't volunteer for anything. My father forced me into the South Korean army. I was born in Seoul in 1932, and I grew up here in the central city. My father was a minor official in the city government or in some business association; he eventually became secretary-general to the vice president of the Republic and an official in various commerce bureaus. So I grew up in relative comfort, and I went to Chong-dong High School, one of the best in Seoul. I wasn't a very good student, so I didn't get into one of the best universities when I graduated in 1950. When the war began I was studying for another round of exams and working part-time.

My memories of the first days of the war are still clear. I remember hearing the sound of firing in the distance, coming closer and closer to Seoul. Then on July 28 there was silence. Some of my friends came to my house and called me to come out in the street. They had red armbands on. Since my father was a government official, I worried about leaving the house, but I did, and I saw three T-34 tanks parked along the street. I also saw the Communist soldiers shoot some South Korean prisoners right there in the street. I ran back into the house.

Sometime that day or the next the Communist police came to our house and arrested my father. A young man who worked in my father's office betrayed him; this young man was the Communist cell leader in our neighborhood. I thought I'd never see my father again. The same day American bombers attacked Seoul, and the city around the railroad station and the military installations around Yongsan caught on fire. As we learned later, my father escaped in the chaos and went into hiding in the countryside. To avoid being drafted into the North Korean army, I left the city for my grandfather's farm near Onyang. Well, we all came home in September after the Marines liberated the city.

I still had a problem, however, because I had received orders to report for military training in the South Korean army earlier in June. This was a routine call-up for mandatory military training since I had been in a cadet corps in high school. Since the war had begun, I suppose I was technically a deserter or something. Who knew? My father thought he did, and he wanted revenge on the Communists, so he called some ROK army officials and asked them to come pick me up for military service. So one morning in October, a jeep pulled up to our house and the army took me away. I didn't have any shoes or personal items, so my father's driver brought me shoes, clothes, some money, a little food, and cleanliness items later to our assembly area at the Pi-won imperial garden. The assembly area was a mess, full of men of all ages and physical conditions. I couldn't believe the army wanted all these people. I couldn't believe it wanted me!

The Chinese intervention in late October sealed Lee Tong-hui's fate—he would be a soldier. The Rhee regime ordered complete conscription, complete mobilization, so complete and so hurried that thousands of Lee's fellow conscripts sickened and died before they ever saw a Chinese soldier. The disaster started with a hurried train trip south to Taegu and then on to Pusan. At first Tong-hui thought a long train ride would be fun; he had never been farther from home than Kaesong and Suwon. The train ride south became a nightmare—no toilets, no food, no heat, no place to sit or sleep in any comfort in a crowded boxcar, little water. The only thing that saved the reluctant soldiers was the slow trip and many stops; they could relieve themselves and buy food from the villagers along the tracks. Fortunately, Tong-hui left home with some money. After nine days the troop train finally reached Pusan.

I didn't know it at the time, of course, but I had become involved in the National Defense Corps scandal, but I was young and healthy enough to survive, and I eventually ended up at the Second Military Training Center near Pusan, a regular army basic training camp. Our barracks had been a primary school. There was no electricity. We had a sixteen-day training schedule, then off to the front to kill the Chinese invaders of our homeland—most likely to get killed ourselves. We learned to shoot the M-1 with only sixteen rounds or two clips per man. That was it. We drilled a lot, did some minor tactics. The instructors didn't know much more than we did, but they had some combat experience. Towards the end of our training we got our field equipment: a U.S. GI overcoat that dragged on the floor, a new M-1, two rice balls, maybe a cartridge belt and canteen, maybe a blanket, and a helmet. The helmets were much too big and heavy. We got canvas field boots; we had never seen anything like them. Fascinating. We were ready to go off to war. I imagine most of my comrades probably lasted two weeks.

I did not go off with the replacement company. The night before we were to depart, the company commander came around the barracks late at night and awakened a few of us and took us to the orderly room. He said he wanted to keep two or three of us for his training cadre and he would "requisition" the new trainers right now. A corporal gave us a test, which included the Chinese symbols for the rules for military sentries. Everyone cheated, but I didn't, and the company commander then told us he wanted honest soldiers, and he chose me to stay behind. So I became an NCO and a trainer. Our battalion commander then learned that my family had some standing in Seoul, so he asked me if I wouldn't like to be an officer, to go to OCS [Officers Candidate School]. I really didn't like the army or officers, but I thought maybe if I went to OCS, the war would be over before I was sent to the front. We didn't think the Americans would lose the war or accept any truce.

The battalion commander later said he thought I should go to the Korean

Military Academy, just reestablished at Chinhae as a four-year course. Four years! Certainly the war would be over before I graduated. I didn't think I could pass the entrance examinations, though, and I told the battalion commander about my academic deficiencies. I took some preliminary examinations and proved what I said was the truth. The battalion commander realized we had a problem, but he thought of a solution, too. He said he could transfer me to a training camp in Chollanam-do [South Cholla Province], and I could take the exams there, where the competition might not be too tough since Cholla schools were so poor. I needed a residence, though, and it happened that I could live with my uncle in Kwangju. He was a famous basketball player who had local influence. That might help, too. So off I went to Kwangju and away from the fighting.

The Grand Evasion worked as planned. Lee Tong-hui went to Kwangju and took the written examinations for admission to the Korean Military Academy. He also had to take an oral examination, conducted by Major General Lee Hyung-gun, who was the commanding general of the Field Training Command.

He was in exile for disobeying orders while he was commander of the 2nd Division in the defense of Seoul, but he was a graduate of the Japanese Imperial Military Academy. He liked to show how smart he was. The one thing I wanted to avoid was talking about mathematics and science, so I told him my hobby was reading the biographies of great men. He thought I meant Japanese and Koreans, but I said no, that I liked reading about British statesmen. He asked me who I thought was a great man and I said Benjamin Disraeli, even though I didn't know much about him. General Lee asked me which book about Disraeli I'd read. He thought I had read something in Japanese, but I told him I read European and British authors, and I gave him some names. I had no idea whether they had written about Disraeli, but neither did he. So I passed the interview, but I still had those written exams. The monitor helped me with the math section. When the results were posted, I had a final total score of 73. It was the highest score in Chollanam-do. I was in!

Lee Tong-hui went to Chinhae to become a member of the famous 11th Class of the Korean Military Academy, a class that included Chun Doo-hwon and Rho Tae-woo, future presidents of the Republic of Korea, and many of the officers who dominated the regimes of Park Chung-hee and their two classmates who succeeded him. The class formed on January 4, 1952, under the kindly observation of their great patrons, General James A. Van Fleet, U.S. Army, and President Syngman Rhee, whom some of them would help overthrow in 1960. General Lee for the first time realized that he had become part of something very important: the first real comprehensive test of an American undergraduate curriculum in the Republic of Korea. He thought it insured that

South Korean officers would be much better educated than any of their civilian peers.

> You see . . . we took the West Point curriculum in its complete form: mathematics, science, engineering, social science, humanities, and languages, the whole thing. No Korean university had that sort of comprehensive curriculum. They still don't today. Our advisor was a Lieutenant Colonel [Robert B.] McLane, who had graduated from West Point [1932] and taught Spanish there. He insisted on real exams, on giving grades that meant something, on even flunking people out, which meant that they went back to the war as common soldiers. We didn't start our classes with much enthusiasm, but we certainly started to be serious students when we realized what the penalties for failure might be. I actually learned that I was much smarter than I thought, but perhaps I simply worked harder. In any event, I became a real soldier and a serious student at Chinhae, and I graduated well up in my class in 1956. Of course, the war had ended by then, too.

Lee Tong-hui became an important member of Korea's first generation of soldier scholars, a concerted effort by modernizers within the South Korean army to be more like their U.S. Army counterparts and to deal with the Korean political elite with equal educational self-confidence—or arrogance, as the case may be. When Park Chung-hee became president, he insured that officers penetrated the most important universities. Lee Tong-hui went to Seoul National University and became one of the first five Koreans to earn a Ph.D. in political science in their native land and the first soldier to do so. He served thirty years as a faculty member of the Korean Military Academy, reaching the positions of department head and academic dean. Since his retirement in 1986, he has championed educational reform in Korea and is often a featured speaker and planner in many Korean associations dedicated to internationalism and educational modernization. The reluctant nonvolunteer of 1950 still serves his nation in many ways.

# 13

## The Odd Couple
## Makes the Great Escape

For Kim Chae-pil, the son of an affluent farmer-landholder and Presbyterian elder of Pyonggannam-do province, war and political oppression had stolen most of his life as a young man. Still a teenager, he had been impressed by the Japanese to be a defense construction laborer on Okinawa, where he ended the Pacific war as an American prisoner of war. Kim liked the kindly Americans and learned some English. His Christianity helped bridge the cultural gap. He also had learned to drive and maintain a truck, his ultimate salvation. In late 1945 Kim returned home and went back to school, but as the vise of Korean Communism tightened, Kim lost his place in school, denounced as a Christian and an oppressor of the people. He was sentenced to be a truck driver, hauling salt from a saltworks to distribution centers throughout the province. One night in September 1947 his ordeal took another turn—for the worse.

After another exhausting day driving his salt truck over mountain roads, Kim Chae-pil came home to find a surprise guest, a Mr. Chai, his favorite middle school teacher. Chai had been banished to a school in Sinuiju on the Yalu River for attempting to keep Kim in school, and had become implicated in a student protest that the Communists had crushed with force. Chai was on the run and headed south for Seoul. He wanted Kim to go with him. The idea stunned Kim. He would be leaving his family. "Seoul was so divorced from our world, as far, as inaccessible as Jerusalem." Kim had considered fleeing south in an abstract sense, but "the reality of my life and our surroundings commanded my absolute attention." At least he could listen to Chai's plan, an overland walk across the border to Kaesong, aided by friends. They talked until they fell into an exhausted sleep. Kim awoke still uncertain about his choice and began to pray. Then, to the howl of the family dogs, a squad of police stormed the Kim home and arrested Kim and Chai amid the screams of the Kim family. Days later, after incessant beating, Kim confessed to antipeople conspiracy and received a sentence of life imprisonment at hard labor. Kim went north, not south.

For three years Kim Chae-pil worked on construction projects around the city of Sinuiju. Like his fellow prisoners, his health failed when the police cut the food ration by two-thirds. The Korean People's Army needed the food more than the traitors. More prisoners died, and Kim thought he might as well lie down and never get up. Then in February 1950 the authorities told him to go home, a complete surprise. He struggled back to Namyang and shocked his family and neighbors. He was alive but looked dead. His mother nursed him back to health, mostly by feeding him. By April he felt healthy and carefree. "It was the happiest phase of my life."

Then the People's Police came again and took Kim Chae-pil away to join the Korean People's Army. His freedom had been nothing but recuperative leave from state service. Kim left home again to his mother's sobs, and before the day's end he had "volunteered" for the army rather than return to prison or worse. The recruiting policeman told Kim and the other "reactionary" youths that their "past crimes" had been forgiven. Kim received orders to a paramilitary unit of the Security Bureau, Ministry of the Interior. His job was to stockpile ammunition for the columns of soldiers, tanks, and artillery moving south into mountain hiding places. He also saw a teenager executed for asking for leave to see his mother. Kim worked hard, drove trucks and jeeps with skill, and listened but said little. When the invasion began, he was a full-time truck driver, and he began to think of ways to drive to the Republic of Korea, provided there still was one. Then one day, Kim fell asleep and ran his truck into a mountain cliff. The truck blew up, killing the guard detail, but a burned Kim survived and staggered back home, where he hid for four months. The police found him again and hustled him off with other deserters. Pyongyang had fallen to the Americans and "puppet troops."

In an orgy of political cleansing, the People's Police rounded up and executed enemies of the state by the thousands, and throughout North Korea anti-Communist partisans struck back. A group of guerrillas found the convoy of deserters stalled on a mountain road to Sinuiju and attacked just as the police appeared, ready to lighten their human burden with a hail of gunfire. Kim survived the battle but could not escape the police, who won the firefight but lost their lust for slaughter. The convoy reached a city in chaos as the remnants of the People's Army reorganized for a last stand to hold the Sinuiju bridgehead for the Chinese People's Volunteers Force, reportedly on the march to the rescue. Instead of a bullet in the head, Kim Chae-pil received another vehicle to drive—a captured American GMC two-and-a-half-ton cargo truck. To prove his indispensability to his officers, Kim immediately started stealing truck parts from Chinese convoys for his own and other vehicles. Within six months he was a trusted member of the KPA, with the rank of senior sergeant. His skilled night driving spared him from American air attacks. He had become indispensable, but he had not abandoned his latent hope that he would someday defect.

One night in late August 1951 Kim Chae-pil's luck began to change for the better, through prayer and quick thinking. With three security officers, Kim and his truck were hauling furniture north to a new People's Army headquarters, but dawn found them short of their destination. They camouflaged the truck and then hiked to a nearby village to eat and bathe. They were drinking from a village well when a very elderly, very excited farmer ran up to them and screamed for help. The farmer had just stumbled across some sort of beast in the woods, something or someone crawling on hands and knees in the bushes, moaning, wearing tattered clothes of some sort, but red-skinned and very hairy like an ape. The farmer had run back to the village in fright, but no villager or the police would confront the beast. Would the comrade soldiers save them? Senior Sergeant Kim Chae-pil was about to meet Captain Ward M. Millar, U.S. Air Force.

The second half of the odd couple had just experienced enough misfortune to qualify as a Korean. Millar, considered "a substantial pilot" by the commander of the 49th Fighter-Bomber Group (F-80's), had been called to active duty in October 1950, from his junior year (studying physics) at Reed College in Portland, Oregon. As a former P-38 pilot, Millar had GI Bill benefits, but with a wife and daughter to support he needed the drill pay of an Air Force Reservist. When mobilized, he flew transports to Japan and then from Japan. He did not like flying C-54s. He also knew that one-hundred-mission combat pilots rotated back to the United States—and perhaps back to civilian life. He had talked his way into the 49th Fighter-Bomber Group, and by the end of May 1951 he had flown twenty-eight missions in thirty days. Then he became mired in squadron paperwork. On June 11 he flew his thirtieth—and last—mission. After his flight struck a Chinese troop concentration north of Seoul, Millar found himself trapped in a burning F-80 with a napalm canister stuck under his right wing and little remaining fuel. Having no time for an escape flight and no taste for disappearing in a fireball, Millar fought his way through a jammed canopy, popped his chute, separated from his seat, and hurtled into a mountain valley. He broke both ankles in landing or in clearing the cockpit. He also landed near the Chinese he had just strafed and bombed.

Ward Millar was about to become part of a select group of three U.S. Air Force pilots who were actually captured by the Chinese and North Koreans and subsequently escaped. During the Korean War 1,690 U.S. Air Force pilots and other air crewmen crashed or parachuted into enemy territory. Only 175 were rescued by helicopter or some combination of air-sea rescue service boats and amphibian airplanes. Another 155 air crewmen most certainly died in observed crashes. The remaining 1,360 became "missing in action." Of this group the Air Force decided that 263 were most certainly captured, and 248 of these officers and airmen returned to American custody during the prisoner exchanges of 1953. In 1955 the Chinese released fifteen more captive airmen they had jailed as "war criminals." Of the remaining 1,097 only three—Captain William D. Locke, First Lieutenant Melvin J. Shadduck, and Captain Ward Millar—survived crashes, parachute rides, and captivity.

When Kim Chae-pil met Ward Millar, the American pilot had already spent eighty-five days behind enemy lines because his broken ankles and the prompt actions of the Chinese had prevented his rescue. Since his first capture he had spent his time lying in Chinese hospitals or escaping from Chinese hospitals while being trucked up and down Korea's west coast. He had been almost always sick as well as crippled, and he was starving to death. He had bartered and sold personal effects to survive and he had stolen food, but his ankles never healed, so when he escaped he had to crawl after walking with extemporized crutches became unbearable. When Kim found Millar, the captain had been loose for ten days and had been reduced to crawling south. With torn and bloodstained jacket and flight suit, wild and matted long red hair, and gaunt face and body, Millar scared Kim, too, but Kim had a pistol drawn and two armed political officers behind him. Millar's only weapon was a wooden cross, a religious symbol, of course, but part crawling stick as well.

In retrospect, the Korean sergeant and American captain could not remember which languages they used to communicate with each other. Millar tried to use pidgin Chinese, which Kim recalled as incomprehensible. Kim thought he asked Millar if he was an American in English, but the captain thought Kim used Korean or Japanese. They agree on one part of the conversation. Kim asked Millar: *ki do kyo?* Christian? Millar nodded. "Jesus and Mary?" Kim said in English. Millar almost collapsed in amazement since he knew nothing of the history of Korean Christianity. He immediately realized he would never escape without help, and now he had found one Korean who might aid him.

Slowly over the next two days the Kim-Millar alliance formed for the desperate mission ahead, a dual escape from North Korea. The obstacles looked insurmountable. Kim realized that Millar could not walk; he would have to ride or be carried. Moreover, Kim had to deceive his three comrades and persuade them to leave him alone with Millar. Kim doubted that he and Millar could either reach the coast or cross Communist lines. Their only hope was to attract American aircraft, convince them they were friendly and required rescue, place themselves where a helicopter could reach and evacuate them, and do all this without getting killed or, worse, recaptured by the Communists. It was a good thing that the odds did not concern them, only survival. The burden of the operation fell on Sergeant Kim.

The most immediate challenge Kim addressed was getting Millar in shape to travel and under his own control. Kim carried Millar back to the farm village and fed him rice and fruit, while refusing to surrender the pilot to a curious patrol of the People's Police. Having promised the police and his escort that he would take Millar north, Kim told his party he would get the truck, which he did. He then drove it into a muddy creek bed and left the ignition on so that the battery would be dead when they finally pulled it out. Kim also tried to get to know Millar better in a conversation in broken English, Chinese, Korean, and dramatic pantomime. They established that Millar might walk a mile a day but Kim could carry him ten. Kim proved his commitment by carrying the dysentery-stricken Millar to an outhouse and washing his scabrous clothes. In the meantime the North Korean soldiers and villagers dragged the truck onto the road. It did not start. Kim flew into a convincing rage and persuaded his escort to accept a new scheme.

Having recharged the battery to prove his special competence, Kim persuaded the three officers that they should take a longer route that would reduce the chance of air attack and produce a smoother ride for the truck and cargo. The route also narrowed the distance to the front. On the night of September 4, the odd couple and the three officers headed south. Everyone marveled at Millar's good humor and new vigor. When the truck reached the point closest to the front, Kim stalled the engine, opened the hood, and announced the truck needed gas. One of the officers marched off to a People's Army depot and returned in a Russian jeep with a barrel of gas and a KPA intelligence officer. Kim decided that he needed to close his dramatic deception and start overland. When all the officers fell asleep, Kim awakened Millar, packed their essential survival gear, including a spare headlight and battery for signaling, and headed into the mountains. Kim became a human *chige,* or Korean A-frame. The air rescue option looked better and better as Kim struggled up a mountain with Millar on his back. Fortune again smiled on the two good men. Kim had learned that an F-51 had crashed nearby two days before, killing the pilot. The Air Force, however, was still sending planes over the crash site. They decided after three nights of using the headlight as an SOS beacon that American planes would not respond to a suspected flak trap. Kim raided a nearby village for a mirror for daytime signaling.

The wanderers were not yet out of the woods. After repeated failures to attract American aircraft, they finally reached a low-flying F-80 with the SOS— or so they thought when the F-80 made an unprovoked wingover. They were thrilled then when four F-80s roared in a couple of hours later—and strafed the village where they had taken refuge. No one was hurt. Now desperate to the point of exhaustion, Kim and Millar went to a clearing the next day, September 10, 1951. Millar put on his orange "Mae West" and flight jacket; Kim trimmed Millar's wild hair and beard. That afternoon they attracted another lone F-80, which circled the clearing several times while Millar danced wildly in the open. Kim stayed hidden, keeping alert for enemy patrols. The race for rescue now changed from a marathon to a 100-meter dash. Four F-80s arrived at the same time a North Korean patrol opened fire from the village. Four Marine Corsairs continued the air strikes, and then four F-51s replaced the Corsairs. Finally, an Air Force Sikorsky H-19A rescue helicopter arrived. As the rifle fire became louder, Kim raced past Millar and almost ran into the rear rotor blade. Millar pushed him toward the door, where a stunned crew chief took aboard an armed North Korean sergeant and a hobbling, bearded scarecrow in the remains of a flight suit. Millar reassured the crew chief that the odd couple was friendly, and off the helicopter roared to an air base on Seoul's Youi-do Island. They were free.

But only fairy tales, not war stories, have completely happy endings. For Ward Millar the war was over, but the ordeal of leg operations and physical therapy had just begun. He returned to flying two years before he could walk or run normally, but he remained in the Air Force a decorated, honored hero. As long as Ward Millar's presence protected Kim Chae-pil, his "brother" as the odd couple called each other, the Korean hero received the grateful thanks of the U.S. Air Force. Korean army counterintelligence agents, however, claimed Kim was a double agent, asserted their jurisdiction, and bundled him off to the Cheju-do Island prison camp, where Kim barely survived repeated beatings and torture from hard-core Communist resisters. He finally convinced ROK interrogators that his religion and defection were sincere.

His status changed to "internee," Kim was one of the twenty-seven thousand "good Koreans" freed in June 1953 by Syngman Rhee's orders to his army's Provost Marshal Command and against American wishes. By 1954 Kim had reestablished his contacts in the U.S. Air Force, which helped him clear his record of all suspicion of treason and gave him a reward for saving Millar. Kim then found a job as a driver for Dr. Pai Min-soo, a prominent Seoul physician and Christian layleader. He could now pray for others' freedom.

# 14

## Sonny

**YONGSAN, SEOUL, KOREA**
**July 8, 1996**

onny Pang, fifty-seven, sits comfortably in his cramped office near his own
fiefdom, the Hartell House, an attractive officers club at Yongsan that caters
principally to the senior American and Korean officers of Combined Forces
Command. In fact, the club is a rendezvous for active and retired senior officers
of the South Korean army, and Sonny Pang is their master of the house. Sonny
Pang, of course, is not really Sonny Pang, and he has never served a day in the
Korean army. Nevertheless, he is a veteran of the Korean War, and he is a survivor. His name at birth, Pong Sun-kuk, did not survive years of Americanization;
for the record, he is Master Sergeant Sun K. Pang, U.S. Army (Ret.), a twenty-
year regular, whose office walls display a large number of autographed pictures
of prominent American political and military leaders and the usual display of
medals. Sonny Pang has a Meritorious Service Medal and Army Commendation
Medal, predictable awards for a senior NCO. The Legion of Merit is more unusual. I first met Sonny Pang in 1991, and the person who made the introduction
was an old friend, Major General Bill Eshelman, USMC, then the J-5 of Combined Forces Command. That night Sonny Pang wore the lapel pin of the 45th
Infantry Division (Oklahoma National Guard). That fact, which Bill mentioned

in passing when he said that Sonny went up to the DMZ almost every week to meditate, suggested that Sonny Pang had known war long before he entered the U.S. Army.

Sonny Pang has told his story often, and I had heard parts of it before, but it loses nothing in the telling, and there is always something new.

I came from a large and relatively well-off family in a village, Hwang-ju, just twenty miles south of Pyongyang. I was born in 1939, one of ten children. Almost everyone in the village was a relative of some sort. My father was a successful farmer. His apples went to the best markets in Pyongyang, which served the Japanese. We raised corn, beans, and rice, too. Even after the end of World War II, when the Japanese left, we made a good living, but the Communists clearly saw my father as a class enemy. We had one advantage, and that was that one of my uncles was an important Communist leader in our district, and he protected our family. Another of my uncles served in the North Korean security forces. Many of my cousins were Communists, and the Communist propaganda in our schools when I was a child was so effective that I probably would have been a Communist, too. The Communists told my father's farm laborers and domestic help that they did not have to serve a class enemy, but many of them stayed and worked anyway. My father built a home for some of our help, which bought us some time with the Communists. Nevertheless, we feared the future. The Communists continued to tell us that the Americans would kill us and rape the girls when we had a war with them and the "Rhee puppet regime."

I was eleven years old when the war began, and except for the fact that many of the young men in our village had to join the North Korean army, I don't remember anything special about the war until October 1950 except some fear of U.N. air attacks, which the Communists said were Russian planes on exercises. We had air-raid drills mostly diving into haystacks. When the U.N. forces crossed the 38th Parallel and marched toward Pyongyang, the whole Communist party structure and security forces came apart. My uncles and their families tried to flee, but many of the local non-Communists took the law into their own hands, killing party members and officials, burning their property, and beating and imprisoning their families. When the South Korean army and police arrived, they and the militia wanted to exterminate anyone suspected of Communist sympathies. My father, who hated Communism, became head of the local home guards, but he used his position to shield my two uncles and their families from the ROK police.

It was a bitter time for all of us. I know that some of my cousins killed some of my other cousins. Then the Chinese intervened, and the tables turned again. Even before U.N. forces retreated south, one of my uncles advised my father to flee south of the 38th Parallel. My father did not take the advice, but my second-born sister's husband, who worked for the railroad, arranged for some of the family to leave. We had no idea that we would never return. We thought the rest of the family would follow us soon, too. My brother-in-law and my sister had just had a baby son, and they feared he would die without better food, which they thought they would find in the south. My sixteen-year-old brother, Sun Cho, went with us, but everyone else stayed at home. I have never seen any of them since late October 1950.

Our ride to South Korea was a nightmare, but at least my brother-in-law's influence allowed us to ride inside one of the cattle cars with reasonable space. The people riding on the roof were not so fortunate. When we started to go through tunnels, many of them were swept off the roof. I remember hearing screams and seeing blood seeping through the roof of the car. We had U.S. Army engineers aboard, and I think they destroyed some bridges after the train passed over them. We all were confused, hungry, cold, and very frightened, so I'm not sure exactly what happened. I do know we got to Seoul, and I remember thinking how well dressed the people in Seoul station were. That should give you an idea of what poor shape we were in. We eventually got as far south as Pyongtaek when we were turned back. My brother and I just wandered around begging and living with other refugees.

We eventually arrived in Inchon on our way back to North Korea—we hoped—since the food and shelter at home, however meager, would have been better than our life in the south. We followed the U.N. lines north as the army fought its way back toward the 38th Parallel. In Inchon we heard that the Seoul fire department wanted to hire new men, so we bluffed our way into the group. I was only twelve but tall for my age, so I managed to sneak into the group. Well, we didn't go to Seoul, but to Uijongbu, where we became laborers for the U.S. 1st Cavalry Division. We built fortifications for the Americans, and they fed us. Then one day a big sergeant called me out of line and asked me if I would work for his battalion. My brother said I should go since these Americans might give me lighter work and feed me better. The last time I saw my brother was when I got into that GI jeep. We drove to another camp, and I got a haircut—GI—my first real shower, complete with soap and a clean towel. Then I got a GI meal, the most food I had ever eaten in my life. The GIs watched me eat with amusement, but then I got sick, and I stayed sick for three days. I still have trouble eating mashed potatoes and gravy.

Sonny Pang, now called simply "Skoshi" by the GIs, worked around the mess hall and did errands for the mess personnel. When the 1st Cavalry Division left Korea for Japan, the GIs arranged for the incoming 45th Infantry Division to keep Skoshi around. Sonny remembers the Oklahoma Guardsmen as even bigger and friendlier than his former protectors.

I thought I was learning English pretty good, but these guys sure sounded strange to me. I missed my own family terribly, but the GIs got me clothes and food from their families. I had it pretty good for a kid. I think this was around December 1951. Anyway, I really felt bad when I learned from some other Koreans that my brother had died with his Korean Service Corps company. These guys said he'd just been found dead one morning in his tent. Someone said he had a heart attack, but, hell, he was only eighteen. I suppose it could happen. Maybe someone else killed him, but who knows. All I knew was that my brother, our father's oldest son, was dead. I couldn't even find out what had happened to his body except that it was cremated and sent to some warehouse in Inchon. His company commander said he had made the proper arrangements, but I really didn't know just what happened. My life with the 3rd Battalion, 179th Infantry went on as usual from day to day. I had no idea what would happen to me.

Learning that an ROK division had moved into the line next to the 45th Division in the "Iron Triangle" sector, Sonny and a friend left camp one day, looking for a meal of rice and *kimchi*. They got their meal, but not safe passage home. South Korean MPs arrested them and demanded their ID cards, which they did not have. When the MPs discovered they were both from North Korea, they were arrested and imprisoned as guerrillas. Sonny believes that he would have been shot without any further cause.

After seven days of beatings, I believed I would die, but then I heard a familiar voice, that of Lieutenant Young, one of our battalion officers. Since he was a black man, he was easy to recognize. The Army didn't have many black officers in those days. He was a first-class guy and very intimidating, very persuasive. He made sure I understood that he had worked hard to find me and rescue me. I promised not to leave the battalion again. Lieutenant Young turned toward me and told me that he had bought my freedom for six bottles of Scotch. That really impressed me, since six bottles of Scotch could buy a lot in Korea in those days.

Sonny Pang finished his war with the 45th Infantry Division as a kitchen helper, interpreter, scout, and jack-of-all-trades for his battalion. Once he found himself abandoned during a short withdrawal when he and a GI fell asleep in a jeep trailer. Finding themselves in no-man's-land, he and the GI started running south, but they soon ran into a jeep load of GIs who had come back to get them when they had been discovered missing. The incident only strengthened Sonny's conviction that he wanted to get to the United States, a goal his GI buddies encouraged with promises of sponsorship and adoption. When the division shipped out, however, Sonny stayed in Korea without sponsors, money, and prospects. He was fourteen years old.

Sonny Pang worked hard to find himself a place in postwar Korea. He had learned enough English and American habits to make himself indispensable to a series of American employers in the club business around Seoul. He also worked as a transportation clerk for the Army and discovered that his sister, brother-in-law, and nephew were still alive. This discovery raised his spirits, but he still wanted to go to America. He kept working and hoping, but he became sick and lost his job. However, he eventually found employment with an American firm that sold liquor to military clubs. Sonny married a Korean girl and kept working. In 1963 a group of American sergeants at Camp Page raised the money and did the paperwork necessary to get Sonny on a plane for America. After two years of family separation and marginal employment in Milwaukee and Chicago, he joined the U.S. Army in order to return to Korea and his family. His undocumented personal history and security requirements delayed his enlistment until June 1966, a year the Army quit being too demanding about volunteers. Sonny requested assignment to Korea, not a choice assignment, and he eventually served three tours in his native country. His family always remained in Korea even if he had to take an "overseas" assignment to the United States. Sonny Pang's son became an officer in the U.S. Army after graduating from Johns Hopkins University with two degrees, in electrical engineering and in computer science. Sonny's two daughters, also graduates of Seoul American High School at Yongsan, have American university degrees.

Sonny Pang's life is still not free of surprises. Just after I met him in 1991, he arranged a Korean pilgrimage for many of his comrades of the 45th Infantry Division. When he rallied with his buddies at a downtown Seoul hotel, he found he was not included on the guest list for a visit to the National Cemetery. Upset, he rushed back to his office and called a Korean general (one of the few he respected) and poured out his complaints about his unjust fate. The general gave him a number to call at the cemetery, but when Sonny reached the man at the other end of the line, his ire had seeped away. Instead of arguing his way onto the invitation list for a grand ceremony, he impulsively asked whether the cemetery official had any record of his brother's remains. He still has no idea why he asked the question. The man on the other end of the line switched Sonny to the woman who answered location inquiries and she asked him questions about his brother's name, family background, and home. Much to Sonny's amazement, she knew Sun-cho's father's name and his place of birth. Sun-cho's ashes had not disappeared into the ocean—the Korean equivalent of a pauper's grave—but now rested in Site 90, Section 17 at the National Cemetery. Although he worries that young Koreans no longer see unification as a national goal, Sonny Pang now spends more time at his brother's grave than he does at the DMZ. He still hopes that he will see unification. "Someday I would like to return to my village in a free and unified Korea, to pray at the tombs of my ancestors and eat an apple from a tree in my father's orchard."

# 15

## Birth of an Army
## and a General

SEOUL, KOREA, December 1994 through
WASHINGTON, D.C., June 2001

The road of discovery that took me to the "real" Jim Hausman started with one of his closest friends and colleagues, Major General Lim Sun-ha, ROKA (Ret.), and the two of them convinced me that the full story of the Korean Constabulary and the U.S. Korean Military Advisory Group (KMAG) had not been told. Early in my research on the postwar American occupation of Korea, I learned that an unknown American captain (a major in 1950) named James H. Hausman Jr. was the brains and moral force behind the suppression of the 1948 insurgency that challenged the creation of the Republic of Korea. From the treatment Hausman received from revisionist historians like Bruce Cumings and Callum MacDonald, I concluded that he must have been the most powerful villain in Korean history, an equal of Hideyoshi Toyotomi in terms of Korean blood callously spilled in the name of tyranny and foreign domination. Later a disaffected Korean expatriate in the United States used the Internet to accuse Hausman of atrocities against Korean civilians and of being a champion of military tyranny. The attacks upon Hausman were, of course, laughable, but they were based on one central fact: More than any other one man, Jim Hausman created the South Korean army in 1946 to 1950.

There was nothing in Jim Hausman's military background to suggest a special magic for forming foreign armies and dealing with postcolonial politicians, let alone the American civilian and military governmental bureaucracy. A pre-1941 U.S. Army enlisted man, he became an infantry officer during World War II and spent most of the war training troops in the United States. He managed to join a late-deploying infantry division that arrived in Europe in time for the Battle of the Bulge, and he was wounded and frostbitten while serving as a battalion operations officer. To remain on active duty—he was only a temporary officer—Hausman volunteered for civil affairs duty in Japan, but found himself in Korea instead. He was a reserve captain, which meant that he could be released anytime as the Army demobilized. The personnel wizards assigned him to duty with the Department of Internal Security, run by an American colonel named Terrill "Terrible" Price, who was trying to organize the Korean National Police and a paramilitary police reserve, the Korean Constabulary. After a short tour as a regimental advisor, Hausman transferred to the office of the Constabulary chief, Lieutenant Colonel Russell D. Barros, a former National Guard officer who escaped captivity in the Philippines to become a guerrilla leader. Working in Barros's office when Hausman arrived (August 1946) was a twenty-three-year-old Korean lieutenant named Lim Sun-ha. In all our conversations since our first luncheon in the KMAG Club in 1994 at Yongsan, Lim Sun-ha has been consistent in his praise for Barros and Hausman, who became Barros's executive officer.

I returned to Korea from Japan after World War II along with thousands of other Koreans, including military veterans. I had been a student in British law and literature at Meiji University when I was forced into the Japanese army along with thirty-five hundred other Korean students majoring in the liberal arts. When Japan surrendered, I was a lieutenant in the Japanese army assigned to administrative duties, since a Korean officer could not command Japanese troops. My family, which came from a town near Wonsan, had always been well-to-do and valued education. As a student in wartime, however, I had to participate in military training, so I was a *hakpyong,* or university cadet, subject to active duty. I was called up in January 1944 to attend an officer candidate school. Some Korean students, especially Choi Hong-hi and Kim Wan-yong in Pyongyang, used the Japanese army as a place to organize a pro-Allied resistance movement and revolt in 1944. After they were released from prison in August 1945, they became Constabulary officers. Just like every other unemployed veteran, I went home and found the Russians and Communists already in control, so I went to Seoul since I heard the Americans were organizing some sort of army there. I thought my English language ability and my experience in the Japanese army would help me get a commission.

Lim Sun-ha arrived in Seoul just as the Korean Constabulary of seven American officers and a former colonel in the Japanese army was screening applicants for commissions and setting up training posts near Seoul. Given the unhappiness of the Korean National Police at seeing a rival organization created and the lust of every political faction (including the Communists) to dominate or discredit the Constabulary, selecting officers was a political as well as a professional enterprise. Many Koreans with Chinese military experience or as guerrilla leaders refused to participate in what they believed would simply be the re-creation of a colonial Japanese army formed by Koreans. In fact, the first 110 commissioned officers who became "the First Class" and "the

**Maj. Gen. Lim Sun-ha, ROK Army, 1953**

Association of Founders of the Korean Army" had military experience, and all but twelve of them had been officers. The inner elite were twelve Koreans who had attended the Imperial Japanese Military Academy. Their competitors were an equal number of graduates of the Manchukuo Military Academy, the source of officers for the multinational Manchukuo army, responsible for the internal security of Manchuria. The officers who served in Manchuria had the advantage of combat experience since they commanded ethnic Korean counterpartisan units; the two most prominent generals of the Korean War, Chung Il-kwon and Paik Sun-yup, were veterans of Manchurian service. The largest single group of new officers were, like Lim Sun-ha, *hakpyong* who had spent a year or so as lieutenants from 1944 to 1945 and seldom were more than twenty-five years old. "As a group we were well-educated, reform-minded, nationalistic, hard-working, middle-class, and ambitious," Lim Sun-ha recalls. "Many of us knew a little English, and we were pro-American." There is no firm evidence on some other factors that shaped these men—especially their uncompromising opposition to Communism—but many seem to have come from Christian families (certainly the Paik brothers did), and they were refugees from northern

Korea. There is no argument about their influence. Seventy-eight of the officers commissioned between January and April 1946 became generals, and thirteen of them served as chief of staff of the South Korean army.

"We wanted to be the officers of a new Korean army, a modern army, an army of a democracy, but we didn't know how to become such an army. Some of us thought the key was working hard, learning all we could from the Americans, many of whom worked much harder than Japanese officers ever did. We expected to handle the troop training, not turn it over to the NCOs, not that we had many of them either." Sun-ha remembers how difficult it was to abandon the ways of the Japanese army. Officers appeared in riding boots, fancy leather belts, and samurai swords; others slapped and kicked their troops for mistakes. A group of sergeants mutinied and almost beat Chung Il-kwon and two other company commanders to death for their brutality, insensitivity, and misuse of military supplies. The American advisors did their best to set new standards, but there were too few of them, and some of the Americans were either too young and inexperienced or simply serving time. The American military government, however, forged ahead with Plan Bamboo, a scheme to create a Constabulary of twenty-five thousand officers and men who could relieve the U.S. Army's XXIV Corps (two half-strength infantry divisions in 1946) of any civil disturbance duties and the protection of economic assets and government property, all targets of theft and vandalism.

The Americans wanted us to expand as quickly as possible, so it was hard to screen people for political backgrounds or to train them except in active units. Companies split to become battalions, battalions to become regiments, and, too soon, regiments to become brigades. Between 1946 and 1950 I was promoted from lieutenant to colonel.

Jim Hausman was the man who kept us on the right track, largely because he had a positive attitude and developed strong personal ties to many of our officers and, eventually, with Syngman Rhee. Jim was a great role model for us; he knew infantry training, army organization, and operations. His relations with the American senior officers were almost always good, because they didn't want to deal with us. He protected us from the Korean National Police, who accused us of being a haven for Communists, which was true to some extent. From April 1948 on we were always at war, and that war continued after the armistice in 1953. We faced the Cheju-do Rebellion and then the guerrilla war that followed the Yosu-Sunchon uprising. Then the Communists sent guerrilla columns across the 38th Parallel, and we had a border war in 1949 and 1950 that really had not ended when the Communists attacked on 25 June. The Constabulary became the South Korean army in December 1948, but we were still a light infantry, counterpartisan force, not a real army with armor and artillery. Jim did his best to send officers to the United States—and I was one of them—and Japan for training with American troops. He tried to rotate units out of the field from the counterguerrilla campaign for training, but it was almost impossible to both expand to one hundred thousand men and improve. KMAG rated one-third of our battalions combat-ready in 1950, and that was a generous assessment.

Lim Sun-ha remembers how personal relations and factionalism made building a cohesive officer corps almost impossible.

The recruitment process for the Second and Third Classes for the Officer Training School was very careless, and these two classes produced some of the most radical and politicized officers in the army. One of them was Park Chung-hee, who was a Communist in those days and a subversive dedicated to the overthrow of the Rhee regime. He was sentenced to death for mutiny and treason, but he was pardoned after June 1950 and eventually returned to the army in 1951. When he became the leader of the military junta in 1960 and dictator in 1961, he got his vengeance on those of us he identified as too pro-American, as northern Koreans, as supporters of Syngman Rhee, and his enemies in 1949. Basically, he forced twenty of us out of the army and cut our pensions. Our biggest problems in those early days, however, were senior officers without troop-leading experience appointed directly by President Rhee. One of his favorites, Won Yong-duk, had been a medical officer in the Japanese army, but more importantly he had wide connections in the elite of Seoul society. Then we had several mutinies after Yosu-Sunchon and defections to the Communists, something like eight or ten officers from the first 1946 group alone. President Rhee played people and factions off against one another. That was his idea of how to control the officers, not to build a professional ethos in the army.

Lim Sun-ha remembers a sense of foreboding that grew within the army in 1950 as he and his fellow officers saw the growing signs of an impending invasion. President Rhee would do nothing to alarm the Americans, and the senior KMAG officers would not take the predictions of disaster seriously enough to press the issue of rearmament in Washington.

We had no illusions about our ability to stop the North Koreans without aircraft, tanks, mines, and heavy artillery. Of course, some of our generals made costly mistakes in the first three days of the war, but the Americans had the same problems we did when they entered the battle—poor antitank weapons, not enough good ammunition, poor air-ground coordination, too few fighting soldiers, and substantial leadership failures. Jim Hausman and I saw it all. He stayed with the ROK army headquarters—which meant Chung Il-kwon after July—and I was in charge of the Korean liaison mission to the 8th Army. With the exception of General [William F.] Dean, the American generals didn't know anything about Korea. They paid hardly any attention to our army since commanding their own army was a challenge. Our relations with the 8th Army didn't improve until General [James A.] Van Fleet became 8th Army commander. During this period I became a general at the age of twenty-eight and commanded the Infantry School. In the meantime, Jim was reassigned to the Pentagon. We missed his influence in dealing with the Americans and President Rhee.

In 1952 Brigadier General Lim Sun-ha became the commander of the ROK 3rd Division, which had fought well from the very beginning of the war. Most of its actions had been up and down the center-east region of Korea as part of the ROK I Corps, U.S. IX Corps, and ROK II Corps. It had fought especially well in the mountains of the Hwachon-Kumsong region, much of which is now a national park and resort area. In early 1953 the division held an advanced position on the eastern edge of the "Iron Triangle," an area known as the Kumsong salient.

In June 1953 General Taylor sent Major General Samuel T. Williams, commander of the U.S. 25th Infantry Division, to serve as temporary deputy commander of the ROK II Corps to make a personal assessment of the ROK army's combat readiness. General Williams judged that Lim Sun-ha did not command the best division in the corps, but that he was probably the best division commander. He and the other division commanders still faced serious problems in coordinating their inadequate fire support with large unit maneuvers. Williams found the entire corps in need of more generous logistical support and personnel reinforcements, but he thought the II Corps was holding its own against steady Chinese offensive pressure even if it had surrendered some of its forward positions along the Kumsong River.

When the Chinese launched their last major offensive of the war, the 3rd Division was in ROK II Corps reserve. General Chung Il-kwon, the corps commander, once again proved that his leadership in actual battle left much to be desired. He detached one of General Lim's regiments from the 3rd Division to reinforce another division, then attached a fourth regiment from another division to the 3rd Division, all in the process of trying to stop an offensive by twelve Chinese divisions. "I had an awful time in this battle because of the corps commander's decisions. My KMAG advisors and I struggled to perform our blocking missions, but the Chinese always held the initiative until General [Maxwell D.] Taylor committed more American artillery and airpower to the battle. At one time President Rhee came to visit the battlefield. I thought I might be relieved. Instead, the president gave me the Taeguk Military Valor Medal. I also received a Legion of Merit from General Taylor for my command of the 3rd Division, and I am proud of that recognition."

After the armistice Lim Sun-ha remained in the army until 1959, when he retired to become active in Korean business. When the business failed, his wife left him, so he moved with his three children to Tokyo for another management position. There he met an American school-teacher, his current wife, Sandy, whom he married in 1971. Happily, in the meantime Jim Hausman returned to Korea in 1956, became a Department of the Army civilian employee in 1959 (his critics claim that Hausman was really a CIA agent), and served as the longtime political advisor and liaison between the senior U.S. Army commander in Korea and the South Korean army. For his imagined influence during the Park Chung-hee years and the coup of 1980–1981, Hausman became the villain of choice for the Korean liberal left, a charge that overlooks the fact that Hausman disliked Park and his closest associates and their use of their intelligence agencies, army security commands, military police, and the national police to corrupt the army and terrorize potential political opponents.

**Lim Sun-ha, 2000**

LIM SUN-HA

Jim Hausman, who had retired to Austin, Texas, in 1981, died suddenly during a routine hernia operation in October 1996. Lim Sun-ha organized the tributes from the South Korean army and represented his nation at Jim's funeral. General Lim still regards the North Korean army as an irreconcilable enemy, encouraged by the false hopes and misleading language from Korea's civilian politicians, who are eager to exploit the uninformed passions of their electorate.

# 16

## The War Goes on
## for Some Koreans

Although the psychological and physical scars of their war still affect thousands of Koreans, there are some who are still *in* the war. They are or were prisoners until the 1990s. In the Republic of Korea the maximum-security prison at Taegu held more than one hundred political prisoners, whose crimes dated to the 1950s. In 1993 President Kim Young-sam decreed that any political prisoner who renounced Communism and pledged not to attempt to overthrow the government would receive amnesty. This opportunity applied to men over seventy years of age, many of whom had lived for years in solitary confinement. Most accepted the president's terms, but some did not. The group profile of the released POWs was fairly consistent. They had been captured from 1951 to 1953 serving in the North Korean army or in the South Korean Labor Party underground organization, and they had been citizens of the Republic of Korean when captured. There was no explanation why they had not been repatriated or released in the 1950s under the terms of the armistice.

In 1994 a patrol boat of the National Fisheries Administration, the Republic of Korea, found an elderly man drifting alone in a small boat off the coast of southwestern Korea near Kunsan. He claimed to be an escaped prisoner of war, and the Agency for National Security Planning (the Korean CIA) immediately took him into custody for interrogation. The man, Cho Chang-ho, was a legitimate escapee from a North Korean coal mine worked by slave laborers; he was also a first lieutenant in the South Korean army who had been captured in May 1951 near Inje at the end of the Chinese Fifth Offensive. Seized when he attempted to escape from a prison camp, Lieutenant Cho had spent the next thirteen years in a slave labor camp in North Korea, and for thirty years after that he had worked as a coal miner. He had developed black lung disease. Being an invalid he was not watched carefully, and he finally reached the western coast and put out to sea, hoping the wind and current would take him south before he died. The Korean government promoted Lieutenant Cho to captain, decorated him, and presented him with forty-three years' worth of back pay. More importantly, Captain Cho learned that he still had six brothers and a sister living in Korea.

After Captain Cho's return, the first known escape of a POW from North Korea, the National Intelligence Service (still the KCIA) announced in 2000 that fifteen more former POWs had escaped from North Korea in the past six years. They were not part of the defector population, which had been small but steady since the 1950s. They, too, had been slave laborers in North Korea until they found ways to escape to China, which had then sent them to South Korea. There was no official explanation as to why these former South Korean soldiers had not been repatriated in the 1950s.

As part of his "sunshine policy," President Kim Dae-jung approved the release of sixty-three "unconverted" prisoners who had been jailed for decades for espionage and subversion, some of the men captured during or immediately after the Korean War. They all had no choice regarding their destination: North Korea. There is still no accounting from either of the two Koreas as to how many Korean prisoners each may still hold.

# Part 2

# THE ALLIES

# 17

# Of War, Mines, and Pheasants

## SHRIVENHAM, SWINDON
## OXFORDSHIRE, ENGLAND, 1987–2001

Dan Raschen went to Korea to hunt pheasants, not Chinese, but the mines got in the way.

I met Colonel Dan Raschen of the Royal Engineers in 1987. Ten years earlier he had retired, after thirty-three years in the British Army, to accept an appointment as a faculty member and infantry weapons design specialist at the Royal Military College of Science in Shrivenham. Our mutual friend, Brigadier Bruce J. Willing, introduced us during our first visit to Shrivenham, a delightful village where one picks mushrooms off the soccer field after a rain. Dan and his wife, Judy, wined and dined us during that first visit, and we have since returned as their guests even though Bruce and Chris Willing have decamped for their retirement home on the Isle of Jersey. One never tires of the Raschens' hospitality, especially Dan's stories of his Korean War service, about which he has written in *Send Port and Pyjamas!* (Buckland Publications, 1987), the second of his four-volume autobiography. The cover shows a ring-necked cock pheasant and red minefield markers. I knew of pheasants in Ohio and mines in Korea and Cuba, and I wondered how they mixed. Dan explained it all in our first visit, largely because we both also like American Marines.

After late World War II service in the engineers of the Indian Army in India and Sumatra, Dan returned to England in 1947 to complete his formal engineering education. Commissioned just before the war with Japan ended, he had become a regular officer in 1946, and the Royal Engineers (RE) wanted him more schooled. After a series of inconclusive postings and educational false starts, he won an appointment to return to Cambridge University, his original school, where he completed a special two-year course for engineering officers in the spring of 1951. The war in Korea found Dan at Cambridge, and, unlike most of his civilian and army classmates, Dan wanted to go to Korea. "I may not have been a very conventional soldier, but I knew that wars were my business. I had already missed the fighting of 1939 to 1945, and now I might do the same again." The Chinese intervention settled the short war problem, so Dan still had his war in 1951, and he volunteered for posting to the 1st Commonwealth Division. He was unmarried, twenty-five years old, eager, more or less fit—though pear-shaped—and more talented at demolitions than construction. Nevertheless, Dan had to lobby rigorously for a posting to Korea, but casualties and a "stalemated" war reduced the enthusiasm of his competitors. He got the assignment by agreeing to an eighteen-month tour, the equivalent of a full three-year overseas tour elsewhere.

Lieutenant Dan Raschen had a personal motive for going to Korea: pheasant hunting. An ardent upland game hunter, Dan learned from army and missionary sources that Korea had more pheasants than England, a statement that proved exaggerated but not much. In England, wartime austerity—still a depressing reality in 1951—had even reached bird hunting, as Dan learned during the disappointing 1950 season. Korea beckoned. Satisfied with whatever combat weapons the British army gave him, Dan looked for an appropriate shotgun because "I considered my own too good to take with me." Fortune smiled. Dan found a gun among the vintage wines in a widowed aunt's cellar in Herefordshire. It was an ordinary 12-gauge double-barrel with interior hammers, and it worked when Dan tested it. Moreover, it came with two-hundred-plus prewar cartridges, a scarce commodity. It was not a handsome gun, but Dan was not a handsome hunter. The gun and cartridges went into Dan's battle kit, which included new, more generous field uniforms to accommodate Dan's more mature college figure. Off the gallant sapper (combat engineer) went to Korea with enough equipage for a Roman legion. Dan checked in with some depot toffs (experts in the rear) at Royal Engineers Chatham for combat tips. *Do learn all you can about mines,* the toffs said, *nasty things the Chinese like to use. So do the Americans and Koreans. Good luck.*

After a routine ocean voyage on a British troop transport, Dan arrived in Kure, Japan, in August 1951 and went to a bleak officers transit camp. "There

were certainly masses of depressed
officers, so goodness knows how the
soldiers felt." Since the Commonwealth 27 Brigade and British 29
Brigade had both taken significant
casualties in the Chinese Fifth
Offensive (April to May 1951), the
British army had deluged its Korean
forces with replacements, far
exceeding requirements. "[T]here
must have been thousands of us . . ."
In fact, the Postings Colonel said the
Commonwealth Division had too
many sapper officers. Since Dan,
however, was the only RE officer in
transit, he could go to battle camp
for two weeks, then go to Korea to
persuade the Commander Royal
Engineers (CRE) to keep him. Dan
thought he could meet the challenge. By late August Dan Raschen,
ardent sportsman and less skilled
mine warfare expert, had bypassed
Battle Camp and talked his way into
the 64 Field Park Squadron (equivalent to a large American engineer

**Capt. Dan Raschen, RE 1952**

company), a support unit. All the other sapper officers he met seemed to be
World War II combat veterans bowed by the weight of their DSOs and MCs.
Before he could settle in, Dan received a further posting to 12 Field Squadron as
"intelligence officer." A fellow Cambridge graduate, Major Howard Stephens,
commanded the squadron, stationed six miles south of the Imjin River. Dan
had never before served in a British army combat unit. And hunting season
approached.

Because September typhoon rains and the new armistice negotiations had
slowed the war to local actions, Dan Raschen saw much of "the front" without
much molestation from Chinese shelling. He conducted engineer reconnaissance missions and decided the sector was a perfect pheasant habitat—but he
saw no birds. Another officer assured him they were there, but before Dan could
continue his ornithological expeditions, he took over a field engineering troop
(platoon) of sixty sappers, most of them "old soldiers" of wide knowledge and

measured energy. Dan threw himself into his varied missions: building a ferry, fixing roads, and helping extract mired tanks and lorries. Always there were the mines—American mines of metal and plastic more or less designed to German standards of unpleasantness, and Chinese mines, crudely made Russian replicas and even more crudely made wooden box mines, almost undetectable with conventional mine detectors. Whoever had occupied the Commonwealth sector—and it had been fought over four times in a year—had not left the usual wire fences and mine signs, let alone minefield maps. In support of 3 Battalion, Royal Australian Regiment, Dan and his troop joined a combat patrol, survived Chinese mortar fire, discovered the ordeal of being stretcher bearers, served as a reserve infantry platoon, and rescued a tank. Dan also broke his only pair of decent eyeglasses and had to wear his ugly gasmask spectacles. No hunting yet for Sapper Dan.

The autumn of 1951 tested Dan's combat engineering skills, first in Operation Commando, the Commonwealth Division's offensive across the Imjin into the mountains to the northwest, then to create the World War I-style defensive systems necessary to hold the division's tenuous perches on Hills 355, 217, and 317. The work involved creating new all-weather unpaved roads (a military oxymoron), bridging the Imjin (a river of legendary flooding), and planting and plotting minefields so that they impeded the Chinese and spared moving Commonwealth infantry, artillery, and armor. Dan saw his fellow soldiers die from Chinese artillery and minefield accidents. He marveled at the range of bravery, ingenuity, stupidity, and carelessness he observed. His major accomplishment was organizing a field of American and British antipersonnel mines with tripwires and flares for a frontline company of 1 Battalion, Kings Own Scottish Borderers. Rigging the tripwires and arming the mines was no job for the inattentive and frivolous. Only Dan and one sergeant proved equal to the task, which could be done either at night or in daylight within sight of the Chinese positions. Dan's troop lost one sapper in a careless accident. Toward the end of the slow project, Dan learned he had been ordered to the engineer regimental headquarters, a reassignment he viewed with a mixture of relief and unhappiness since he thought his colonel did not respect his soldierly virtues.

From October 28, 1951, until his departure for England in February 1953, Captain Dan Raschen found several forms of excitement and fulfillment as a liaison officer and intelligence officer for 28 Engineer Regiment and the Commander Royal Engineers. The new posting "turned out much more pleasantly than I had ever dared to expect." The headquarters was organized in the Imjin River valley, heavy with trees and long grasses. On an armed walk on October 29, Dan bagged the first of fifty-one pheasants he was to shoot in Korea—without a dog and using a friend's unfamiliar shotgun. "Yes, there were pheasants in Korea!" Duty, however, was not just pheasant chases. Dan earned his keep by conducting aerial reconnaissances, checking roads and bridges within the division sector, investigating friendly and enemy minefields, and working with American and Korean engineers, most memorably those of the U.S. 1st Marine Division. The Marines gave Dan one of their distinctive herringbone twill cotton utility hats so that Chinese observers would not be tempted to fire mortar shells at a distinguished British VIP in a beret. Dan spent a great deal of time working with the "gunners" to see that engineering barriers were covered by artillery barrages and counterattack

Col. Dan Raschen, RE (Ret.) 2002

routes were not. His work eventually put him in the office of the Commander of Royal Engineers at division headquarters.

Dan also established himself as an important personality in the sapper mess. He impressed the Regimental Sergeant Major with his deftness in making hors d'oeuvres and his commanding officer with his dexterity in removing champagne corks. His rat-elimination campaign, mounted with a self-mixed poison, received general approbation, until writhing rats rained down from the headquarters straw roof or decayed out of sight but not out of scent. On one dark night Dan charged out of the division operations tent, became night blind, and ripped a nasty seam in his thigh upon colliding with a long, sharp metal tent post, thus shedding "as far as I know, the only blood seen in Divisional Headquarters in the entire conflict." The wound sparked much debate: To which hospital should Dan go for repairs? The vote was for the Indian Field Hospital, known for its excellent curries. The division medical officer, however, sent Dan to the U.S. Army 8055th MASH for sewing, which forced a night jeep ride across three division sectors, a journey designed to inflict more serious wounds. Dan's medical odyssey ended with six stitches and several days of unsympathetic recuperative care from two "nurses from hell." Because Americans were allowed no liquor and were provided with only scanty gowns, a desperate message went forth to Dan's division headquarters colleagues: *Send port and pyjamas!* The relief expedition found him before he transferred to a Canadian hospital, even more inhospitable, so he escaped by feigning recovery and sped back to the division, only to be bedridden again.

The hunt season of 1952 to 1953 found Dan Raschen at his best—energetic, enthusiastic, and knowledgeable. As a reconnaissance and intelligence officer, Dan knew where the pheasants were and where the mines were not. The Commonwealth Division hunts became so memorable that senior officers from all over the U.S. 8th Army curried invitations from the GOC, the tall, regal Major General A. J. H. Cassels, CB, CBE, DSO. Armed with his restocked and repaired shotgun, Dan became the master of the Imjin Hunt Club, with the entire 28 Engineer Regiment at his beck and call for guides, beaters, drivers, and service personnel. He marked false minefields to discourage poachers, notably neighboring gunners. He worried about shotgun shells, always in short supply. His biggest frustration: no bird dogs. He had lobbied for the British army to send mine dogs to Korea, which it did. The dogs proved marginally useful in their military specialty, but resisted retraining as pointers and retrievers. Otherwise the pheasant campaign on the Imjin put many a bird into the division's messes. The hunting exceeded Dan's wildest expectation but ended (according to British law) on February 1, 1953, with the Imjin valley less about one thousand pheasants, according to Dan's report home on January 25, 1953. With his second pheasant season in Korea behind him, Dan spent a dangerous week among the minefields, orienting the engineers of the U.S. 2nd Infantry Division, which arrived to allow the Commonwealth Division to move to a reserve position. With his curiosity about war fully satisfied, Dan then packed for home.

Almost fifty years later the hills north of the Imjin-gang are now defended by two Korean armies. The river still floods, often washing mines old and new toward the sea. The pheasants patrol the fields and woodlands in legendary numbers through the minefields of the Demilitarized Zone, a bird sanctuary. In Shrivenham, Dan Raschen still helps organize the annual local pheasant hunt.

# 18

## The Belgians

The two retired Belgian lieutenant colonels introduce themselves, apologize for their inability to speak English well, and talk quickly in French and Dutch to my host, Lieutenant Colonel Luc de Vos, international military historian in four languages and esteemed professor at the Royal Belgium Military Academy. Our guests, Julien van Cauwelaert and Gaetan de Buck, are former officers of the Belgian battalion that fought in Korea and are members of the Fraternelle du Corps de Volontaires de Guerre Belges pour la Corée, an association of veterans that enjoys the patronage of the Belgian monarchy and armed forces. Van Cauwelaert (Flemish) and de Buck (Walloon) served in the battalion as infantry officers, van Cauwelaert as a company commander and de Buck as a platoon commander. Both received decorations for valor, and de Buck was wounded on a patrol in December 1951. In appearance, manner, and perspective they are professional soldiers.

With Professor de Vos translating to speed the interview—actually both officers know a good deal of English—we spend much of a warm Brussels morning discussing a cold war long ago, but the Belgians bring it alive without much prodding. Van Cauwelaert discusses how the battalion was formed.

Our motivation was simply to help the Americans, who had liberated us in World War II. America was a NATO ally. Besides, the British, Dutch, and French were going to send troops to Korea, so why shouldn't we? We were curious about serving in an American army since our historic military experience came from either France or Great Britain. We really didn't think much about Korea being a United Nations war, and fighting Communism as some sort of crusade didn't mean much either, even though we were Catholics and had a cross in our cap badge. Our NATO army was just taking shape, so we didn't send a regular battalion. I was already an officer, a captain, at age twenty-four, a former member of the Resistance and the Free Belgian army, formed in 1944. I had been a reserve officer since March 1945. All our soldiers were volunteers. They wanted to serve their country by fighting in Korea for liberty and democracy. Professional soldiers go to war when their country commands them, but we were something more than just professionals. We believed in our mission and looked forward to our deployment when Crown Prince Baudouin presented us the colors of the Korea Battalion.

Both van Cauwelaert and de Buck, also a World War II veteran and an officer since the age of nineteen, volunteered to join the cadre of professional soldiers who formed the Belgian battalion, officially known as the 1st Battalion, Corps de Volontaires pour la Corée, and named "Kamina" for the transport that took it to Korea. The colonels agree that the soldiers generally fell into two groups, veterans of the old and new Belgian armies and the Resistance, and young men who were relatively uneducated, unemployed, or caught in poor jobs, such as

J. VAN CAUWELAERT

**Capt. Julien van Cauwelaert, 1951**

farm labor. They hoped that military service would improve their employment possibilities. Both groups included men seeking an Asian adventure, a new type of colonial military service.

The Belgian government also gave the volunteers an additional benefit: One year's service for the Korean War would be judged the equivalent of two years' obligated service under Belgian conscription law. Satisfactory combat service would be an important factor in selecting officers and NCOs for the new, expanded Belgian army. Army personnel officers screened three thousand volunteers and took only seven hundred, although the battalion had an authorized strength of nine hundred. Only three former members of the Waffen SS tried to enlist, and they were rejected. In the platoon from Luxembourg, however, the Belgians found several former members of the Wehrmacht, but they all had been reluctant draftees (so they said) under a Nazi fiat that all Luxembourgers were really Germans and therefore subject to conscription. In nationality terms, the Belgian battalion was carefully balanced—half Flemish, half Walloon—but organized into linguistic rifle companies to make communications easier. The headquarters and weapons companies were mixed.

**Col. Julien van Cauwelaert**

Colonel de Buck remembers the rigor of the predeployment training, but still believes the training period was too short. "It took most of September and October 1950 to form the battalion, but by mid-October we had moved to an isolated barracks in the Ardennes for field training, especially in physical fitness. We needed a great deal of infantry training, especially commando-style training, since we had former sailors, airmen, and all sorts of army occupational specialists. Of course, these men had many other skills we used to good effect in maintaining the battalion. We fired our weapons often, including live firing with real artillery support. We did not do enough training for night operations."

The Belgian battalion arrived in Korea on January 31, 1951, when it became clear that no one was going home for Christmas except as a corpse. After some service in the U.S. 3rd Infantry Division, the Belgians went into battle as a fourth infantry battalion in the British 29 Brigade Group. They thought they were as good as the three British infantry battalions, but that the British tank company (a squadron of the King's Royal Irish Hussars) and the 45th Field Regiment, Royal Artillery, did not give timely, effective support. Since the Belgians came to Korea with World War II British weapons and uniforms, 29 Brigade looked like a good home, but the Belgians quickly concluded that being a fourth battalion in an American infantry regiment might be more educational than remaining a patronized part of a British brigade. The British were moving toward the formation of a Commonwealth Division, so a change of parentage seemed timely. The Belgians became a permanent battalion in the U.S. 3rd Infantry Division on August 21, 1951.

Colonel de Buck judged collaboration with the British as good, but the Belgians eagerly switched to American uniforms and weapons by October 1951. They studied American operational practices. "We were especially impressed with the American artillery." Colonel van Cauwelaert agrees.

> The 3rd Division artillery battalions sent us forward observers, and our own officers learned to call for fire in English. Planned fires worked best. Emergency firing was not always good, too many language and operational barriers. In March 1952 my company held a hill under Chinese attack, largely because of American artillery fire, but the Americans, misinformed by an air observer, thought the outpost had fallen. They were going to blast the entire hill as soon as it became light. Fortunately, our battalion commander saw Belgian brown berets—we didn't like American helmets—in the trenches and barely got the fire mission stopped. I lost a quarter of my company dead or badly wounded in that battle. I don't know how many men we lost to our own artillery, but we certainly lost some. It was unavoidable. Incidentally, GIs often tried to steal our berets as souvenirs. We didn't like that, not only for national pride, but for survival. No Chinese or North Koreans had caps like ours!

> The Belgians thought that the 3rd Division treated them well, but they found many things about being American allies interesting—some good, some not so good. American rations were memorable. The C-rations were tolerable but boring; only the fact that they came with cigarettes, chewing gum, candy, and toilet paper impressed the Belgians. Cooked rations, brought up by Korean carriers in Marmite cans, were more tolerable but still boring. The bread was awful. In reserve the Belgians happily cooked and baked for themselves. The Belgians questioned American creature comforts. They thought rear area showers and

G. DE BUCK

**Lt. Gaetan de Buck, 1948**

medical care were outstanding; they marveled at American largesse in jeeps and trucks. Van Cauwelaert still wonders about some American military priorities. "We willingly split up the battalion to provide companies to man combat outposts. I was on one such outpost in November 1952— remember the Chinese were attacking all of us in the western sector— and I received a call that the Korean porters were going to bring us the full U.S. Army Thanksgiving dinner. We had plenty of food. I insisted that the Koreans bring us more ammunition, water, grenades, and barbed wire, but not food. I had quite an argument, but I got what we needed."

Col. Gaetan de Buck, 1998

The Belgians respected their counterparts in the 3rd Division and formed friendships for life, nurtured by continued contact with "their" American division when it served in Germany for three decades after the Korean War. They learned American military terms and soldier slang. "I knew more English in 1953 than I do now," van Cauwelaert laughs. He remembers good relations with the Koreans. "We were always short of soldiers, so we took our share of KATUSAs [Korean Augmentation to U.S. Army soldiers, see glossary]. We expected to use them in support roles, but some of them became very fine soldiers. They are members of our veterans group and wear our Belgian brown berets and Royal Army cap badges. They are comrades." The Belgians knew about Catholic missionary activities in Korea, and their priest-chaplains supported orphanages and relief work with Army and church money. The Belgian officers do not recall any racial incidents of importance. As for other allied troops, they insist that the Belgian battalion was more soldierly than its Dutch counterpart in the rival U.S. 2nd Infantry Division.

As the morning wanes and the room warms, we are approaching the end of the interviews. I press the Belgians about their thoughts on the war and its impact on them. "I worried about the Americans rationing ammunition in 1952 to 1953," van Cauwelaert says. "Would they be reliable allies in Europe? Would they stand up to the Russians for many years? As for our service, I was disappointed that our own people had no interest in the war after we returned. Some of our officers were jealous of us. Many combat veterans left the Army, even though they could have stayed, because they were unhappy and felt unappreciated. I don't think we were discriminated against in the Army. One of our battalion commanders became the Army commander, and we had our share of senior officers. And we did learn much about the U.S. Army."

"I think what I remember most often," Colonel de Buck adds, with a slight Gallic shrug, "is that we felt we could have kept advancing north in 1951. We could have won the war."

# 19

## Diggers

CANBERRA, AUSTRALIA
July 1995

Some people shudder when I tell them that Korea was a great war for me, and Vietnam was, too. For a professional soldier, a war is the only place to learn one's business, and I started my education in Korea."

Major General R. A. "Ron" Grey, Australian army (Ret.), laughs easily as we chat over a very good nouvelle cuisine lunch at the exclusive Commonwealth Club. The view over Lake Burley Griffin is spectacular now that the winter rain has rushed off to the coast of New South Wales. The Australian wine is even better than the view. It is a peculiar setting to be talking about war, but it is a great way to do research.

One of the most respected senior officers of the post-World War II Australian army, Ron Grey is sixty-four and looks ten years younger, aided by ageless brown hair, spare eating, and a busy life with his family, which includes my good friend and fellow Korean War expert, Dr. Jeffrey Grey, Australian Defence Force Academy. General Grey returned once from military retirement in the 1980s to serve as Chief Constable of Australia to reform a national police tainted by corruption. He is a no-nonsense organizational leader, who is as crisp with me as he is with Jeff. He is a man accustomed to giving orders that are

RON GREY

ROYAL CONSTABULARY OF AUSTRALIA

**Lt. Ron Grey, 3 RAR, 1952**

**Police Commissioner of Australia
Ron Grey, Maj. Gen. (Ret.)**

obeyed, but I think his staff officers would have found him easy to work for since his guidance is given with clarity and no sign of ego.

General Grey entered the Australian army upon graduating from the Royal Military College, Duntroon, in 1951. After additional training he joined the veteran 3 Battalion, Royal Australian Regiment (RAR), Commonwealth Division, in the summer of 1952. The division was then defending the Kaesong-Munsan corridor along the Imjin-gang north of Seoul. Lieutenant Grey took command of 12 Platoon, Company D, 3 RAR.

> Of course, we were waging a patrolling war with the Chinese when I arrived. The Chinese were very good, and they had good artillery placed in tunnels in the hills, virtually impossible to destroy. We all operated at night to avoid artillery fire. Unlike the Americans, we considered the isolated Combat Outpost Line an invitation to disaster, so we kept the Main Line of Resistance strong points well manned instead, but we needed aggressive patrolling to keep the Chinese outside the wire. You may be sure they'd control No-Man's-Land if we let them.
>
> We would patrol most often with one officer and a half platoon, about fifteen men, and find a laying-up place during the night. Then three-man groups would prowl about, seeking information. Capturing a prisoner was virtually

impossible unless you ran into a Chinese patrol, which meant a fight. Night skirmishes, of course, are no fun for either side, lots of wild firing and showers of grenades. I was wounded on one such occasion by grenade fragments in my leg, arm, and forehead.

General Grey remains matter-of-fact over coffee, but part of his right eyebrow is plowed under by scar tissue. Having had a similar wound inflicted upon me as a child, I am sure General Grey saw his way back to his lines in a red haze. "I was bunged up enough to go to a U.S. Army hospital in Japan. One day a very well-turned-out American general came through the ward passing out Purple Hearts. He did the general bit, talking to the troops, boosting morale. He gave me a Purple Heart, too, which, of course, I couldn't wear, but I thought it would make a fine souvenir. Later some nurse came back into the ward and demanded I return the medal since I shouldn't have it. That irritated me since I certainly had earned it."

General Grey returned to 3 RAR to finish his tour as the commander of an 81-millimeter mortar platoon. Almost twenty years later he commanded 7 Battalion, Royal Australian Regiment, in Vietnam. "I remembered how dangerous the Chinese had been in Korea, and I assumed the Vietnamese could use rockets as well as the Chinese used mortars and grenades. We dug in and organized complete positional defenses for our base camp and on operations. People who fought only in Malaya did not and got roughly handled. Korea taught me that no enemy should be lightly regarded."

# 20

## Commander,
## *Renmin Zhiyuanjun*

The interrogators worked in shifts on the old man, beating him, kicking him, depriving him of sleep and food. He vomited and defecated and bled. His ribs were cracked, a lung punctured. But he would confess nothing. "I fear nothing!" he shouted. "You can shoot me! Your days are numbered. The more you interrogate me, the firmer I'll become." He insisted he had always been loyal to Chairman Mao Zedong, but his loyalty demanded he give the chairman sound military advice, not indulge his every martial whim, usually bad ideas from his court of party advisors. For such sturdy values the old man had fallen from grace in 1959 and then into the hands of the interrogators of the Gang of Four. At seventy-four years old, the man was facing his last battle, and he was losing. Losing his life, certainly, but not his self-respect or the love of thousands of his former comrades, even when he died alone in an army prison hospital, soiled, degraded, abandoned, and in pain. He never confessed. He was a marshal of the People's Liberation Army and former commander of the Chinese People's Volunteers Force, and his name was Peng Dehuai.

After a childhood of poverty, periodic starvation, begging, and part-time work as a cowherd, coal miner, and dike builder, Peng Dehuai, peasant boy of Hunan Province, finally escaped the grinding labor of virtual serfdom by joining the Hunan army as a common soldier in 1916. He was seventeen years old. His strongest memory of his "non-childhood" was the hopelessness of peasant life

106

and his old great-uncle's romantic tales of the Taiping Rebellion (1851–1864) and how the Taipings preached equality and economic rights for the poor. His private's pay of six silver dollars a month (less two dollars for rations) went home to support his grandmother, sickly father, and youngest brother. He kept one dollar for himself. Caught in a complex civil war for control of southern China, Peng proved a valiant, resourceful, and durable soldier. He survived his first extended interrogation and torture in 1918 when he was caught spying. He also became a spokesman for the rights of the enlisted men. He participated in the Changsha Mutiny when one hundred thousand soldiers demonstrated for back pay. He saw the Hunan army generals break the protest with bogus promissory notes and worthless educational vouchers. In 1920 Peng became a temporary company commander, and he used his unit to kill tyrannical landlords. He met other radicals and read books about fighting injustice. The next year he left the army to return to farming and rural reform, but in 1922 he seized a chance to attend the Hunan army's officer candidate academy. He was carried on the rolls of two different companies, thus drawing double pay, which he shared with two other officers, but it gave him money for his cause, the Save-the-Poor Committee. In the meantime, the Hunan army joined the National Revolutionary Army of the Republic of China (1925, Canton) for the Northern Expedition of 1926 against the warlords.

The violent confusions of the next two years (1926–1928) brought Peng Dehuai, who had become a regimental commander at twenty-nine, into the Chinese Communist Party when the Quomintang split into right-left factions and Chiang Kai-shek crushed the Canton uprising. Another pay dispute began a new wave of radicalism in Peng's division, and he became a key leader of the Pingjiang Uprising (July 1928), a major victory for the Communists, that created a firm political base and army in Hunan, Hubei, and Jiangxi provinces. The rebel forces—renamed the 5th Army of the Communist field forces—then defended their domain against a Nationalist expeditionary force, but had to fall back to avoid crippling casualties. Peng had fought and lost his first major battle, but he had learned much about being a proper Communist commander.

For the next twenty-two years Comrade Commander Peng Dehuai advanced in the ranks of the People's Liberation Army and the Chinese Communist party. He kept Communism alive in west-central China under pressure from Nationalist and Japanese armies. He reorganized his army as a guerrilla force of only fifteen hundred hard-core revolutionaries and took part of his force into the mountains to meet Mao Zedong and Zhu De, the legendary 4th Army commander. Always on the move, Peng's army kept the revolution alive against five Nationalist army "anti-bandit" campaigns. Peng became one of Mao's most trusted and dependable commanders, the master of the Hunan-Hubei-Tiangxi

YI XIAOBING

**Peng Dehuai (second from right) meets Kim Il-sung near the front, 1951**

border area. He held the ground that allowed the Red Army to escape from southern China in 1934 and begin the Long March. Peng's forces held the post of advance guard on the Long March. In 1935 Peng attended his first Central Committee meeting. A future patron, Liu Shaoqi, joined Peng's army as political director. Peng found himself in a complex cooperative-competitive relationship with Lin Biao, the army's outstanding field commander. He forged new alliances with warlord armies in western China to fight the Japanese and became deputy commander of the 8th Route Army when it formed in 1937 as the central Communist field force. Throughout all the political maneuvering, Peng followed Mao's positions, although he sometimes disagreed and several times "misunderstood" and "misinterpreted" Mao's line of limited cooperation with the Nationalists. At the end of the War of Liberation (1946–1949) Peng was deputy commander of the People's Liberation Army and commander and political officer of the 1st Field Army and the Northwest China Military Region, with his headquarters in Xian.

Peng Dehuai was no stranger to the debates in Beijing about how to protect the People's Republic of China from a renewed American-Japanese alliance to dominate China and roll back the Revolution. He certainly knew about the creation of the Northeast Border Defense Army (NEBDA) in Manchuria in July 1950 and about how three crack PLA armies and support units had been transferred to that army. By August 1950 the PLA had strengthened this force with extensive antiaircraft units. The NEBDA approached three hundred thousand frontline combat troops. The 13th Army Group headquarters, which had been planning to capture Taiwan, moved north to take over operational control of the expeditionary force. Peng, however, was not invited to the crucial October 2 meeting of China's key leadership: Mao Zedong, Zhou Enlai, Liu Shaoqi, and Zhu De from the Politburo Standing Committee and Gao Gang (the party boss of Manchuria) and PLA Acting Chief of Staff Nie Rongzhen.

Despite his knowledge that key members of his inner circle had serious reservations about saving North Korea from the Americans, Mao was determined to intervene. He did not, however, have a field commander due to the fact that his favorite, Lin Biao, pleaded incapacitating illness. Lin's health was indeed precarious, but the prospect of fighting the American armed forces had deepened his indisposition. Mao had had Peng in mind for the command since August. The key issue was the same one that bothered Lin Biao: Would the Soviet Union provide an air force to protect his army in Korea, the modern weapons, and the logistical support that the Chinese needed to stop the American and South Korean armies? With Stalin's commitments still vague, Mao sent for Peng on October 4 and brought him by plane to Beijing for another emergency meeting of the Chinese leadership. Peng arrived late and said nothing. The next day Mao checked Peng's enthusiasm for intervention and judged it sufficient to name him commander, which was announced at another meeting that afternoon. Peng then publicly supported Mao's decision to intervene as critical to China's future. His confidence in victory—not clearly defined—helped move the group to immediate action, even without firm Russian promises. Peng's comrades complimented him on his energy and strength of conviction.

Peng Dehuai did his best to give Mao Zedong a decisive military victory, but no such triumph followed five major offensives (October 1950–May 1951) for the very reasons Lin Biao and others feared: American air attacks and artillery savaged the light infantry divisions of the Chinese People's Volunteers Force; logistical support was inadequate, causing ammunition and medical service to be uncertain; the motorized mobility of the U.S. 8th Army confounded Chinese plans; the South Korean army did not collapse but became bigger and sometimes better. Mao bombarded Peng with gratuitous advice, and so did the Russians. The North Koreans proved stubborn allies, unwilling to concede any territory for tactical advantage. Every one of Peng's offensives produced dramatic but fleeting battlefield victories; only the Second Offensive produced real strategic change, the end of United Nations Command's mission to unify Korea. Mao wanted the CPVF (Chinese People's Volunteers Force) not just to chase the Americans back to Seoul, but to send them packing for Tokyo or Los Angeles as well. Peng tried to convince the chairman that his lack of air support, supplies, and mobile heavy artillery made this war aim impossible. After the Fifth Offensive fell apart in May 1951, Peng finally won over the majority of Mao's advisors. With much unhappiness, Mao accepted a war of attrition.

Given his personal commitment to the Korean intervention, Mao Zedong did not like his force commander telling him that the Americans and South Koreans showed no signs of losing the war. After the failure of the Fourth Offensive (February 1951), Peng went to Beijing and told Mao that some sort of solution status quo ante bellum, secured by negotiations, was the best China could hope for. Mao ordered the Fifth Offensive, with seven hundred thousand Chinese and Korean troops and lasting forty days, the largest and longest Communist offensive of the war. Peng believed the only justification for the attack was that it prevented United Nations Command from undertaking a second amphibious landing and overland drive toward Wonsan. The Chinese army suffered eighty-five thousand casualties and showed signs of real demoralization. Peng called the offensive one of only four operational errors of his career, but Mao gave him no other option. The alternate strategy of attrition allowed the Chinese to reduce their expeditionary force and exploit their strengths: stealth, field fortifications, camouflage, night operations, concentrated artillery and mortar barrages of short duration but upon very precise targets, and combat patrolling and raiding.

Mao's faith in Peng Dehuai's generalship slipped away with the hope of crushing United Nations Command. However unfairly, Mao may have held Peng responsible for the death of his oldest son, Mao Anying, who served as Peng's secretary and Russian translator, in an American bombing attack in November 1950. Peng began to rely more on his immediate staff and deputy commanders to deal with Beijing, where they most often saw Zhou Enlai and Nie Rongzhen. Peng could not avoid all conferences with Mao, and after the failure of the Fifth Offensive, he spent several protracted stays in Beijing for medical reasons. Mao pushed his Korean commander to the decision-making margin, but Peng accepted his role with good grace and focused on providing better weapons, food, medical services, and living conditions for his troops. Zhou Enlai directed the armistice negotiations through his personal representative at Panmunjom, Li Kenong, his first deputy foreign minister. The affairs of the CPVF fell to a committee of senior officers at headquarters: Deputy Commander Deng Hua and Chief of Staff Xie Fang (the Chinese delegates at Panmunjom), Yang Dezhi (director of operations), Du Ping (head of the political department), and Hong Xuezhi (chief of logistics). To their credit these officers served Peng loyally. For example, they shared credit for the digging of underground tunnels, caves, and fighting positions they later claimed rivaled the Great Wall, underground.

Peng did his best to square the attritional strategy with Mao's belief in a special strategy of People's War. He stressed the revolutionary nature of protracted warfare and "extremely favorable conditions" that would allow the CPVF to continue the war as long as the chairman dictated. Peng continued to insist that people were the key to military success: "Combat depends mainly on soldiers. Capable soldiers have always been the most important thing." Peng's sincere devotion to revolutionary principles gradually improved his relationship with the chairman. In August 1952 Mao praised Peng's execution of the attritional strategy. When Yang Dezhi decided the CPVF should mount a major offensive on the U.S. 8th Army in the autumn of 1952, Peng supported the concept and helped convince Mao that the Battle of Shangganling represented a major victory for the re-formed, rearmed CPVF. Peng and his deputies concluded that Lao Mei (the Americans) had no taste for real war and would soon make significant concessions to end the war. The Chinese believed they had won the Korean equivalent of the Battle of Verdun.

Peng remained distant from the course of the armistice negotiations in 1953, but he approved of Mao's instructions to launch one more offensive. After Stalin died in March 1953, the Russians quickly told Mao that they wanted a negotiated end to the Korean War. Mao knew his military assistance agreement was in peril if he delayed approving an armistice agreement too long. Peng agreed that the South Koreans needed more instruction on their military weakness. He approved a cascading series of CPVF offensives, from April to July 1953, that hammered American and South Korean divisions. When an armistice was finally signed on July 27, 1953, Peng signed the agreement at a Chinese camp near Panmunjom. He later took great satisfaction in the fact that the UNC commander, General Mark W. Clark, signed the document and remarked that he was the first American general to agree to end a war with no official victor.

In the postwar period Peng Dehuai became Minister of Defense and advocated rapid military modernization and the creation of a high-technology military-industrial complex, all of which required good relations with the Soviet Union. The PLA could not remain a peasant army. Peng's aggressive advocacy of military modernization led to his final confrontation with Mao Zedong, and when Peng criticized "the Great Leap Forward" economic program, his fate was sealed. By 1959 he had lost all his important military and political positions for "right deviationism." At that point China's greatest modern general became a target for victimization, not a hero of the Revolution or the man who had given China its first victory (however partial) over a Western military force. His reward was humiliation and a painful death without the care of even a person to wipe his face or give him a bedpan, because the chairman said it should be so. Only years later was Peng's reputation rehabilitated, well after Mao's death.

# 21

# A Doctor in Korea

Don Beard stands out in any crowd, even the Australian veterans of the Korean War who have turned out for the Chief of Army's annual history conference that this year, no surprise, focuses on the Korean War. At seventy-five Don Beard appears to have held on to every inch of his 6'5" of height without weighting his bayonet-straight body with extra "stones." In appearance—dapper, clipped mustache—Don Beard could be a retired general. Indeed, he clearly chats easily with General Sir Thomas J. Daly, KBE, CB, DSO, one of the former commanders of 3 Battalion, Royal Australian Regiment (3RAR), which provides the largest and most vocal group of "mates" at the conference. Don Beard draws a crowd as well as standing above it; the veterans ebb and flow around him for a word or two, punctuated with many handshakes and laughs. The easy comradeship has a special touch: Don Beard is 3RAR's family doctor.

Colonel Donald Beard was born in 1925 and attended university and medical school in his native Adelaide, South Australia. Still in university when World War II ended, he felt guilty about not leaving college while still a teenager to serve in the Second Australian Imperial Force in the waning days of the war with Japan. Don recalls that he also felt he needed a break from the intensity of med-

The senior officers of the 3d Battalion, Royal Australian Regiment: Capt. Donald D. Beard, MD, RMO, is third from the right. Lt. Col. Ian Bruce Ferguson, the commanding officer, is fifth from left.

ical education when he volunteered to serve as an Army medical officer for the Australian contingent in the British Commonwealth Occupation Force (BCOF) in Japan, 1948–1949. As a captain and medical officer on a one-year contract, Beard went to Kure, Japan, and then extended his tour by six months in the temporary rank of major while he arranged to return to his medical education as a resident in surgery. (Doctor Beard eventually completed his residency in surgery and board certification at the Royal College of Surgeons in England and Scotland.) In June 1950 Don finished his BCOF tour and packed for home. At the boisterous hail-and-farewell party, graced by some exuberant Red Cross women, the celebrants learned a war had begun in Korea. Don returned to his post at Kure, remembering the party as the beer worse and the women less attractive than he thought at the time. He remained in Japan as a hospital medical officer until the autumn of 1950. The commanding officer of the hospital asked him to volunteer to go to Korea as the medical officer for 3RAR, an assignment that would require his return to the rank of captain. Don thought he had no option but to "volunteer," however reluctantly. A war was not part of his career plan.

I learned to be a real doctor and a decent human being in 3RAR. I flew to Taegu with orders to the battalion, but I couldn't find anyone who knew where it was. Of course, the whole 8th Army was in some disarray after the withdrawal from North Korea. Since I had a hangover, I wasn't in any hurry anyway. I started from the U.S. Air Force base at Taegu and headed north until I learned where 3RAR could be located south of Seoul. I found it at the end of December. When I joined the battalion, I thought its esprit was terrific. It had withdrawn, but had not been defeated in battle. The biggest immediate problem was coping with the cold weather. The battalion did not have adequate cold-weather gloves or shoes, because our army had no recent winter war experience. The CO [Lt. Col. I. Bruce Ferguson] was desperate to do something about the mounting number of frostbite casualties, since we were not receiving replacements. I don't recall exactly how I got my brainstorm, but I decided to distribute as much American shaving cream as I could find—Barbasol—because it contained lanolin. Australians didn't use brushless shaving cream in those days, so I tore the labels off and announced that it was a special frostbite-prevention and treatment lotion. I don't know whether the lanolin really worked, but all that rubbing and flexing of hands and feet certainly helped. Everyone felt better, and the CO thought I was a pretty good RMO [Regimental Medical Officer].

From the perspective of the CO of A Company, Major Ben O'Dowd, Don Beard had come up with a perfect treatment for frostbite. In his own memoir, *In Valiant Company* (University of Queensland Press, 2000), O'Dowd praised Beard for coming up with a consistent treatment for frostbite that could be administered in the company rather than at the Regimental Aid Post (RAP). Any "digger" who felt inclined to go to on sick parade knew that he would simply get more strange lotion and be told to rub it into his feet when he changed socks, a daily requirement. Peeling off wet socks in the dead of winter was no barbecue, but the hard-working hands and numb feet all profited from the exercise. O'Dowd and his men also discovered that the magical cream slowed the effects of frostbite and reduced the chance of having bare hands freeze to the metal of their weapons, which often required maintenance work that could not be done with gloved hands. Within weeks better gloves and boots helped reduced the danger of exposure.

During the winter of 1950–1951 the weather and terrain caused me more concern than the Chinese. We didn't have many casualties during our slow advance north under General Ridgway, but we really didn't have enough medical personnel to handle even our low number of casualties. I don't know why, but we didn't have any Korean Service Corps bearers to help carry the stretcher cases down from the hills. Like any Commonwealth infantry battalion, we used our bandsmen for stretcher bearers, but I ended up using some of them as medical orderlies, too, since we rated only one medical orderly per company. The Americans would normally have four or five. I asked the Catholic padre and the Salvation Army representative to help, and they did a

**Col. Donald D. Beard, MD (Ret.) at Kapyong, Korea, 2001**

great job. I also had a young man from North Korea, Kim Young-choi, to do general work around the medical post, and he was both industrious and loyal to a fault. He is now an Australian citizen. Our real saviors were the members of the Indian Army's 60th Parachute Field Ambulance Unit. Not only did the Indians evacuate our wounded promptly by jeep to a U.S. Army Mobile Surgical Hospital (MASH), but the CO, Lieutenant Colonel A. G. Rangaraj, would suddenly appear at my side to help stabilize the most serious cases. Doctor Rangaraj and I have been friends ever since, and I visit him in India. He just made a parachute jump at the age of eighty-five. I certainly valued his advice, too, since he was ten years older than I and had lots of World War II experience.

Doctor Beard and I continue our conversation over coffee during the conference and during lunch with occasional breaks as Don speaks to his many admiring mates from 3RAR.

Our biggest medical problem that winter—other than frostbite—was pneumonia. I actually saw our men spitting blood into the snow, and if I saw someone with that kind of problem, back he went to an American MASH with no argument, because the pneumonia could kill you, or at least ruin you for life, if you didn't get some rest and warmth. I got a touch of pneumonia, too, but I treated myself and stayed with the battalion, since we didn't have another RMO to call in. I didn't feel very well, but I wasn't out in the hills all the time like the troops either. I struggled to make our evacuation system better, but it sometimes took all day to get a casualty down to the RAP and back to a MASH. I know that we lost some men in transit.

Like the rest of 3RAR, Don Beard remembers the Battle of Kapyong (23–25 April 1951) as the battalion's finest hour during his service in Korea.

The battle ruined our plans for a splendid ANZAC Day on April 25, since we had invited the Turks to participate and thought we were in for a grand time with some tough adversaries who were now our gallant allies in Korea. The Chinese offensive spoiled all that. You've read about the battle and talked to others about it, I assume. [I had and even walked the battlefield in 1998.] From my perspective, the biggest problem was that the CO had our headquarters—including the RAP—much too exposed, so we were in constant danger of being overrun and had to use too many key headquarters personnel to man defensive positions. Fortunately we had an American tank company [Company A, 72nd Tank Battalion (Medium)] more or less attached to the battalion, and it helped defend the HQ. The bad side of this arrangement is that the Chinese also wanted to destroy the tanks, so they drew more attention than we needed. I know that we could not have evacuated many of our wounded from the company positions if the tanks hadn't gone forward at some risk to provide covering fire and some shelter for the stretcher bearers. The Chinese actually stopped firing to let us get some of our wounded back to the RAP. I still regret that we didn't have enough time and skill to treat the wounded promptly and properly. We had too few trained orderlies and too many casualties at Kapyong. We handled our mates too roughly. When I went back into the Army in 1968 to set up the medical organization for the Australian force in Vietnam, I insisted that we properly man each RAP with trained personnel, and I think we did.

Doctor Beard finishes his story as the conference draws to a close. He left the battalion in the summer of 1951 to return to his medical education, a much older and wiser young doctor of twenty-six and still bothered by the effects of pneumonia. He believed he had provided good medical care to the "diggers" and that he had helped make 3RAR one of the best battalions in the entire Army, a judgment that will find little challenge from either veterans or historians. After a lifetime in medicine, developing an international reputation as a trauma surgeon and cancer specialist, Don Beard believes his mates of 3RAR are the finest people he has ever known. Clearly his mates feel the same way about Doctor Donald Beard, AM, RFD, ED, QHS, BS, FRCS, FRACS. They still call their RMO just "Doc Beard."

# 22

# The Thais

My escort from the U.S. Defense Attaché's Office, Captain Peter Huddle, USAF, and I drive to the manicured compound of the Supreme Headquarters, Royal Thai Armed Forces, in search of a Colonel Krit, who is to lead us to the headquarters of the Thai-Korean War Veterans Association. Arranged by Colonel Edward C. Mann III, USAF, I am to meet with some retired officers of the Royal Thai Army who served in Korea. I am vague on their ranks and importance. We race around Bangkok trailing Colonel Krit's car. Captain Huddle, a Japanese American who thought he was going to Vietnam before he was diverted to Thailand, tries to remain philosophical about his wasted year in Vietnamese language school. Our grand prix ends when we roar into a modest compound that appears to be a cross between a Buddhist temple and a mansion; it is the third home of the Thai-Korean War Veterans Association. Our host, Air Vice Marshal Sommai Menaruchi, cordially greets us and gives us a quick briefing. The association, which has a commercial license so it can raise funds, tries to help Korean War veterans, although it can identify only about twelve hundred of the some ten thousand soldiers who served in Korea. It is a point of contact for other nations' veterans organizations like the VFW (Veterans of Foreign Wars). It works with the Koreans on maintaining the Thai monument at Unchon, South Korea.

I meet the president of the association, General Chaveng Youngcharoen, also retired but at age seventy-eight every bit the very impressive general and political insider he had been while on active duty. Beginning his military career in 1944, just as Thailand's wartime alliance with Japan began to dissolve, he commanded a company that maintained order in the wake of the Japanese surrender. In addition to his Korean War service (1952–1953), General Youngcharoen served with Americans several times and graduated from the U.S. Army Command and General Staff College in 1957. Twelve years later he commanded the Thai expeditionary force in Vietnam after liaison tours in Seoul and Honolulu. Through most of the 1970s he served in key staff and political billets in Bangkok, including chief of staff to the supreme commander of the Thai armed forces. For thirteen years he was a member of the national legislature. Trim, handsome, and vigorous, General Youngcharoen has organized this worthwhile meeting. He has invited seven other retired Thai generals to tell me about their Korean War experiences. He translates when necessary, which is not often, as I sit in front of the panel of veterans. I feel slightly like I have been court-martialed, but the generals are as eager to tell me about their war as I am to hear their stories.

General Youngcharoen fields my first question about why Thailand volunteered so quickly (June 30, 1950) to provide ground combat troops to United Nations Command. Historically pressed by the British in Burma and India and the French in Indochina to join some sort of colonial protectorate, the Thai monarchy and military oligarchy chose to collaborate with Japan in 1941 and 1942 in ridding Southeast Asia of its European overlords. The Japanese would have conquered Thailand anyway, so an alliance of a sort seemed the better part of valor, but Thailand quite properly worried that the victorious Allies might not respect its sovereignty. The Thais saw the United Nations and the friendship of the Americans, who refused to accept Thailand's declaration of war on the United States, as the best guarantors against foreign domination. The Korean War provided Thailand with an unparalleled opportunity to prove its new global citizenship and to become a partner with the U.S. Army in what it hoped would soon be a military alliance. Every part of the Thai armed forces sent units to Korea, but the Royal Thai Army sent the largest contingent, a battalion combat team, and lost 125 of the 129 Thai servicemen who died in Korea. Since independent Thailand has been a military ally of the United States on a treaty basis since 1954, the political gamble worked, even though Thai combat losses in Vietnam (351 deaths) made the Korean expedition seem a minor affair. For the officers in front of me, the Korean War must have seemed puzzling in 1950.

For Lieutenant General Surapol Tonpreecha, handsome, soft-spoken, and articulate, the Korean War provided his first experience with command and combat as a platoon commander in the 1st Company. "Our 1st Battalion came from units throughout the Royal Thai Army. We were supposed to be the first battalion of a new regimental combat team, the 21st Infantry, but the Americans really didn't want allied units that big. They said that battalions attached to American infantry regiments were easier to train and supply, and I suppose they were right. So we never got larger than a reinforced battalion." Thailand also sent a liaison group to United Nations Command, led by a prince, Major General Pisit Dispongsa Diskul, who amazed American officers by arriving with an entourage of eleven officers and a field camp supplied by Abercrombie and Fitch. When the 1st Battalion, 21st Infantry arrived in Pusan by ship on November 7, 1950, it found itself assigned to rear training areas and routine security missions while it acclimatized itself to the Korean winter and its officers trained to use American artillery and air support. The 8th Army, then struggling to meet the Chinese in North Korea, did not seem to have enough liaison officers. It also had no time to ease the Thais into the war. On November 26, the battalion was in Pyongyang, attached to the 187th Regimental Combat Team (Airborne). It was just as confused as the Americans about the massive Chinese offensive against the 8th Army.

General Tonpreecha remembers that winter vividly:

We Thais had no experience with such harsh cold. Our wool American uniforms, even when cut down for our small bodies, were too heavy, too cold when wet. We could hardly stand up, let alone walk. We didn't have adequate cold weather clothing until we developed our own later in the war. And the food was so foreign to us. The rice was poor, so we imported Thai rice. We bought firewood from the Koreans at almost any price, but at least we paid. In total confusion we retreated south with the Americans to Suwon, which we reached on December 14. We wondered what we had gotten into.

The Thai battalion then joined the 1st Cavalry Division, which gave the Thais its big yellow division patch to wear and provided ample liaison officers to continue the postponed course in American tactics and fire support procedures. The Thais provided much-needed security patrols and posts. In early April 1951 the Thai battalion finally went into combat with the 5th Cavalry in the hills south of the Hwachon Reservoir and lost its first man killed in action to sporadic Chinese fire; eleven more were wounded. General Tonpreecha remembers the operation as unexceptional. The fighting around Seoul in May 1951 was sharper, but the Thais both attacked and defended against the Chinese with good results, especially at Hill 452 near Ponghak-dong and Unchon, now the site of the Thai memorial. The general thought the Thais had been good soldiers.

In July 1951 the first Thai battalion returned home, replaced by a second battalion of volunteers and stiffened by veterans of the first Thai battalion who had not yet completed a full tour. This pattern of rotation insured a major infusion of new soldiers, but also made certain that battle-tested veterans joined the ranks to share their experience. Major General Prayool Nootkan-janakool commanded the "second rotation" battalion. He is now balding, but looks fit, laughs easily, and pushes his glasses back up his nose as he reflects upon the war he inherited in the summer of 1951:

> We joined the 8th Cavalry Regiment while the division was in I Corps reserve, then moved into position on the Main Line of Resistance [MLR] on 31 July. We occupied a ridge northwest of Yonchon in the "Iron Triangle" area. The truce talks were getting started—and it rained all the time—so we didn't do much more than run patrols and work on our fortifications. I admired the Korean laborers in the Korean Service Corps, usually older men who carried big loads on their A-frames. They carried everything: barbed wire, food, water, sandbags, stakes, ammo. If they got fired upon, they dropped their loads and ran for the rear, but we didn't blame them since they always came back when the artillery fire stopped. My problems? Well, we never did get our three-hole latrines to conform to U.S. Army dimensions and sanitary standards. On the other hand, we got to enjoy U.S. Army food prepared in kitchens and carried in insulated containers to our positions. Whenever we got a really good meal—ice cream, steaks, real eggs—we knew someone wanted us to attack a tough position, usually with a night combat patrol. Senior American officers would visit the battalion when an operation was about to begin. Lots of smiles, lots of handshakes. The more VIPs, the more handshakes, the more dangerous the mission.

In October the Thai battalion participated in Operation Commando, which ended with the battalion in new positions on T-Bone Ridge and the Alligator Jaws, battlefields for the next eighteen months. Twice in November the Chinese tried to capture a Thai outpost on Hill 179 and failed both times. The second attack almost captured the hill, but the defending platoon fought off two Chinese companies and some tanks at the cost of eight dead, fifteen missing, and about the same number of wounded. The platoon commander died heroically and received an American Distinguished Service Cross. American artillery fire helped the Thais, who fought at close quarters despite the fact that almost every man in the platoon was a casualty.

Major General Pratuan Kittirat, an artillery forward observer in the second battalion, knew how seriously American gunners took their business. Still young-looking, almost impish, General Kittirat is bearded and dark-haired. His English is especially good:

> I came to Korea before the second rotation to train with the Americans to become a forward observer (FO). The battalion commander asked me if I'd been to Fort Sill. I hardly knew where Fort Sill was, and I said no. He immediately assigned me to one of his lieutenants and told us to work on calling fire missions in English. We did it in three stages: face-to-face, by telephone, and by radio. I really learned how to call for artillery fire in English and under pressure. It was the best training I ever had. Actually, I already spoke some English, but it was British English and none of the Americans could understand me. Once I joined the battalion, I thought I did a good job, thanks to that tough American commander.

During the winter of 1951 to 1952 the 1st Cavalry Division left Korea to become theater reserve in Japan, so the Thai battalion first went to the 3rd Infantry Division and then became part of the U.S. 9th Infantry Regiment, 2nd Infantry Division. It passed a quiet winter in the mountains northwest of Kumhwa. The next spring this battalion left for home and was replaced by the "Third Rotation Battalion," the last of the Thai all-army volunteers. General Youngcharoen arrived as the battalion adjutant and personnel officer, and he tells the story for his rotation despite the presence of General Akapol Somroop, who says little but says it carefully and precisely and with a touch of humor. General Youngcharoen keeps calling the former artillery FO the "third rotation" hero without being very precise about what General Somroop did. I find the story later in Korean and American accounts.

In the autumn of 1952 the Thai battalion went into a portion of the MLR studded with memorable names: Old Baldy, Outpost Eerie, and Snook Hill. The central outpost position was a low, ugly ridge called Porkchop Hill. General Youngcharoen insists that the 9th Infantry had good intelligence of a major Chinese offensive in November. He praises the tough professionalism of the regimental commander, Colonel Julian J. Ewell, a very demanding airborne commander in World War II and an unforgettable division and field force commander in Vietnam. General Youngcharoen pronounces Ewell's name "Evil," an inadvertent nickname that American GIs and Vietnamese would find descriptive. Ewell set the terms for the defense of Porkchop, a prime objective for the Chinese. The Thais would get no American reinforcements and would not mount counterattacks of their own; the company on the outpost would have to save itself with the help of the fire of seventy-two artillery pieces of every caliber from 8-inch guns to 4.2-inch mortars. After two probing attacks, the Chinese assaulted the hill three times in battalion strength, supported by their own improved and ample artillery. The first two attacks cost the Chinese about one hundred dead in the wire and the Thais twelve dead and sixteen wounded.

On the night of November 10–11, 1952, the Chinese made their most determined attack, with a regiment of probably eight hundred. Manning the trenches with two platoons, the Thai company commander kept two full platoons safe in deep bunkers and counted on artillery to break the attack. Lieutenant Akapol Somroop called in the American artillery, and shells burst above and within the overrun position. The two protected platoons then broke the remaining Chinese with an attack with grenades and bayonets. More than two hundred Chinese died inside the wire, with perhaps another hundred dead on the slopes. The American intelligence estimates placed total Chinese casualties on Pork-chop Hill at more than one thousand in the three attacks; the Thais lost twenty-five killed and seventy-six wounded. Twelve Thai soldiers received Silver Stars, among them Lieutenant Somroop. General James Van Fleet presented the medals and called the Thais "Little Tigers," a nickname that stuck.

The Thai battle for Porkchop Hill (not the fight enshrined by Hollywood and Gregory Peck) marked the last dramatic combat action for the battalion. The "fourth rotation" battalion representatives—Major General Pradit Nilsorn and Lieutenant General Amporn Kumpiranont—listen to the others' stories, but do not add much to the account, and time is fast approaching for lunch. The "fifth rotation" battalion commander is also present—Major General Parti Yoskrai—but the general has been silent, slowed by a stroke. His eyes indicate that he approves of the others' accounts. All the other generals and some young aides treat General Yoskrai with tender and affectionate care. During lunch, which included *Popeye's* chicken in my honor as I yearn for *satay* and *pad thai,* we continue the talk. Like other old soldiers, the generals remember their first war with affection and some awe. They are still comrades with the Koreans and the Americans.

Accompanied by a new escort, Commander George Flax, USN, we drive to the depot of the 21st Infantry Regiment (Airborne) at Chon Buri, southeast of Bangkok on the Bay of Siam. The purpose is to visit the Korean War Memorial and the regimental museum. The post is neat if spartan by American standards; the soldiers are giving the whole post a martial manicure and paint job in antici-pation of Queen Sikirit's annual visit to "her" regiment. From the buildings and grounds, we estimate that the 21st Regiment is still not a three-battalion orga-nization. We are greeted by the regimental commander and exchange pleas-antries over tea and pastries. George and I then learn that we will place a wreath on the Korean War Memorial, complete with musical honors. We manage to avoid embarrassing ourselves in military bearing, coached by the deputy regimental commander, who then shows us a very nice, small museum in the English regimental tradition. The uniforms, weapons, and displays are properly labeled in Thai and English, and there is a diorama of the last Chinese attack on Porkchop Hill. What strikes me are the regimental photographs. Almost every one of them shows Thai soldiers huddled together in a Korean winter. We know what the Thais remember most—being cold. Even in Chon Buri in August, I shiver a little from my own memories of climbing Heartbreak Ridge (safely) in December 1994. It must have been the air conditioning. We return to the heat of a Thailand summer and drive back to Bangkok, sweating comfortably.

# 23

## Soldier of Orange

**WEERT, THE NETHERLANDS**
**January 2000**

A professional soldier for his entire adult life, and now seventy-seven years old, Colonel Leendert C. Schreuders is a professional veteran, the secretary of Vereniging Oud Korea Strijders (VOKS), the memorial and service association for Dutch Korean War veterans who served in the Netherlands Detachment United Nations (NDVN). The name of the Dutch battalion in the U.S. 8th Army hardly rings with martial tones. In Korea the NDVN was the only active unit of the van Heutsz Regiment. It is now one of the airmobile infantry battalions of the 11th Airmobile Brigade and is quartered at the Oranje Kazerne at Schaarsbergen, a village near the historic city of Arnhem on the Lower Rhine River. The van Heutsz Regiment is the most decorated regiment in the Dutch army. It is a memorial to the Dutch colonial army.

The Dutch tributes for Korean War service are displayed in Oranje Kazerne. The central monument is truly international. It carries the insignia of the U.S. 2nd Infantry Division and the U.S. 38th Infantry Regiment, the American parent organizations for the NDVN. In addition to the names of the Dutch soldiers who died in action in Korea or those still missing in action, the memorial also honors the Korean soldiers who served and died in the NDVN as KATUSAs, or Korean Augmentation to the U.S. Army soldiers, and the porters of the Korean Service Corps. The number of KATUSAs who died fighting as adopted Dutchmen is twenty. Colonel Schreuders considers it a major accomplishment of the Vereniging Oud Korea Strijders that, since the founding of VOKS in 1977, an annual official remembrance ceremony is held at the monument with the ambassador of the Republic of Korea and the Minister of Defence and the chiefs of staff of the Netherlands or their representatives attending.

Leendert Schreuders remains energetic and fit as a retired colonel of over forty-years of active service. He speaks rapidly in fluent English, a product of boyhood schooling, one

**Lt. L. C. Schreuders, RNA, 1951**

year's service as a volunteer in the British Cheshire Regiment, and a lifetime of international soldiering for the North Atlantic Treaty Organization and the United Nations. His home office for VOKS is covered with the inevitable but prized photographs, citations, plaques, and memorabilia that colonels accumulate. Colonel Schreuders publishes the association booklets, gives lectures at military institutions about leadership, arranges meetings and group visits to Korea and remembrance ceremonies, provides counsel to veterans in distress, and ensures that the Ministry of Defence remembers the soldiers of Orange who so gallantly opposed Communist aggression. He was one of the founders and a board member of the Veterans Platform, an assembly of forty veterans associations, and is the Dutch member of the International Federation of Korean War Veterans Associations.

Schreuders knows a good deal about aggression. When he was sixteen, in 1940, his hometown of Ede (pronounced Eh-dah) was overrun by the Wehrmacht. The first dead soldiers he saw were the Dutch defenders of Ede; in September 1944 the dead soldiers were British when the 1st Airborne Division tried to retake the Lower Rhine bridge in Operation Market Garden. Dodging forced labor in Germany, Leendert Schreuders joined the Dutch Resistance in 1943, was arrested twice, but escaped twice when gathering information about the

German activities, transmitting messages and transporting weapons. Following the German surrender in May 1945, as an acting NCO he trained resistance members for service in the new Dutch Army. His service in the British army (1945–1946) earned him an appointment as an officer candidate, and in 1947 he became an ensign in the Dutch army. He then organized and trained a company for service in the Dutch East Indies, and as the senior ensign he took the company to the Pacific, where he fought assorted guerrilla bands until the Netherlands withdrew from an independent Indonesia. He returned to the Netherlands as a first lieutenant in 1950, an experienced and skilled troop leader. Unlike the British army, Schreuders asserts, the Dutch army officers trained their own platoons and lived close to their troops.

Lieutenant Schreuders had been in the Netherlands only five months when the North Korean army crossed the 38th Parallel. He and other Dutch soldiers thought the Netherlands had a duty to the United Nations and the United States—a new NATO ally—to send troops to Korea. The Dutch government, however, was overwhelmed with the task of raising its NATO contingent and thus showed no urgency in sending a token unit to Korea. Schreuders laughs as he recalls the Dutch volunteers' direct approach:

> We took matters into our hands when a delegation of soldiers went to the American embassy to volunteer. The government really didn't want to raise even a battalion, the minimum force the Americans would accept. In fact, we didn't raise a full battalion since we had only two rifle companies, not three. When the defense minister called for volunteers, he said that there would be only a two-week recruiting period. Nevertheless, something like fifteen hundred serving soldiers or recent veterans volunteered for a minimum of one year's service in Korea. We took no untrained soldiers. I'd guess that seventy percent were wartime veterans. The volunteers were very fit, had no disciplinary records. We could have sent a full-strength battalion, but Dutch policy limited us to 636 officers and men. Because we demanded the highest mental and physical standards, only forty percent of the volunteers were accepted. We were partly idealistic, partly adventurers . . . well trained . . . accustomed to war . . . fit . . . with excellent relations between officers and men.

Schreuders sailed for Korea with the NDVN on October 26 as the second-in-command of the support (heavy weapons) company and as such the battalion reconnaissance officer for Lieutenant Colonel M. P. A. den Ouden. The Dutch believed they were sailing off to a war that had ended. They also thought the weather in Korea must be mild since the peninsula had roughly the same latitude as the Mediterranean. They were wrong on both counts.

Learning about the capacity of Siberian winds to ruin one's lust for combat and discovering that the Chinese had created an altogether new war, the NDVN became a fourth battalion of the 38th Infantry on December 13, one of the regiments ruined in the Chinese offensive along the Chongchon River and the retreat through "the gauntlet" to Kunu-ri. The Dutch themselves received an augmentation of one hundred Korean soldiers and one ROK lieutenant, all combat veterans. The Koreans were integrated throughout the NDVN, not established as a third rifle company.

We communicated with the Koreans in English, most military commands and swear words. The first group of Koreans were good soldiers. The next group—about eighty new conscripts—were not good soldiers until we trained them. We knew the U.S. Army of World War II was a fine army. The American army in Korea was not its equal, too many young officers and men, not enough hard training, too careless in the field. We knew about American weapons since we trained with them on the ship coming over, but we had no winter clothing. We had lots of heavy weapons, though, and vehicles that had been abandoned by the Americans. We needed all those jeeps to carry our heavy machine guns, 81-millimeter mortars, and recoilless rifles. The American food was all right, but we didn't get the potatoes and gin we wanted. The fruit cocktail was popular. I remember the special 1950 Christmas dinner. We received warm fried turkey in containers, but we kept changing positions—three times, I think—so the turkey froze before we ate any of it. The dinner included ice cream—well, it didn't melt, I can tell you! In any event, when we started to advance in January we didn't have much contact with the Chinese. Some small skirmishes, patrol actions. Before 12 February we had only five deaths. Then we met the Chinese in strength.

As part of the U.S. X Corps, the 2nd Infantry Division deployed widely to support an advance north by two South Korean divisions along the axis Wonju-Hoengsong-Hongchon in central Korea south of the 38th Parallel. Much of the 38th Infantry provided security for the reinforced American artillery battalions and tank companies supporting the South Koreans. The NDVN remained in defensive positions near Hoengsong with the regimental headquarters and an ROK reserve regiment. On the evening of February 11, the three leading divisions of two Chinese armies fell upon the forward positions of the ROK 8th Division, and in the next twenty-four hours rolled up not only the 8th Division but the better part of the 38th Infantry and its artillery and tanks. Those Americans and Koreans who survived the frontal attacks and the ambushes along their route of withdrawal flooded in great confusion through and around Hoengsong during the night of February 12–13.

The commander of the 38th Infantry received permission to rally his remnants at Wonju while the Dutch battalion and a tank company held back the Chinese. Lieutenant Schreuders and his standing reconnaissance patrol—

L. C. SCHREUDERS

**Col. (Ret.) L. C. Schreuders leads the Korean War Veterans Parade, Wageningen, the Netherlands, May 2001**

mounted on heavily armed jeeps—went south to find the first fallback position near Wonju. While Schreuders was gone, a Chinese regiment attacked the Dutch defenders sometime around midnight; one Chinese unit, dressed in American coats and helmets, penetrated the battalion headquarters by pretending to be retreating Koreans. One of the Dutch Korean soldiers recognized the ruse, and the night blazed with gunfire and grenade explosions. The NDVN headquarters fought off the infiltrators, but only at great cost, including the loss of Colonel den Ouden, killed in a grenade exchange. Of the thirteen Dutch soldiers who died that night or later, four were officers and four were noncommissioned officers. The two infantry companies and the support company held their positions while the last American survivors flowed around the town and away from the battle. The NDVN fell back unpursued around 0200 but did not reassemble until it reached an airfield outside Wonju. Returning from his patrol, Schreuders ran into the first Dutch soldiers on the Hoengsong road, and they told him the battalion had been wiped out. He doubted that extensive a disaster, but he admitted that the losses of the night battle were shocking enough. (Thirty-seven Dutch and Korean soldiers of the NDVN were wounded in the fight.) More unhappy times lay ahead.

We had not recovered from the Hoengsong battle—remember we had no replacements—when we received orders to defend Hill 325. Well, the Chinese attacked first and drove back the American ranger company we were supposed to relieve. So we had to take the hill back before we could defend it—and it was a crucial position that dominated the road and railroad west to Seoul. We thought our Company A had occupied the hill, but the company commander went to the wrong hill and he would not move without direct orders from the acting battalion commander. In the meantime the regimental commander insisted that we attack Hill 325 even with only one company. Our commander protested, but to no avail. Well, it took us two days and more losses (nine KIA [killed in action] or DOW [died of wounds], ten wounded, five breakdowns) to take the hill from the Chinese. We were also strafed by the U.S. Air Force and even had napalm dropped on us, but fortunately the tanks did not explode. We could not have taken the hill without superior U.S. artillery; we had the artillery fire a mix of high explosives and white phosphorus shells with delayed fuses, and we charged among the Chinese just after all these shells went off. We called them "cocktail" fires, a deadly mix.

Colonel Schreuders recalls that by April 1951 the battalion had been hardened by its battles and the terrible weather conditions. It also had only around 440 men in the field.

In March and April we had rain, snow, more rain, sleet, mud everywhere. One time I went on a patrol in waist-deep snow. Once we went six weeks without a change of clothes. We all had lice, but we got used to them. We tried to make ourselves as comfortable as possible—fires, small huts—but the Americans did not since they seemed to think that suffering was the same as soldiering. By now the Dutch government had accepted that it had a real battalion in a real war, and the Ministry of Defence started a flow of replacements to the battalion, including enough men to form the missing third rifle company, which arrived at the battalion the 28th of May. When the Chinese attacked again in late April we again had to cover the retreat of the 38th Infantry. There was only one road for the regiment, so we retreated through the hills without transport. We lost our one radio jeep in a river, so we lost contact with regiment and division, and they thought we had been wiped out. My soldiers carried one mortar, one recoilless rifle, and several heavy machine guns. We had one day's food for a three-day operation, and many of our soldiers became exhausted from lack of sleep, water, and food. Just before we finally reached an American position, we had forty soldiers collapse. The officers and sergeants used bayonets and rifle butts to get them moving, but we left no one behind. When we got to the American lines we received three days' rations and much attention from journalists. We had had only one day's rest when we were ordered to attack Hill 1251, so our commander refused the order since the hill was defended by hundreds of Chinese.

As the Chinese Fifth Offensive staggered to a halt in May 1951, the U.S. 2nd Infantry Division attacked north toward Inje as part of the X Corps's general advance. The NDVN and the 38th Infantry then held Inje against two Chinese divisions that were attempting to break out of an encirclement. The Dutch suffered twenty more dead in two days (May 30 and June 1, 1951) of fighting, but held the position and earned their third U.S. Presidential Unit Citation. Colonel Schreuders recalls that two U.S. transports were hit by friendly artillery fire and crashed in the Dutch zone without survivors. "We were all pretty hardened, insensitive by June 1951. We thought ghoulish humor was best, like the arm of a Chinese soldier that kept popping out of the mud as trucks ran over his body. Someone said he was waving us forward, others that he beckoned us to retreat."

The Dutch battalion faced more battles before Colonel Schreuders returned to the Netherlands on October 1, 1951. The NDVN fought around the now-famous Punchbowl battlefield, at Bloody Ridge, and eventually, Heartbreak Ridge. By war's end 3,418 Dutch soldiers had served in Korea, 554 for more than one tour, and 123 of them had died from enemy action. Another 381 Dutch soldiers had been wounded, ninety-one seriously enough to be discharged and pensioned as permanently disabled. Colonel Schreuders emerged unscathed. "I was frankly quite surprised that I had not been wounded or killed." He gazes out his office window at the bright winter day in silence as if he were looking for snow-covered mountains thousands of miles and fifty years away.

# 24

## Soldiers of the People's Republic of China

Thanks to the masters of military fantasy who make movies in Hollywood, the universal image of the Chinese expeditionary force in Korea from 1950 to 1953 is that of a "horde" of semicrazed coolies, most of them unarmed or lightly armed at best, hurling themselves with fanatic desperation, fueled by drugs or alcohol, at the embattled soldiers of the U.S. 8th Army. It is usually night and very cold and the Chinese attackers plod toward their inevitable deaths to the sound of gongs, whistles, and bugles as flares light the snow and American artillery crashes into the Chinese infantry. If the Americans are overwhelmed, it is only because they run out of ammunition and cannot fire fast enough. It is the Alamo legend, gone to Asia.

If the moviemakers, on the other hand, work out of Beijing, the gallant if simple peasants and workers of the *Renmin Zhiyuanjun* (Chinese People's Volunteers Force) endure crushing and cowardly artillery fire and air strikes and close with the Americans (or "puppet" South Koreans) and win the battle because of their moral superiority. The enemy is craven, eager to surrender, and without honor or unit pride. The common American soldier is a poor white, a Latino, or an African American slave laborer who has been sent to a war designed by Japanese and American capitalists eager to reestablish the Greater East Asian Co-prosperity Sphere and to destroy the Chinese Revolution. This army of mercenaries and ignorant conscripts cannot stand against the ardor of the Chinese soldier, whose spirit will always prevail over Western firepower. It is Beijing opera outdoors with guns and explosive special effects. If the reality had been like the movies, the war—one way or another—would have been over by New Year's Day, 1951.

The Chinese soldiers of the Korean War represented Chinese society in mid-century—which meant poor, unskilled, and numerous—with the vast majority of the people still tied to the cycles of rice cultivation and village life. In a study of over ten thousand Chinese prisoners in 1951, United Nations Command intelligence analysts created a collective portrait of the Chinese soldier. Most (67 percent) were unmarried and half were younger than twenty-six, while all were younger than thirty. The majority of the prisoners were unskilled laborers or semiskilled workers with virtually no mechanical skills. Forty-four percent of the soldiers had no formal schooling, and another 40 percent had attended some formal school in grades one through six. Except for their military service, all of it in China, they had seldom traveled outside their home province. They knew a great deal about their country, about their Revolution, their army, and their leaders, and almost nothing about anything else. They had traded one structured, hierarchical, authoritarian system for another and sensed no special unhappiness except that they had been captured. They fought when, where, and as long as they were told to fight, and prospective death seemed part of the natural order of life.

The Chinese soldiers who appear in epics written by the People's Liberation Army's political department have inexhaustible energy and high morale. In *A Volunteer Soldier's Day* (1961), *Living Amongst Heroes* (1954), *Racing Towards Victory: Stories from the Korean Front* (1954), and *The Best Prose Writings on the Resist-America Aid-Korea Movement* (1990), the Chinese soldier prevailed because he was physically and mentally tougher, qualities that the ideology of Revolution had given focus. Western technological superiority would not prevail. The American and South Korean troops had fallen in love with their automatic weapons, trucks, and sleeping bags. According to one Chinese soldier, "I had never met such flabby enemies. They glanced back repeatedly as they ran. Seeing that we were catching up with them, they began to throw away their things, such as blankets, overcoats, and miscellaneous articles. Finally even cartridges and rifles were abandoned, as these encumbered their movements. How they must have regretted their parents had not given them more legs!"

Locked in battle, the U.N. troops howled like wolves, gibbered like monkeys, bleated like sheep, fought like cornered rats, and died like dogs. Whether the allusions were born in barnyards or astrological calendars, the portrait of the enemy provides not just the obligatory dehumanization, but stresses the fact that Chinese soldiers were stoic comrades who suffered in silence and willingly sac-

**Having come in from the cold, seventeen Chinese soldiers bask in captivity, Hamhung, November 1950**

rificed their lives for their squads. In one tale, a Chinese soldier burns to death silently so he will not reveal his squad's assault position. The Chinese authors became especially rhapsodic when very large, hairy Americans surrendered to gallant Chinese youths half their size. When the Americans unleashed their air-power and heavy artillery, the Chinese soldier responded with guile, patience, and endless hours of work with a pick and shovel as the Chinese army disappeared into Korea's mountains. They were buoyed by their commitment to save the innocent Koreans from the murderous Americans, who specialized in killing women and children in cowardly air attacks.

The U.S. 8th Army knew its enemy well, at least after the Chinese had fought it to a standstill in three offensives. The operations and intelligence staffs of the 8th Army published periodic but numerous "Combat Notes and Enemy Tactics," and in November 1950 the "Combat Notes" paid a good deal of attention to the Chinese expeditionary force. The Chinese were hardy, capable of living on scanty rations, fast marchers, and determined fighters. They were not good shots except at close range, but they used machine guns well and liked employing hand grenades in close combat. The Chinese preferred to fight at night, when the concealment of darkness enhanced the cover provided by Korea's rugged terrain. The Chinese also preferred ambushes and quick attacks of isolated units and inattentive artillery batteries, truck convoys, and service units.

If the Chinese charged, they did so only when they had already found a hole in the enemy's position. The usual procedure was to probe, probe, probe until grenades had eliminated American machine guns and compromised a positional defense. If the Chinese actually launched a mass attack, the first three or four waves were inexperienced troops with few weapons; they created the ammunition shortage then exploited by experienced Chinese mortar men, machine gunners, and heavily armed and well-trained assault companies. The "hordes" were expendable.

As the fighting continued into the spring of 1951, the infantry divisions of the 8th Army and the South Korean army finally came to grips with a central fact: Their infantry would have to defeat the Chinese infantry. For example, American units established battalion-sized positions, not defenses in depth by isolated companies, and all units organized themselves for all-around defense or to repel sudden attacks upon reserve units and the lines of supply. American units now understood that the chance of survival increased if they did not attempt to withdraw—an invitation to disaster—or to rush to the aid of endangered units, for the Chinese army had mastered the technique of quick marches and violent ambushes. The overwhelming fact was that the Chinese army had serious problems arming, equipping, feeding, and treating its soldiers. Whatever his powers of endurance, the Chinese soldier was human and could not fight without inevitable exhaustion and collapse.

The Chinese People's Volunteers Force suffered 149,000 combat-related deaths and 230,000 wounded, according to the statistics compiled by the PLA's medical department. Western historians think the figures are still too low and do not adequately account for deaths from lingering wounds, diseases, hunger, and exhaustion. For political purposes, Chinese troops made much of the notion that they treated U.N. prisoners humanely on the battlefield. While based on some fact—released POWs made good propagandists—Chinese soldiers were more interested in looting the rolling PX and commissary the 8th Army had become in 1950 to 1951. Because the GI surplus donated by the defeated Nationalists disappeared quickly in 1951, in addition to scarce ammunition and weapons the Chinese placed high premiums on cold-weather clothing, food, and medical supplies. American soldiers often found Chinese dead wearing American uniforms under their cotton-padded outer clothing; since American gloves and boots did not fit well, the Chinese suffered from frozen hands and feet even more severely than their enemies. Many a Chinese attack stalled when the troops foraged through abandoned American trucks and supply dumps, much like the Confederate armies who lost the initiative at Shiloh and Cedar Creek.

In the face of increasing hardship as its supply lines lengthened, the Chinese People's Volunteers Force struggled to maintain its morale and cohesion, in del-

icate condition after the bloodlettings of April and May 1951. Digging a sub-
terranean Great Wall helped distract the survivors as new units moved to the
front. The frontline units finally received the family of Soviet weapons the Chinese had so eagerly awaited since the autumn of 1950. The Chinese political
officers addressed another problem with vigor: the mistreatment of the North
Korean population. The Chinese soldiers punished the Koreans for starting the
war, largely through the confiscation of shelter, fuel, and food. Communists or
not, the Koreans still regarded the Chinese as traditional invaders who were as
numerous and rapacious as ever. Changing the campaign to a war of attrition in
a relatively established combat zone just north of the 38th Parallel simplified
the Chinese problems with troop control.

The Chinese army political department officers knew they faced a continuing challenge: to insure the loyalty of the rank and file, which included a
substantial number of former Nationalist and warlord soldiers. Aided by agents
of the Nationalist regime on Formosa, United Nations Command intelligence
officers estimated that such "galvanized" Communist soldiers were probably
overrepresented among the Chinese prisoner-of-war population (twenty-one
thousand at war's end), but their interrogations suggested that the CPVF needed
a very tight system of supervision and group self-regulation.

One of the prize POWs for his ability to describe the oppressive system of
control was Private Wang Tsun-ming, a former lieutenant in the Nationalist
army. Wang's family was part of the small middle class of Shensi Province in
northwest China. His father held a county government post, ran a clothes shop,
and owned and farmed a sixteen-acre farm. The Communists arrived in 1938
and took over local political control; Wang's family fortunes swooned under official pressure and the Communist party empowerment of the dispossessed and
angry peasantry. Traditional moral codes and social relations became the target
of "new thinking." As the crisis built, Wang joined a Nationalist youth group and
then the Nationalist army in 1947 and served two years in the 181st Regiment,
61st Division, a Shensi organization that finally capitulated in December 1949,
two months after the establishment of the People's Republic of China. Wang
bore the onus of being a member of the landlord class and an organizer of
his regiment's continued resistance to the Communists. Wang first went into
solitary confinement and then found himself shipped off to a special camp to
reeducate former Nationalist officers. It was March 1950.

Wang proved to be reluctant student at the Lianghshan Political Military
Academy, but the endless round of lectures and discussion of the virtues of
Marxism and Maoism eventually bludgeoned him into passive cooperation.
The most destructive technique was the continued fragmentation of social rela-
tions by a system of informers and group humiliations in which self-confessions

turned into increased assaults upon individuality and personality. Repeated
threats of retaliation against Wang's family helped mold him into a "new man."
He learned that "the Communists want to kill without having the victim's blood
on one's hands. This meant that they wanted physical and mental liquidation of
oneself by oneself, so that no one could say that they had done it, but rather the
person had brought it upon himself by the nature of his previous actions." Day
in and day out Wang found himself writing and talking about his past until he
believed that he had lived a life of unpardonable evil. To reinforce this lesson,
Wang had to watch the execution and mutilation of two former regimental and
battalion commanders after his group had been asked to vote upon their guilt.
Finally in January 1951 Wang "graduated" to become a private in a mortar platoon in the PLA 31st Division. He arrived in time to participate in the exchange
of the platoon's 81-millimeter mortars (American) for 82-millimeter mortars
(Russian) of inferior quality, but blessed by being made in a Socialist factory.
He also trained on Russian antiaircraft guns.

When his division entered Korea in March 1951, Wang and the other soldiers
heard that the North Koreans were doing all the fighting and that they would
only guard POW camps along the Yalu. However, they then learned that they
would march south to the front and do so rapidly; the company commander
shot two stragglers as examples. Wang himself had a severe case of diarrhea and
remained with a large number of sick soldiers, many of them untreated, until
May. When Wang rejoined his regiment, he learned that most of his comrades
had already died in battle. On May 20 he walked away from a carrying party
and, armed with a U.N. surrender leaflet, walked toward an American position
across a mountain range. He knew where the Americans were because they had
a searchlight on. When he approached an American outpost with his hands
high, a GI promptly shot him in the leg, but the GIs then apologized, treated
his wound, and gave him candy and cigarettes before sending him to the rear.
Wang survived captivity to become one of the fifteen thousand Chinese soldiers
who refused repatriation. He chose Formosa as his new home, and he rejoined
the Nationalist army and eventually became a lieutenant colonel—but only
after he had survived another three-month rehabilitation program that had
some similarities with the Lianghshan Political Military Academy.

The fate of Chinese POWs who returned to China was cruel and long-lived.
The survivors of the 180th Division received special persecution since, surrounded and out of ammunition and food, four thousand Chinese soldiers of that
division surrendered as a group at the end of May 1951. It was the only significant
mass surrender of Chinese soldiers in the Korean War. Zhang Da, a deputy company commander, was one of the prisoners. A dedicated Communist, he resisted
the "education" programs run by Chinese Nationalist agents and American mis-

sionaries on Cheju-do Island, the site of the Chinese POW camps. To encourage his defection, Chinese Nationalist interrogators tattooed his left arm with the slogan "Fight the Chinese Communists, Oppose the Soviet Union." Zhang cut away the tattoo with a knife he made. His honor intact, he chose to return to China as a repatriated POW, only to face thirty years of systematic discrimination. A university graduate, Zhang found work only as a poor high school teacher. He lost his party membership; his fiancée and a party official denounced him and then married each other. During the Cultural Revolution, Zhang's students denounced him as a traitor and spy; for ten years Zhang lived in a cowshed and worked on collective farms. Finally, in 1980—largely from agitation by the veterans themselves and a handful of senior officers of the People's Liberation Army—the Chinese government issued Document 74, which admitted in guarded language that the POWs who chose to return to China had done their duty in the Korean War.

Zhang Da appreciated his tardy vindication. "I'm lucky," he told an interviewer fifty years after the war, since he had survived combat and an operation on one of his legs while he was held on Cheju. An American doctor had saved his leg from amputation. "I lived through it all. But my biggest complaint is still about the Communist Party. They don't respect history . . . If you don't face your history, you're going to repeat it."

# 25

# The Russians:
# Allies of a Sort

In the heyday of glasnost it appeared as if the Russians were prepared to tell all about their participation in the Korean War. Whenever they visited South Korea, both Mikhail Gorbachev and Boris Yeltsin took with them official Soviet documents about Russian relations with China and North Korea, just as they might take bottles of the best vodka and Russian nesting dolls *(matryoshka)*. Just as too much vodka might dull the senses, too many telegram exchanges between Mao Zedong, Kim Il-sung, Stalin, and the Soviet missions in Beijing and Pyongyang left Western historians historically befuddled. The documentary evidence told a great deal about Soviet foreign policy in the early Cold War, but the documents often raised even more questions because of their silences and omissions. Interpreting the documents has been a growth industry in Russia and China studies centers in the United States and Western Europe, especially for the historians associated with the Woodrow Wilson Center's Cold War International History Project in Washington, D.C. The evidence is better than nothing, but it is hardly satisfying.

The incomplete nature of the Russian story begins with the political conditions that prompted Gorbachev and Yeltsin to open the file cabinets. First, they wanted to curry economic favor with South Korea and to demonstrate that Josef Stalin and Kim Il-sung were absolutely guilty of the charges of aggression brought against them in 1950. A second factor was the deteriorating relations between the Soviet Union and the People's Republic of China, a rivalry that produced exchanged recriminations about the Korean War, botched by either Stalin or Mao Zedong, depending upon what you read. Of course, the Chinese saw the war as a victory (however partial and costly), and they were delighted to blame the incomplete war's outcome upon Russian cowardice and limited military assistance. Anti-Stalinism in Russia coincided with anti-Maoism in China, so Russian documents generated Chinese responses. Another phenomenon in Russia added a different dimension to the new openness about the Korean War: the revolt of the veterans of the Afghanistan campaign. Just as their Vietnamese counterparts in the United States encouraged more "revelations" from other Cold War veterans, including Korean War veterans, the *afghansi* campaign for recognition and benefits encouraged Russian veterans of the Korean War to admit their participation and to trumpet their own grievances. As Russian veterans told their stories to Western historians and media types, they verified or enlarged upon the material from the Soviet state archives. Some Russian-reading Western scholars actually got to see some real documents before the Russian foreign ministry and the Russian armed forces closed their file cabinets after the death of General Dimitri Volkogonov, the former chief of military history of the Red Army and Boris Yeltsin's personal defense advisor. The Chinese criticism became muted as relations between Beijing and Moscow improved in the late 1990s, and the North Koreans had never said a credible word throughout the entire glasnost period, except those from North Korea who had been driven into exile in Russia and China by an ungrateful Kim Il-sung.

The only aspect of Russian participation in the Korean War that comes close to openness is the Soviet defense of Chinese airspace and a limited amount of North Korean airspace. The guidance for Russian MiG-15 interceptor pilots was that they had to stay north of the Pyongyang-Wonsan Line and not fly over the West Sea, because Allied air-sea rescue units might capture them if they ditched. Soviet air units could not fly combat missions from bases within the Soviet Union, but had to redeploy to bases in Manchuria, which they shared with the infant Chinese and North Korean air forces, who were trained by Russian pilots and flew Russian aircraft. The Russian aviation expeditionary force in Manchuria numbered perhaps twenty-six thousand at peak strength and included combined arms base defense ground forces, antiaircraft artillery regiments, ground control-intercept (radar) units, aviation maintenance units, and all the administrative structure necessary for a complex and demanding air campaign. The senior headquarters, established in late 1950, was the 64th Fighter Aviation Corps, commanded in its formative years (1951–1952) by Lieutenant General Georgi Lobov. The Soviet air defense of the Chinese-North Korean borderlands simply extended a Soviet commitment to China's air defense that accompanied the Treaty of Friendship, Alliance, and Mutual Assistance (February 1950). In fact, the Russians had started an aviation defense and assistance mission to China in 1949 and had developed a major air and naval base at Port Arthur under the terms of the 1945 treaty Stalin had extracted from a desperate Chiang Kai-shek. Part of the Russian commitment was to train and equip an air defense force for the People's Liberation Army. In June 1950 the PLA Air Force (PLAAF) established its first mixed aviation brigade with Russian-trained pilots in Nanjing, far from Korea but close to the Communists' next objective, Formosa. Thus, the Soviet aviation intervention in the Korean War included the rapid expansion of the PLAAF and the subterfuge that the air defense of Manchuria and Korea was entirely a Chinese and Korean affair.

As the North Korean invasion began to falter in August 1950, and the growing effectiveness of the U.S. Far East Air Forces became obvious, Stalin authorized the strengthening of the Soviet air defense forces in the Maritime Province and Manchuria. He appears to have been convinced by his own theater commander, Admiral Nikolai Kuznetzov, that the aggressive American airmen might attack Soviet airbases. Stalin sent General Lobov, one of the senior commanders of the *Protivovodushnaia* (PVO), or Air Defense Force, to Vladivostok. As the start of a general pattern of aviation redeployment, the 151st Fighter Air Division (General Ivan Belov) went into position at Shenyang (Mukden), followed by two additional fighter divisions divided between bases at Port Arthur, Tsingtao, and Antung. Two more fighter aviation regiments (roughly thirty-two to forty aircraft per regiment) reinforced the Russian air units in Manchuria in September and early October 1950. These units, however, were already in theater and few of them were equipped with the MiG-15 jet interceptor.

As the war went even worse in September and early October, General Lobov and Admiral Kuznetzov argued with Stalin that they required the best PVO MiG regiments if they were to engage the Americans. They played on Stalin's fear that the Soviet military mission in Pyongyang—accompanied by support troops and some antiaircraft batteries—would be captured by the advancing Americans and Koreans. Stalin warned the chief of the military mission that he "must take all measures to prevent any military adviser from being captured." As the Russian military mission withdrew—part of it departing with Kim Il-sung to Kanggye and the rest of Sinuiju-Antung on the Yalu River—Stalin authorized the creation of the 303rd Fighter Air Division (General Ivan N. Kozhedub, a World War II ace), formed from first-line MiG-15 regiments stationed throughout western Russia to protect Moscow and the Soviet industrial heartland from American bomber attacks. Perhaps as many as 70 percent of the Russian pilots were World War II veterans, but only a handful were proven aerial warriors like Colonel Yevgeni Pepelyaev, who today is credited with twenty aerial kills in the war and thus ranks as the leading Soviet ace. (The Soviets counted an air kill as a kill, regardless of aircraft type, according to World War II practices, while the Air Force tended to count only MiG-15s as worthy of an ace, but then the American pilots did not have much else to shoot at.) Although Lobov remained in overall control of Soviet air operations, he retained command of the 151st Fighter Air Division and all units associated with the PLAAF, while Kozhedub and the 303rd Fighter Air Division retained some autonomy and absorbed incoming air regiments from the Maritime Province and the PVO forces in western Russia.

With Chinese ground force intervention largely assured and the North Korean government in whining death throes, Stalin authorized the commitment of Soviet fighters against the Far East Air Forces [FEAF] bomber force, then in a full fury of bombing Communist supply lines between the Yalu and Pyongyang. Neither the Chinese nor the North Koreans thought that the Russian rescue effort would change the course of the war partly due to the fact that Stalin refused to allow any offensive air efforts directed at the United Nations Command ground forces because he feared aerial retaliation. In fact, U.S. Air Force fighter-bombers had already struck Soviet bases by accident and with little official remorse thereafter. Lobov used these incidents to force his argument with Moscow: "I broke a lot of the rules, and I got the pilots to help." The Russians, however, started by playing by Stalin's rules. Lobov's pilots dressed like Chinese airmen and put PLAAF markings on their MiGs; Kozhedub's pilots (who had taken over the mission of training the North Koreans) also dressed like officers of the PLAAF but flew MiGs with People's Air Force insignia. The Russian pilots were supposed to conduct their airborne conversations in Chinese or Korean, but this quaint linguistic rule of engagement dissolved in combat like a contrail. Laughing at the idea of foreign language cue cards in his cockpit, Colonel Pepelyaev later said: " It was impossible in the heat of battle to use a foreign language you hardly knew . . . we forgot not only the Chinese commands, but the Russian words, too—except for obscene curses . . . we just decided to ignore the order. The top brass started complaining, so I told them to come and fight themselves."

Lobov also complained that his immediate operational mission—to stop American bombing of military and industrial targets in the Yalu River valley—required a reactive force posture. He could not order his MiGs into action until he had positive reports of incoming strikes; his limited reaction time meant that part of his interceptor force had to remain on strip alert. A MiG cockpit in summer replicated a sauna, and in winter, a dip in the Volga. "We had to sit stewing in our cockpits for hours on end," Lobov later told a Western interviewer. "We had to be on duty, waiting, but the Americans could choose the time. This was extremely demoralizing . . . I could never prepare a mission in advance, and it was very tough always having to give orders at the last minute over the radio. Many pilots fell sick. We did not have the state-of-the-art flying suits which the Americans enjoyed." Lobov was correct about the American use of early G-suits to keep blood flowing to the brain in high-speed, erratic flight, but his real problem was that the F-86 had a controlled-temperature and pressurized cockpit. Dependent upon ground control intercept (GCI) directors to make an intercept, the radarless MiGs had little option but to take off in large flights, head for altitudes above the ceilings of American aircraft as quickly as possible, and then make mass plunging attacks in the hope that the escorting F-86s would be drawn off and thus leave less-capable escorts like the F-80s and F-84s and the B-29s vulnerable to the MiG's devastating cannon fire.

The Russian pilots thought of the skies they shared with Chinese and North Korean pilots as inherently unfriendly. The Russians also learned that Chinese and North Korean antiaircraft artillery shot at anything with wings. Lobov resisted the diversion of his pilots and service personnel to supporting the PLAAF and only cooperated enough to avoid a clash with Moscow. He knew Stalin's plan: build a PLAAF and PAF strong enough to move into North Korea and then conduct offensive air operations against United Nations Command. He simply believed neither the Chinese nor the Koreans would ever have such a force. The Soviet pilots felt the same way. "It was obvious that the Chinese had many losses and very few victories," Pepelyaev said. The Chinese were dangerous in the sky from the time they took off until the time they landed; their accidents, including midair collisions, made the Russians so mad that they insisted they would not fly unless the Chinese were grounded. The major problem with the North Koreans was their antiaircraft fire. Pepelyaev recalls that he made at least one attack upon an offending KPA triple-A battery. Another irritant was the Soviet practice of rotating PVO squadrons into the war without adequate predeployoment training. Lobov "complained a lot to Moscow. Train them! Train them!" He eventually delayed releasing veteran pilots until they had flown some missions with the newcomers.

For all their discomforts, the Russian pilots made major daylight B-29 raids costly enough that FEAF Bomber Command chose the Royal Air Force [RAF] option: bomb only at night in small groups or one-plane sorties. Such bombing choices ensured almost absolute survival for the bombers since the Russians had no real night interceptor force. It also meant that the targeting depended upon precise guidance systems that were still in their technological infancy and that depended upon radar guidance systems that might reveal the bomber's position to a bold MiG pilot. When the United States started to expand the acceptable target list in late 1952 to prize economic targets along the Yalu, FEAF returned to large daylight raids, although it carefully husbanded the B-29s and deployed Air Force and Navy fighter-bombers against most of the targets. The campaign included a change in American F-86 employment, a more liberal definition of "hot pursuit" that allowed aggressive Sabre pilots to chase targets well into Manchuria and even to attack MiGs in the process of taking off and landing. Lobov could not get Moscow to let him mount some sort of retaliatory mission like a bomber strike from Vladivostok on the most forward American airfields in Korea. The PVO response was to call back the disaffected veteran pilots of the 64th Fighter Aviation Corps and to replace them with squadrons of young, eager pilots who sought aerial glory in 1953. They actually did nothing but provide easy targets for the "MiG Mad" F-86 aces and would-be aces who crowded into MiG Alley in the war's last months.

The limited Communist air victory in Korea, defined by American bomber losses and new knowledge of how to counter American aircraft of all types, came at a high cost for the Russians and produced controversial claims of success. The Russians admitted losses of 335 aircraft (virtually all MiG-15s) and the lives of 125 pilots. The Russian claims for destruction of U.N. air forces clash with Chinese claims—and the North Korean claims are pure fantasy. At issue is to whom and how did the U.N. air forces lose 1,300 aircraft. The Russians claim to have shot down 1,097 aircraft in aerial combat and to destroy another 200 with anti-aircraft fire, which means that the Russians claim all the kills. The Chinese claim to have shot down 330 UNC aircraft of all kinds in the air and 413 with ground fire, which comes close to duplicating the Soviet feat of a clean sweep. Even assuming some statistical elasticity, the U.N. air forces lost no more than 200 aircraft in aerial combat and around 800 to ground fire with around 70 aircraft lost to unknown enemy action. The claims have not yet been reconciled. The Russians stoutly believe that the enemy had no illusions about the identity of their most dangerous foe. As Colonel Pepelyaev boasts: "The Americans knew perfectly well all about us." And he is correct, but the Truman administration had no taste for candor, and the air war received the same denial treatment as many other aspects of the Korean War.

# Part 3
# THE AMERICANS

# 26

## A GI in Pyongyang

**PYONGYANG, October 1945, and
CHAMPAIGN-URBANA, ILLINOIS, 1998**

The C-54 transport from Guam to Tokyo carried only two passengers, but they seemed to have a great deal in common. They both had spent their childhoods in Seoul, they both spoke Korean, and they both were Christians. But there the similarities ended. One of the passengers was a distinguished Korean gentleman of seventy, a legendary champion of Korean independence and modernization, and a foe of the Japanese. When cold or in distress he rubbed his hands, badly damaged by torturers when he was a young man and known as one of the best calligraphers in Korea. He had once been president of the Provisional Government of Korea in China until his colleagues deposed him. He had taken his cause and his supporters to the United States, where he established a political base in Hawaii and a lobbying enterprise in Washington. After Japan's surrender he had tried to return to Korea, but the generals and the diplomats in Washington wondered about the wisdom of sending one of Korea's greatest political agitators to that part of the country under U.S. Army administration. The old man was Dr. Syngman Rhee.

The other passenger was eighteen-year-old Richard F. Underwood, a private in the U.S. Army. Like Syngman Rhee, he too was going home, but to some sort of military assignment. If Syngman Rhee was white-haired and bent, Dick Underwood was tall, slender, blonde, handsome, and nearsighted. Since he had enlisted in the Army after graduating from a New York City high school, his military career had taken some extraordinary twists. Instead of going to basic training, he had been transferred immediately to the Office of Strategic Services (OSS) for training as an advisor to Korean guerrillas. The Japanese surrender ended this assignment, so Dick received orders to join the U.S. Army Military Government in Korea (USAMGIK), orders he requested and received through the OSS. Army personnel officers discovered he was too young to be overseas without basic training, but another official ruled that his case was exceptional and worthy of a waiver, which was granted. He ran out of flights bound for Korea after he reached Guam, where he writhed with impatience and sweat until he found his salvation in a lonely old Korean man eating in the air terminal snack bar. Dick Underwood knew who Syngman Rhee was—and, more importantly, Syngman Rhee knew Dick's family, for they were the Underwoods of Korea. Rhee told Dick Underwood that General MacArthur had sent a plane for him and that it would take off in thirty minutes. Dick volunteered to help Rhee with his luggage and run errands for him in exchange for a seat. He bluffed his way past the dispatcher and helped Rhee board—and they were off for Tokyo.

Although when comparing himself with his three older brothers and his younger sister, he viewed himself as a black sheep, Dick had plenty of Underwood ingenuity, energy, and courage. His grandfather, Horace G. Underwood, was the second Protestant missionary to come to Korea in 1885. In the next sixty years the missionary Underwoods advanced Christianity, modern education, Western medicine, and traditional Calvinist ethical behavior. The Underwoods learned the Korean language in the streets, in the schools, and in high society, but they never went native. They had sufficient family wealth (from the Underwood typewriter) so that they could live well in Western-style homes, and they spent their holidays sailing and hunting with verve and abhorrence of error. They did all they could to protect the Korean Presbyterian Church from Japanese oppression, a growing problem in the 1930s. After Pearl Harbor they had been sent packing by the Japanese and returned to New York City, their American home. While Dick continued his schooling, his older brother, Horace G., entered the U.S. Navy as a Japanese language and intelligence officer. James, twin of John, joined the Navy as a chaplain. In October 1945 Dick's father, Dr. Horace Horton Underwood, was already in Seoul as a civilian employee of the USAMGIK, rebuilding Korea's educational system.

On the flight to Okinawa and then to Tokyo, Dick concluded that Dr. Rhee might not have been fantasizing when he told Dick that "MacArthur has sent

The Underwoods of Korea, Seoul 1945 (left to right): Lt. Horace G. Underwood, USNR; Dr. Horace H. Underwood, civilian employee, War Department; Specialist Grade Three (T-3) Richard F. Underwood, AUS

for me . . . General MacArthur has sent a special plane for me because he wants me to be president of Korea." As he thought about the trip years later, Richard Underwood, distinguished headmaster of Seoul Foreign School, "regretted that I didn't have the maturity or wisdom to really engage Dr. Rhee in meaningful conversation. I could have learned so much if I'd only had enough sense to take advantage of this golden opportunity." After his success with the trick that got him on the airplane, Dick was not inclined to press his luck. When the transport reached Tokyo, Dick dodged the group of officers who had come to meet Rhee. He grabbed his duffel bag and faded into the crowd like a good former OSS agent and looked for a plane that would take him to Seoul.

After working on some knotty problems in determining the real ownership of abandoned Japanese property and requisitioned Korean property—and even recovering some household goods looted from his own home—eighteen-year-old Dick Underwood, now a T-3 or staff sergeant equivalent, received a surprise assignment. He was to proceed by a special train under Russian supervision to

RICHARD UNDERWOOD

**Mr. And Mrs. Richard F. Underwood**

Pyongyang and join the American military mission to the Soviet 25th Army, the occupation force in northern Korea. The mission consisted of a U.S. Army lieutenant colonel and major, either Poles or White Russians, who worked either for G-2 (Army intelligence) or the Counterintelligence Corps. The only thing Dick learned for certain about the two officers was that both spoke Russian fluently and one was a homosexual. Dick's cover story was that he would serve as their driver and Korean language interpreter. They already had a Russian staff sergeant to perform these duties, a former Frontal Aviation captain who had been condemned to death for protesting Stalin's management of World War II while drunk, but who had been pardoned so that he could join an assault penal battalion on the Eastern Front. He had miraculously survived and praised Stalin fervently for his humanitarianism, which Dick found appalling. In any event, Dick's actual mission was to make contact with Korean Christians in Pyongyang and to collect political information from them as well as data on the conduct of the Russian occupation. The assignment was not without its challenges and ironies.

Early in his tour in Pyongyang Dick Underwood grasped the inherent dangers of his situation in several episodes. First, he drank a glass of clear liquid in a Russian mess, only to discover it was vodka. It was his first drink. He learned from a Korean shop owner that a Russian officer had shot one of his own men for stealing the Korean's watch. He learned that the Russian soldiers believed that the American-made cars, jeeps, and trucks of the 25th Army had all been made in Russia, the official line; Dick discovered that these soldiers could not tell the difference between written English and written Russian, so pointing out to them such names as *Ford, Chevrolet,* and *GMC* had no meaning. To move more freely around the Pyongyang area, Dick modified his American uniform (at the suggestion of his commander) to look like a Russian soldier. He learned that at best this thin disguise terrified most Koreans, who literally threw themselves into ditches when they saw his staff car approaching since Russians enjoyed running over Koreans. At worst he ran the risk of being assaulted by Korean street gangs at night. His fluency in street Korean saved him on a number of occasions.

Agent Underwood established contact with sympathetic Koreans by attending Christian church services. When he established his identity, Dick began to receive photographs, sketch maps, and written reports on Soviet economic "reparations," the systematic dismantling and transportation of industrial facilities out of Korea. He heard about Russians shooting Koreans who had protested the looting. He actually saw the Russians using hand-powered crosscut saws to "harvest" telephone and telegraph poles to be used as lumber. Passing material in church, however, became too obvious, so Dick started to make arrangements to meet his contacts after dark, which meant risking curfew violation, not to mention being caught with incriminating documents. Now Dick's success depended on his ability to bluff the North Korean "blue shirt" police into believing that he was a Russian. He had practiced a set of phrases noteworthy for their profanity and racial slurs, provided by his officers.

One night as he was returning to his billet through a Pyongyang park, "I suddenly came face to face with two blue shirts. They swung their burp guns at me and yelled an order to stop. They were almost as surprised as I was. The difference was they had held the guns, while I faced them. All those hours of rehearsal paid off. I let loose with a string of Russian sounds, just the way I'd practiced. What fun! The two blue shirts snapped to attention, gave me a big salute, and waved me on my way." When the adrenalin drained away, Dick realized he had had a close call. He and his mission officers decided that "my nocturnal wanderings" should end. "It was thrilling, and then some, but enough is enough." When Dick received orders that took him back to Seoul, he accepted them with relief.

Dick's last assignment in USAMGIK was to the intelligence section of the Department of Internal Security. During his period of duty, his Korean colleagues intercepted a boatload of arms sent from Chinnampo in North Korea to a contact in the Mapo-ku section of Seoul. The same Koreans, a lieutenant and a sergeant, intercepted a bundle of letters sent from North Korea to some officers and men of the 14th Regiment, Korean Constabulary, stationed in Yosu. The letters were official instructions on how to start a general uprising to stop the creation of the Republic of Korea. Some small guerrilla groups were already active in the Chiri-sans, and the Constabulary senior officers knew that the two Cholla provinces were hotbeds of resentment over the suppression of the People's Committees in 1945 and 1946. The Korean intelligence officers saw an unparalleled opportunity to rid the 14th Regiment of Communists. The loyal troops would simply arrest all the soldiers to whom the letters were addressed and shoot them on the spot or at least throw them out of the Constabulary. The staff of the American military governor, however, ruled that this plan did not meet any reasonable tests for legality, and nothing was done. A year and a half later, Dick, now a college student in America, did not find the Yosu-Sunchon revolt very surprising, but he wondered why nothing had been done to purge the Communists from the 14th Regiment. He found it ironic that the U.S. Army had become so interested in the rights of Asians after enthusiastically depriving one hundred thousand Japanese Americans of almost all their constitutional rights from 1942 to 1945.

Richard F. Underwood returned to the United States in February 1947 to leave the Army and prepare to attend Hamilton College, the academic home of the Underwoods. Little did he know that he had seen the early stages of the Korean civil war; that in the next three years his mother, Ethel von Wagoner Underwood, would be murdered by Communist assassins; that his father would soon become crippled by a heart condition that would kill him in 1951; and that Second Lieutenant Richard F. Underwood, U.S. Army, would return to North Korea as an intelligence officer and then end the war serving as a Korean language interpreter for the United Nations delegation at Panmunjom. When he started his freshman year at Hamilton College in September 1947, he was puzzled why no one ever believed any of his stories about Korea.

# 27

## The Ambassador
## as Soldier

**SEOUL, KOREA**
**July 1996**

Ambassador James T. Laney is a good old country boy made good; he also *does* good. Korea has profited from his commitment to the country throughout his adult life. His background is a striking contrast to his predecessor, Donald Gregg, a confidant of George H. W. Bush and the former CIA station chief in Seoul. Jim Lancy has all the necessary credentials to impress the Clinton White House: modest roots in Wilson, Arkansas, and three degrees from Yale University, the last a doctorate in divinity. He began his career as a minister as the chaplain of Choate School, in Connecticut, and then became the pastor of a Methodist congregation in Cincinnati, Ohio. He came to Yonsei University as a missionary faculty member in Christian ethics in 1959 and stayed six years, the tumultuous time of the fall of Syngman Rhee and the creation of Park Chung-hee's authoritarian regime. Before his career in Christian education ended—in the institutional sense—Jim Laney taught at Vanderbilt University, and later served as president of Emory University, where he became a respected Atlanta civic leader and confidant of Jimmy Carter. He continued to return to Korea and to Yonsei and watched his students lead the movement to civilian government. My own alma mater, DePauw University, gave him an honorary degree for his incomparable record as a teacher and living example of Christian ethics

JAMES T. LANEY

**Agent James T. Laney, CIC, AUS, Seoul, 1947**

in public service. Jim Laney, however, did not start his love affair with Korea as a missionary, but as a U.S. Army counterintelligence agent.

Ambassador Laney's corner officer in the American embassy on Sejong-no is adequate for his high station, but is a bit too palatial to catch the ambiance of Jim Laney's first Korean experience in 1947 to 1948. I sip a Coke, the proper drink to find in the office of a gentleman from Atlanta, and listen. Ambassador Laney, age sixty-eight, is craggy, wrinkled, and good-humored as he recalls Seoul almost fifty years ago:

I must have been one of the last kids drafted under the World War II law. In 1946, I left Yale University during my sophomore year at the age of nineteen and went into the Army. After six weeks of basic training I received orders to go to Korea to be a counterintelligence agent. I didn't have the slightest idea what that meant except that I didn't have to be part of the "real Army," which was all right with me. I don't think I wore a uniform the whole time I was in Seoul. I really wasn't sure what my status was except that by the time I left Korea I was receiving sergeant's pay. I guess I did become an instant lieutenant once to be an aide to General [Albert C.] Wedemeyer when he visited Seoul in August 1947. I suppose someone looked at my file and decided that a kid drafted out of Yale must be qualified for any kind of duty that had "intelligence" as part of its title.

I joined the 971st Counterintelligence Detachment in January 1947 and served in it until I left Korea and returned to Yale in April 1948. My first assignment was to help keep track of the Russian delegation to the meetings of the U.S.-USSR Joint Commission. To tell the truth, there wasn't much to this duty, but I did get to know the city. I also got to know something about the military government and the Korean police. First, I have no doubt that First Lieutenant Harold Bertsch was the power behind the throne with General [John R.] Hodge. I always wondered how a lawyer from northern Ohio got so much influence, but I never figured it out. As for the Koreans, I thought that Cho Pyong-ok, the head of the Korean National Police, was an able and honest person, who had great difficulty getting control of a police department that had learned its lessons from the Japanese much too well. Cho was strictly an exile politician, and he had a hard time breaking its bad habits. The metropolitan police in Seoul were nominally a part of the Korean National Police, but it was really an independent force run by Chang Tae-sang, a real SOB. The city police of Seoul were certainly effective, but they were also the most brutal and corrupt police force with which we dealt.

In 1948 I became responsible for investigating the murders of leading Korean political figures, which had become a real problem. The biggest issue was the assassination of Yo Un-hyong, who was certainly a credible challenger to Syngman Rhee for the presidency of South Korea. We got the murderer, but he never implicated anyone else, although we felt certain that this murder had been influenced by other Korean politicians, perhaps Kim Ku or Syngman Rhee himself. We never did find any connection between these murders and the South Korean Labor Party, meaning the Communists. I thought we had a trail of implication that reached close to Rhee and Kim Ku, but the chief of staff of the military government told us to forget the investigation since the elections of 1948 were in process.

We also shifted our investigative effort toward the Communists in 1948. Their own intelligence effort was very impressive. We found diagrams of all the U.S. Army installations in Korea, and we felt that the Communists might actually attack American bases. We knew that their infiltration of the security services was widespread. We had so much evidence or rumors on conspiracies to overthrow the government—even before there was one—that we could hardly keep them straight. I brought two conspirators from Pusan to Seoul by train; why I took this risk I don't know, but they disappeared during their first night in Seoul. I could imagine what it must have been like to be a peace officer in the American West after this experience.

Throughout all this excitement, I remained very impressed by Syngman Rhee. I went to services at the Methodist church in Chung-dong, which was the seat of Methodism in Korea. Many American soldiers went to church there, too. Dr. Rhee attended services regularly with his wife, and he always talked with those around him. We all found his command of English very impressive. Even before he became president, we thought he certainly acted presidential, but not dictatorial.

It's hard to imagine how hard times were for everyone in Korea in 1948. I thought the grace and patience of the Korean elite I met were exceptional. I imagine the fact that they were Christians impressed me. On the other hand, we spent a lot of time worrying about our own problems of survival. My own most acute sense of deprivation came from the lack of fresh milk. We hated the dried milk, but we loved the officers who brought back blocks of frozen

**Dr. James T. Laney, President
(Emeritus), Emory University and
Former U.S. Ambassador to the
Republic of Korea**

whole milk from Japan. I hate to think about all the time we wasted on such matters.

I don't recall any special time or event during my military service in Korea that gave me the conviction to become a missionary here. I do remember that I found the Korean intellectual elite, the professors and artists, very impressive and very Christian. I had the sensation that somehow I had become introduced to the sort of people who had been Christian martyrs in the time of Simon Peter and Paul. I was still a very young man when I left Korea and returned to Yale, but I guess that initial experience in 1947 to 1948 must have had a pretty dramatic influence on my own intellectual and spiritual development.

Ambassador Laney seems slightly embarrassed by this modest bit of reminiscence, but his personal account echoes the experience of hundreds of Americans who joined their own lives with the fate of the Republic of Korea. Not fifty yards from the home of Dr. Horace G. Underwood, there is a Japanese maple tree memorialized with a plaque as being planted by Ambassador Laney more than twenty years before. The sign is just another example of Korean male chauvinism since the tree was actually planted by Berta Laney, the ambassador's wife. One is tempted to shift to French to reflect upon the changeless nature of change. Jim Laney, however, is living proof that the Korea of the 1940s is not the Korea of the 1990s.

# 28

## Advisors to the
## Korean Constabulary

Of all the assignments they might have found in the postwar U.S. Army, First Lieutenant Robert G. Shackleton (USMA, 1946) and Second Lieutenant Ralph Bliss could hardly imagine that they would become advisors to an Asian cavalry unit. However, that is exactly what they did in 1948 to 1949 as the two-man advisory team to the 1st Cavalry Regiment, Army of the Republic of Korea. The unit they advised started as the 1st Reconnaissance Troop, an independent unit of two officers and two hundred enlisted men stationed in the Seoul area under the direct operational control of the Headquarters, Korean Constabulary. The concept for such a unit came from Colonel W. H. Sterling Wright, the chief of staff of the Provisional Military Advisory Group, and Captain James H. Hausman Jr., operations advisor or de facto G-3 (see glossary) for the Constabulary. Wright and Hausman saw the need for a mobile strike force stationed near the capital and available to intimidate rioters with mounted soldiers and heavy weapons. An infantry Constabulary company was redesignated a reconnaissance troop in April 1948 with Shackleton its advisor. Bliss joined the unit a few months later. The unit was the cadre of an eventual cavalry regiment, fleshed out as equipment became available and the unit was trained.

The advisors had uneven enthusiasm about their assignment. An infantry officer, Shackleton wondered why he had been posted to a cavalry unit, whether the mounts ate hay or burned gasoline, but the duty was better than retraining

157

ROBERT SHACKLETON

**1st Lt. Robert Shackleton, USA, Seoul, Korea, 1949**

American soldiers who contracted venereal disease in Korea, his assignment in the U.S. 7th Infantry Division. Colonel Terrill E. Price, the director of the Department of Internal Security, gave Shackleton no sympathy and no advice on how to organize a cavalry unit without a table of equipment and organization or even a vague idea of what equipment it would eventually be issued. A cavalry officer, the nineteen-year-old Bliss had lobbied for the advisory assignment since he had been placed in a port management (stevedore) battalion of African American soldiers stationed at Inchon. In August 1948 he "escaped this dreary duty" for the 1st Reconnaissance Troop, stationed in an abandoned warehouse on the northern bank of the Han River near Susaek-dong. The troop had been armed with cast-off American infantry weapons, .30-caliber and .50-caliber Browning machine guns, and some very used jeeps and trucks signed over by units of the 6th and 7th Infantry Divisions as they deactivated or departed for new stations in Japan and the United States. Shackleton and Bliss could hardly imagine how they would turn this unit into two planned squadrons, one equipped with vehicles (the M-8 Greyhound scout car, armed with a 37-millimeter cannon, or the White half-track) and the other squadron mounted on real live horses. When Shackleton went to Colonel Price for more guidance, Price told him to leave his office and take his problems to Captain Hausman, who at least provided some general guidance. Shackleton and Bliss were perplexed about how a cavalry unit could be trained efficiently without translated American field manuals. Meanwhile Shackleton drew up a table of organization and equipment for the projected mechanized and horse units.

The troop's inability to start its twelve-week training program on time for equipment shortages was not critical since 60 percent of the troop were sometimes sick from contaminated water taken from the Han River. At least the American lieutenants could mount a field sanitation program to cure their troops of a form of trotting that did not require horses. Shackleton and Bliss also learned that their two Korean lieutenants spoke virtually no English, so they could not do any instructing until they received some kind of translation help. In the meantime they collected more weapons and ammunition from the departing Americans, and the Korean troops cleaned and familiarized themselves with their vehicles (jeeps, half-tracks, and trucks) and weapons. One of the biggest challenges was teaching the Korean soldiers to drive. Shackleton "sweated blood every time they departed the post in convoys." The Korean officers disliked asking for help, but with patience and tact Shackleton and Bliss found they could make their points about training and maintenance. The troop received a new commander in the summer of 1948, a Major Kang, but he was an absentee commander who gave little to the unit except noninterference.

Eventually Shackleton got lucky. One day a young Korean civilian approached him and stated in excellent English that he wanted to join the unit. Shackleton swore the man into the unit on the spot. The man, Chang Bong-chung, rose through the ranks to become a major general in the Korean army and a lifelong friend to Shackleton and Bliss until his death in 1998. With the addition of Chang and a Lieutenant Kim, another English speaker, training and advisory activities took a vigorous turn in June 1948.

The Yosu-Sunchon Revolt of October 1948 provided the 1st Reconnaissance Troop with a critical opportunity to prove its worth. As soon as Constabulary headquarters learned that the 14th Regiment and its civilian sympathizers had seized two cities and employed weapons equal to those of the Constabulary infantry brigade sent to crush the rebellion, the senior American advisor, Brigadier General William L. Roberts, ordered the troop to load its vehicles on a train and head for Sunchon as quickly as possible. The troop deployed with ten half-tracks, fifteen jeeps, and some weapons carriers and trucks for supplies. All the half-tracks and jeeps had at least one, and often more, machine guns as their main armament. The troop arrived to find Sunchon recaptured but the drive on Yosu stalled by rebel gunfire. The troop took over the advance into the city of Yosu and played the leading role in the city's recapture on October 26 after three days of fighting. The troop also suffered about 25 percent casualties (ten killed in action, fifteen–twenty wounded in action), and Shackleton and Bliss were proud that their soldiers did not shrink from close combat. Shackleton was moved to the point of tears when he reviewed the unit at a parade in Seoul after the fighting. Some of the troopers were a few months from civilian life, but they had served with distinction.

The American advisors had other worries. Their men were rough in their treatment of civilians caught up in the fighting, and they had been especially tough on surrendered members of the 14th Regiment. Shackleton later estimated that his soldiers may have killed as many as three hundred civilian non-combatants during the fighting in the streets of Yosu. Most of the casualties came from indiscriminate machine-gun fire at snipers. This was a tragic result of the troopers' lack of thorough training. The atrocities committed by the Communists, on the other hand, sickened Shackleton when he saw the bodies piled up around Sunchon, but he and the other American advisors would not accept the angry reprisals their Korean loyalists wanted to inflict on prisoners. "The memory of the piles of dead in Sunchon never left me. Henceforth the terms *Communist* and *butchers* were to me synonymous." Ralph Bliss had the dubious honor of being memorialized in a picture taken by the prize-winning war reporter and photographer of *Life* magazine, Carl Mydans. Bliss is the young, thin, taut lieutenant standing behind a Korean widow as she wails over the body of her husband, a murdered policeman of Sunchon.

After it returned to Seoul and the rebellion shifted into a protracted guerrilla war in the Chiri-san Mountains, the 1st Reconnaissance Troop began to prosper. Its American counterpart in the U.S. 7th Infantry Division trained it in early 1949 and turned over its arms and vehicles before leaving for Japan. The unit expanded to eight hundred officers and men and divided into two squadrons. The motorized squadron, principally advised by Shackleton, formed two companies, each equipped with sixteen M-8 scout cars, sixteen half-tracks, and around thirty jeeps, as well as supporting trucks. The horse cavalry squadron, Bliss's special project, took more work. Korea was not rich in good horses since those left from the Japanese occupation had either gone to work as carthorses or into a pot. Bliss gathered some mounts from the Seoul racetrack, private owners, and butcher shops. Horses were so scarce that Bliss drafted a plan to use oxen to carry supplies when the squadron deployed into the mountains to chase Communist guerrillas. The horse squadron (which never became larger than a company) actually found itself performing in parades, festivals, and government ceremonies, almost daily events in Seoul.

Except for releasing some antique McClellan saddles and training manuals discovered in the warehouses of the 1st Cavalry Division, the U.S. 8th Army in Japan did nothing to support Shackleton and Bliss. As their relations with their Korean counterparts matured—aided by the assignment of a fine regimental

ROBERT SHACKLETON

**Pvt. Chang Bong-chung and Lt. Kim of the Reconnaissance Troop, 1949**

commander, Colonel Lee Ryong-moon—the American advisors became increasingly aware of the tension in Korean-American relations. At the policy level, the American advisors believed that the United States was not properly supporting the Korean army, much of which was actually at war with the Communists. They were incensed by the lack of help from MacArthur's FECOM (Far East Command) staff as well as the 8th Army. At the working level, the U.S. Army's order prohibiting off-duty fraternization with Koreans stood as a monument of insensitivity. Shackleton was twice arrested by American MPs for eating dinner in a restaurant with Korean officers. Shackleton recalled that the MPs seemed shocked that he was also eating Korean food. Shackleton found it infuriating that Americans would become social lions with the Japanese, former wartime enemies with a stunning record for atrocities, while the same Americans "treated the South Koreans like untouchables. Our nonfraternization policy deeply offended Koreans."

On the positive side, the Cavalry Regiment—for such it became in 1949—moved to better quarters when it took control of a former Japanese cavalry post in Seoul's Sobingko district. The training situation improved. One problem was the continued upheaval in the army. On one memorable morning the Americans discovered that the military police detachment had "seceded" from the

ROBERT SHACKLETON

**Maj. Gen. Chang Bong-chung, Robert Shackleton, and Ralph Bliss, Korea, 1970**

regiment and set up a special all-MP compound. The cavalry MPs had seized a barracks and set up two loaded machine guns. Astonished by the event, Shackleton and Bliss vigorously objected, consulted with the regimental commander, and then reported the facts to Colonel Wright. Shackleton sorted out the episode:

> We later learned that this was a Korean MP power play to institute an independent MP channel throughout the Korean army, depriving unit commanders of their control over their organic MP units. Colonel Wright stopped the effort dead in its tracks, and our regimental commander immediately regained control over his MP unit. The machine guns and their crews disappeared by mid-afternoon. This episode was an example, I understood, of Japanese military methods, which some Korean officers wanted to emulate. I remember it as an instance when the Advisory Group exerted a decisive influence in avoiding a potentially nasty development in the Korean army.

Both Lieutenants Shackleton and Bliss departed from the 1st Cavalry Regiment and Korea in the spring and summer of 1949, turning their advisory assignments over to a major and a couple of junior officers. Shackleton left the army in 1949 and joined the Foreign Service, where he specialized in political-military affairs. Although he claims, "I never took to military life," he served as politico-military officer in the U.S. Embassy in Saigon (1968–1969), Bonn, and eventually as the U.S. Army and Air Force representative to the German states of Hesse and Rheinland-Pfalz (1977–1991) and as a political advisor to several U.S. Army senior commanders in Europe. He continued to believe that the Korean War might have been prevented if the United States had made a serious effort to create an effective Korean army ("We did a poor job . . ."). Ralph Bliss remained in the army to retire as a lieutenant colonel.

In June and July 1950 the 1st Cavalry Regiment fought as separate detachments with four different South Korean divisions. The M-8s and half-tracks were no match for North Korean tanks and self-propelled assault guns. The South Korean army's official history of the defense of Seoul provides no evidence that the "Independent Cavalry Regiment" had any impact on the losing battle. The horse-mounted squadron went to war as foot reconnaissance teams and also disappeared in the debacle north of the Han River. When the regiment re-formed during the defense of the Pusan Perimeter, it became a standard infantry regiment in the Capitol Division. Shackleton and Bliss never learned what happened to the Korean soldiers they knew in their year's service with the regiment except that Colonel Lee had been killed in action late in the Chiri-san campaign (1949) and Major Kang had been shot for cowardice in 1950. Survivors of the regiment, such as Major General Chang Bong-chung, always believed the regiment was inadequately armed to meet the North Korean assault. Shackleton in later years concluded the U.S. advisory effort was a failure. It did not, he thought, provide the necessary tools and training to the South Koreans to defend themselves. "The integrity of South Korea was subsequently secured only at the cost of American lives and huge suffering by the Korean people." When Shackleton proposed a memorial to the Cavalry Regiment in 1997, for which he and Ralph Bliss would pay, he found the ROK army disinterested. The Korean defense attaché in Washington finally told him that too many regiments had been destroyed in 1950 to memorialize only one.

# 29

## Early Casualties

**NATIONAL MEMORIAL CEMETERY OF THE PACIFIC**
**"THE PUNCHBOWL," HAWAII**
**June 2000**

I went to "The Punchbowl" the middle of Puowaina Crater, an extinct volcano, to attend a Korean War fiftieth anniversary commemoration that honored the veterans of the 5th Regimental Combat Team (RCT), U.S. Army. Reorganized at Schofield Barracks, Oahu, in June 1949, the 5th RCT was a Hawaiian regiment of World War II veterans and local recruits when it sailed for Korea. Now, fifty years later, its exceptional service was to be memorialized with a special monument on the lip of the Punchbowl, where one can see both the cemetery and downtown Honolulu. It is a place named by the Hawaiian *allii* as a hill of sacrifice to honor warriors.

Robert M. Alip tells me that he and his high school friends climbed to the Punchbowl before World War II to see American soldiers practicing shooting. After the war they watched burials. Alip is not a former member of the 5th RCT, but he is active in the Veterans of Foreign Wars, and this is a VFW event, too. He is an elfin warrior—perhaps 5'3"—wiry, active despite a neck brace, and deeply tanned, which sets off his white mustache and goatee. From the greetings of other veterans, Alip is clearly well known and liked. He tells me he does not feel well and fears losing weight, but despite the heat he shows no signs of fading away.

What's my family background? Portuguese, Chinese, Filipino, maybe Hawaiian, pretty typical here. I graduated from high school in Honolulu in 1948, but I had no money for college, and jobs were scarce. I joined the Army like a lot of Hawaiians. I enlisted to save money, get GI benefits, and travel to Japan. I ended up in Company H, the weapons company of the 2nd Battalion, 19th Infantry, 24th Infantry Division. We were stationed in southern Kyushu. In the spring of 1950 we had a mix of training, athletics, and passes off post. It was good soldiering.

On the morning of 25 June, all that changed. Since it was a Sunday morning, reveille was supposed to be late, 0700 or 0800, I suppose. A lot of us were hungover from a big party in the town of Beppu. Suddenly some sergeants turned on the barracks lights and started yelling about some war in Korea, and we were on alert. Well, we sobered up quickly. We spent the day cleaning and packing gear. I remember we took a break and heard a good briefing. Apparently the war wasn't going well for the ROKs. Our regimental commander, Colonel [Guy S.] Meloy, talked to us, too. He said we didn't have any movement orders yet, but we would. He thought we'd be back in Japan in two months. He also said some of us wouldn't come back at all. That was very sobering.

The 19th Infantry was the last regiment in the 24th Division to leave Japan. I think we went aboard an old LST [landing ship tank] on July 1 and landed at Pusan on July 4th. An ROK army band was on the docks playing American patriotic songs, but the songs sounded strange, and we sure felt strange on that particular Independence Day. We'd already heard that our other two regiments had been badly shot up. I wondered about all the talk about an easy war.

Three comrades in Japan before battle: Nick DeStefano (KIA), Pvt. Richard Alvarez, Pvt. Robert M. Alip, 19th Infantry, 24th Infantry Division

On July 16, 1950 Alip's regiment occupied positions along the Kum River, north of Taejon. His machine gun section, attached to Company F,

HONOLULU TRANSPORT

**Robert M. Alip**

prepared firing positions near Hill 200. He thinks he remembers ROK soldiers on the right, GIs from the 34th Infantry on the left. Neither group stayed very long when North Korean shells started falling, and he could see tanks crossing the river.

I was part of a .30-caliber, water-cooled Browning machine gun team. Water for us and the gun was not plentiful. We didn't have enough rations, either. The big problem was ammo. We had only two boxes of belted ammo, five hundred rounds. Luckily the machine gun ammo was in cloth belts, not metal links, so we could reuse the belts. The reserve ammunition, however, was boxed as five-round clips for the old M1903 Springfield rifle. So we had to take the bullets out of the clips, stick them in the empty belts—which jammed easily—and hope we could load the belts fast enough to keep firing. Ammo was so short—and some of it had rusted in storage—that our ordnance people wouldn't issue it, so we had to run back under fire for our resupply.

We couldn't stop the North Koreans. The tanks kept crossing the river, shooting at our hill but not paying much attention to us. The North Korean infantry came after us with grenades and burp guns [the Russian PPSh41 submachine gun] of which they had plenty. Our infantry fell back around our machine gun, then we ran out of belted ammo, so we started firing our M-1s. At one point I think the platoon sergeant and I were the only ones shooting. During one lull I realized I was wounded, shot in the shoulder and maybe elsewhere. I was bleeding, in shock, and dehydrated. I told the medic I could still walk—barely—so he tagged me and sent me down the hill. At the aid station someone jammed compresses into the wounds and gave me a shot of morphine. The next day the medics were loading wounded into jeeps and trucks for a retreat, and I got in a truck before the morphine knocked me out. The medics took us to Taejon. Later some other wounded guys told me they had to fight their way through several roadblocks before we got to relative safety in Taejon. The wounded were evacuated by train to Pusan. My war had ended.

Sometimes I run into some VFW guy who was a Korean War vet from 1950. We start talking, and he says he knew four or five buddies who died in Korea. Hell, I bet I knew fifty!

# 30

## A Korean from Hawaii

**HONOLULU, HAWAII**
**June 1996**

Tai Soon Lee, age sixty-seven, and I met in the coffee shop on the grounds of the Hale Koa, the U.S. armed forces' luxury hotel on Waikiki Beach. It is a strange place to discuss the Korea of the 1940s and 1950s, but Lee served two tours there. I found him through the veterans' groups so active in the Hawaiian Islands, a place where veterans cherish their service records, in part because they challenge the anti-Asian racism that plagued Hawaii in the past. I had started my quest for a Hawaiian witness hoping I could find a Japanese American veteran of World War II who fought in Korea with the Hawaii-based 5th Regimental Combat Team. My contacts suggested, however, that Lee would make a great interview, and they were correct. Retired from the U.S. Air Force in 1971, Lee has devoted his second career to veterans' affairs in and out of the state government. Born in Lanai in 1929 to a Korean cane cutter who had become a skilled worker and a Japanese mail-order bride who arrived only to find her fiancé dead, Lee knows well the problems of Hawaii's Asian citizens. Yet he remembers how proud his community was of its World War II veterans. That pride and the lack of work on Lanai in 1946 pulled Lee toward the Army, but his father would give him permission to enlist only if he met one condition.

Tai Soon Lee's broad, friendly face wrinkles with a smile when he remembers his father's injunction: You will go to Korea!

My father didn't want me to go to Japan and just get into trouble with the other GIs, and he wanted me to find his family. I don't know what my mother thought, since she had family in Japan, too. Hell, I just wanted to get off Lanai, get a start on learning a real job. The Army was delighted to have me, since it had to send replacements quickly to Korea to replace all the guys who were rotating home. I was seventeen years old and thought I could handle anything, especially in Korea, since I spoke both Korean and Japanese as well as English. After five weeks of basic training I shipped out for Korea and ended up on the 38th Parallel just north of Kaesong, working as an interpreter and intelligence clerk.

We screened refugees from the north—some from as far as Manchuria—for information about the North Korean, Chinese, and Russian armies. I thought we got some pretty good stuff on unit identifications, locations, and other observable things. Our most important conclusion was that the North Koreans intended to fight along the 38th Parallel as early as 1948 since they built a whole set of new roads that had no commercial purpose, and the refugees saw military construction everywhere. Our own outposts had to deal with guerrillas and Communist border police commandoes, so we kept pretty alert. The Communists had a field day attacking isolated Korean National Police stations, so it was no surprise when the ROK army arrived since our sector was pretty active. After Korean independence in 1948 we went to Japan, so I got there after all, but I never made contact with my parents' families. I returned to Hawaii to be discharged in June 1949, but the job situation was still lousy, so I extended my enlistment and ended up with the 5th Infantry at Schofield Barracks as a personnel clerk. Then I switched to the 555th Field Artillery Battalion, which was part of the regimental combat team. I was still in the Army as a corporal when the war began in June 1950. We had no hint that this war was coming.

Alerted for Korean duty in early July, the 5th RCT scrambled to prepare to deploy. It took in new recruits with virtually no training, but it also joined about one hundred or so World War II veterans who volunteered even before the reserve mobilization. Since three Hawaiian National Guard infantry battalions had served in World War II (including the famous 100th Infantry Battalion, which became part of the *Nisei* [Japanese American] 442nd Regimental Combat Team), the number of veterans, some active reservists, did not represent a massive response, as Lee remembers.

We were glad to have veterans of any sort, but I don't recall much fuss then about combat veterans from the 442nd RCT. We had a real racial mix and experience of all sorts, but we didn't have enough real fighters, so many of the regulars and veterans who held support jobs ended up in infantry battalions and artillery batteries. I wouldn't say we were wild about the idea of being combat soldiers since we *were* veterans. We had to train on the ships, which meant really just shooting weapons, but I guess that put us ahead of a lot of units. I still had my clerk's job, but I volunteered to be a truck driver, an ammunition hauler, too.

In addition to this job, I became an interpreter again and found myself in charge of a Korean working party. I was now a sergeant. When we went into action in August 1950, our artillery battalion got partially overrun, and our headquarters battery and two of the firing batteries suffered about 45 percent casualties. There seemed to be no safe rear areas since we always had infiltrators and guerrillas around. I got into a couple of firefights and got wounded when a burp gun blew all kinds of sharp rocks into my legs, a close call. So I got a Purple Heart, which I would have traded for my typewriter and some safety. Anyway, we hung on, and in September we started north when the North Korean army collapsed.

When the 5th RCT crossed the 38th Parallel, Sergeant Lee immediately noticed a difference: North Korea still had trees on its mountains. After a tumultuous welcome in every South Korean village as the Americans drove north, Lee found little more than trees in North Korea. The enemy army had disappeared and the villages seemed deserted. When the regiment passed through Pyongyang, Lee found the modern buildings surprising. Danger, however, still lurked off the roads. Once, Lee's battery went to see the bodies of GIs who had been shot inside their sleeping bags. He remembers that the Commonwealth brigade, especially the Australians, shot first and asked questions later. Any casual violence against Koreans distressed him. Nevertheless, he found some humor in his conversations with "real" Koreans, who told him that his Korean vocabulary and idioms dated back to the reign of King Sejong. They had no trouble believing that Lee's father had immigrated in 1910. Considering the devastation in North Korea—the product of the air raids—Sergeant Lee had no urge to change places with the newest victims and refugees. Then the Chinese intervened, and the 8th Army soldiers became road people, too.

After the Chinese attacked the ROKs and the 1st Cavalry Division near Unsan in late October, we knew we had a new war, whatever MacArthur thought. I remember how relieved we were in early November when we turned off the road for the Yalu River and stopped the advance. The weather had turned cold—and we Hawaiians really felt it! Boy, we hated the cold! MacArthur came up for a visit, and he looked cold, too, and he didn't stick around long. Although the Chinese didn't hit the I Corps too hard, we weren't surprised when we headed back south. General Ridgway may have outlawed the use of the word "bug-out," but we sure drove fast. The roads were a mess, especially south of Pyongyang. There were accidents everywhere, fires, supply dumps being pillaged by GIs and Koreans, food scrounging, gasoline stealing, even occasional gun battles over the right-of-way and loot. Of course, we had guerrillas harassing us, especially at night. I remember when a big ammo dump blew up in Pyongyang—I think our engineers did it—and the sky rained unexploded shells and bullets as well as burning debris. It was a good time to keep your helmet on—and I still had mine and used it. I don't think our morale was poor. We were happy to get out of the grasp of the Chinese, but we assumed we would get reinforcements and fight our way back in the spring.

When we started our counterattacks later that winter, the regiment did very well, as least as long as the veterans were there. When the rotation policy started in the spring of 1951, of course, the combat infantrymen and artillery FOs [forward observers] went home first. Our replacements also ended the Hawaiian character of the regiment since they came from everywhere, reservists and draftees. They were good soldiers, but they had a lot to learn. Personally, I'd had enough of the Army and the war when I left for home in August 1951.

Still unimpressed by the job opportunities in Hawaii, Lee switched from the Army to the Air Force in 1954 and became a technical sergeant (personnel administration) before retiring. He regrets that he never married and had a family, but service life did not favor family stability. He also had a problem with Japanese and Korean parents who did not consider him quite right for an honorable marriage because of mixed parentage. In any event, Tai Soon Lee thinks of himself as a Hawaiian and loyal American and he has earned that right.

# 31

## Expatriate Veteran

**SEOUL, KOREA**
**August 1996**

The heat and humidity give the rice a green aura as we drive up the new superhighway ("MSR 1" in military parlance) that runs along the north bank of the Han River to the estuary the river shares with the Imjin. This is the historic "Western Corridor," one of the invasion routes to Seoul that runs from Kaesong, now in North Korea, through Munsan and into Seoul. It is a measure of South Korean confidence that this superhighway to the Imjin-gang exists at all. At Freedom Bridge, however, the Korean War begins again, and the security is tight through the Joint Security Area to the camp of the Neutral Nations Supervisory Commission (NNSC), where the Swiss and Swedes find less and less to do, shunned by the North Koreans and ignored by the South Koreans. I am making a second speaking trip to the NNSC mess, which is always a treat since the NNSC knows how to make boredom enjoyable. My driver on this trip, however, is special: Master Sergeant John McCarthy, U.S. Army (Ret.), a continuous resident of Korea since his retirement in 1969. John is a natural salesman, and I find it perfectly believable that American companies that do business in Korea find his expertise invaluable. One of his clients is the Heineken Corporation, which explains his popularity with the Europeans trapped at Panmunjom.

McCarthy knows his territory, largely because he fought over most of it in 1950 to 1951.

> I grew up in Dorchester, Massachusetts, a town that has sent boys into the Army since the Revolution. I joined the Army in 1949 at the age of seventeen. The draft didn't have anything to do with it. It was a family thing, and most of my male relatives had been in World War II. I came to Korea in July 1950 as a rifleman in Company I, 3rd Battalion, 29th Infantry Regiment, an independent regiment based on Okinawa. We were a very green unit, not in good physical shape, probably about half new recruits [actually 400], and armed with new weapons we had never test fired. The only thing that saved us was that we had some good officers and veteran NCOs.

John McCarthy drives his Hyundai sedan with skill and ease as he talks about one of the biggest disasters the 8th Army suffered, in July 1950. Thrown into battle as an attached regiment of the 25th Infantry Division, the 29th Infantry was further divided into battalion task forces for a futile series of counterattacks in southwestern Korea, designed to bolster the ROK forces falling back before the NKPA's crack 6th Division. The 3rd Battalion received vague orders to "retake" Hadong, a key city on the road to Chinju, which leads to Masan and then Pusan. The battalion had a special guide, Major General Chae Pyong-duk, who had just been replaced as ROK Army chief of staff, but who had not fled the field. John McCarthy remembers the Hadong disaster well, but without special passion.

> We walked into an ambush, and I suppose Company I would have been wiped out except that we were at the rear of the march column in battalion reserve. When the fight started, most of the command group, Weapons Company, and Companies L and K really got hammered. General Chae got killed, too. Most of the battalion command group became casualties immediately. I remember all the noise, the yelling, the artillery and mortar shells exploding everywhere. We went forward to try to clear a hill, but we took heavy casualties and couldn't advance. It seemed as if everybody was running for his life. My platoon stayed pretty cohesive, but I think we lost all our company officers. I remember our company commander, Lieutenant Makarounis [First Lieutenant Alexander G. Makarounis], covering our withdrawal, and we never saw him again. [Captured at Hadong, Lieutenant Makarounis escaped from the North Koreans in October 1950; he has now been nominated for a Medal of Honor by Colonel Lewis W. Millett, the former president of the Medal of Honor Society and a fellow Korean War hero from Massachusetts.] The survivors of the battalion gathered at Chinju, and we went into the under-strength 19th Infantry as composite companies in two different battal-

ions. Our morale—at least the Company I guys—wasn't too bad. We thought we could do better next time, and we wanted to get some revenge on the North Koreans.

The Hadong affair destroyed the 3rd Battalion, 29th Infantry. Other units eventually recovered the bodies of more than 300 GIs from the stricken field, and 100 more remained missing, most of them captured and doomed to die in captivity. When all the survivors could be mustered and counted, the battalion had about 350 effectives left, the rest wounded and missing. The remnants remained with the 19th Infantry for awhile, then re-formed as part of the 27th Infantry Regiment, which did not have a third battalion. John McCarthy was glad to be a "Wolfhound," one of the two truly outstanding regiments in the 8th Army of 1950, commanded by the legendary Colonel John L. Michaelis, a World War II paratroop officer and future Army general.

We became part of the Wolfhounds and saw plenty of action in late August and September, the most notable being at the "Bowling Alley" north of Taegu. I don't remember much about the battles. When we broke out in September and went north—actually west in our case—I recall seeing discarded North Korean equipment and vehicles and plenty of POWs. I was surprised that we took women prisoners, who claimed they were all nurses. Well, the North Koreans must have had great medical care! I didn't see any atrocities or wanton destruction. We just drove from city to city, welcomed by happy crowds everywhere. Across the 38th Parallel, we got cold and saw plenty of destruction, but even when the Chinese intervened, we managed to get away without real problems.

John McCarthy considers himself a lucky man, and the statistical realities of war suggest that his good fortune is indeed unusual. "I came to Korea a PFC [Private First Class] and left a Staff Sergeant, a squad leader, and I served in the infantry the entire time. I was never wounded, a real miracle. I was in Japan on R&R when the Chinese offensive of April 1951 began. I left Korea in July 1951."

I ask John about his first impressions of Korea and the Koreans. His response is matter-of-fact: "It's hard to remember. I'm married to a Korean, a wonderful woman, and I've lived here so long I feel comfortable. And we feel the same way in the States, where our daughter lives now. I liked the Koreans and saw how much they had suffered. As for the KATUSAs in our company, they were a mixed bag. A few were fighters."

John McCarthy never doubted that the war was worth fighting, and he remains active in veterans' associations and other Korean-American friendship groups as well as the international community in Seoul. "Any veteran who thinks we lost or fought a useless war should come to Korea. I'm proud that we gave the Koreans another chance to build a better life for themselves and their children—and they did!"

# 32

# The Making of a
# Special Forces Officer

**QUEBEC, PROVINCE DE QUEBEC**
**August 1995**

Colonel John E. "Jack" Jessup, U.S. Army (Ret.) and I are at the annual meeting of the International Commission of Military History, military historians from more than thirty countries, most of whom work for their armed forces. This colloquy is another clash of national historical "party lines," in this case about peacekeeping. Jack Jessup and I first met at a similar conference twenty-one years ago, and I have listened to his most excellent war stories ever since. He has impressive academic credentials (a Ph.D. in Soviet history), and his last troop command was the 3rd Infantry, "The Old Guard," the Army's Washington ceremonial regiment for promotions, retirements, and burials. Jack's uniform drips medals for combat valor and distinguished service in one Cold War brushfire after another. He has no medals for being in Budapest in 1956 or Tehran in 1980. Jack has had a rich mystery life as a Special Forces officer, but he began his life in the beaten zone as an infantry lieutenant in Korea in 1950. At the time of our talk Jack is sixty-eight and still scuba dives, but he has given up skydiving. He clearly enjoys telling his Korean War stories, New York City accent intact.

**1st Lt. John E. Jessup, USA, Korea, 1950**

After I served as a boy Navy frogman in the last year of World War II, I went to college at the University of Maryland on the GI Bill. I became a second lieutenant, infantry, with a regular commission when I graduated in 1948 and went to OCS. I was twenty-one. After OCS I went to the Infantry School and then to Fort Knox to be an instructor in an experimental Universal Military Training Unit. When the war began, I got orders to the 5th Regimental Combat Team [RCT] in Hawaii, but I didn't join the regiment until July 1950 when it reached Sasebo, Japan, on its way to Korea.

Although the 5th RCT eventually made a reputation for steadiness in combat, it did not arrive in Korea with its ranks full of ardent soldiers. Jessup remembers the press-gang methods the 5th RCT used to fill its ranks. First, it joined some two hundred prisoners in Japan, GIs who had missed their units' deployment to Korea. The replacement officers served as their armed guards. This "dirty two hundred" filled the rifle companies. The regiment also raided the over-strength 24th Infantry, offering its African American soldiers one jump in rank if they joined the 5th RCT. The temptation worked.

We were a pretty rough lot. When we left Sasebo for Korea on a Japanese coastal transport, we had prisoners in the ship's brig, some of whom had mutiny on their minds. The 24th Infantry's NCOs helped keep the peace. So did the Japanese sailors. We had one prisoner badly beaten by a female Japanese coal stoker when he assaulted her, and another went blind from bad booze. Even aboard ship some of the thugs, who were no longer handcuffed, beat and robbed other GIs. What could we do with them? Send them to Korea? Fortunately, the 5th RCT had picked up some Hawaiian veterans of all races before sailing. The *Nisei* were the best known, and they were great soldiers. I had a PFC in my platoon who had a Distinguished Service Cross won in the "Go for Broke" 442nd RCT in World War II. Of course, the Communists picked up on our *Nisei* members and said we were really the Japanese army coming back to Korea. Seoul City Sue gave us a whole broadcast as the new Japanese army.

Jack went into combat on August 6 as the commander of the 2nd Platoon, Company E, 2nd Battalion, 5th RCT. He thought climbing the hills was more challenging than combat. He spent much of his time looking for withdrawal routes or "bug-out boulevards." He remembers that his company always got to burn down villages, taking "Arson Easy" as a call sign. His platoon also looked for Russian weapons, especially mint condition PPSh "burp guns" with 1950 markings to prove Soviet sponsorship of the Korean People's Army. One time the company took positions behind the 24th Infantry just in case it withdrew without orders. On another occasion Company E learned that the 8th Army band was protecting its flank—not reassuring news. Jack was lucky because one of his soldiers had grown up in Korea, a missionary's son. The pastor's son was good with villagers, and he could get good intelligence and extra food. Jack's company had to defend huge frontages without much artillery and no air support. His platoon took three and a half hours to climb one hill and fifteen minutes to run down the slope under North Korean counterattack.

Col. John E. Jessup, USA (Ret.), Washington, D.C., 1995

The next time the KPA attacked again it was at night. A rainstorm set off our flares and land mines. I was taking a crap and shot one KPA soldier from the squatting position with my carbine. We also had a Bren gun and carrier, which gave me some extra firepower . . . our own little tank, sort of. We stole it from some Brits who weren't looking. Things did not get better. We found ourselves in some apple country near Taegu in September, backing up the 1st Cavalry Division. There was no front to speak of, guerrillas and KPA patrols everywhere. We were very nervous, shot at anything. We burned down a village by mistake. We used *National Geographic* tourist maps, so it is no wonder we got lost.

On September 16 Jack's company attacked a hill that had been bombed by B-29s. Company E was supposed to clean up the "remnants," but found the KPA battalion to its front largely unscathed and fighting mad. The attackers became the attacked. Fighting in a driving rainstorm, caught between two KPA companies, and mortared constantly, Jack's platoon held its position, losing all but seven of its twenty-five soldiers. During the battle an American tank machine-gunned Jack's platoon, killing a Chinese American sergeant. Jack tried to kill the tank gunner, but could not get a clear shot before another NCO tackled him. He was then hit by mortar fragments in the back and by a bullet in the stomach. He thought he'd been gut shot, but the bullet had hit a C-ration can of mixed fruit, so the mess was not his intestines. It was a good thing, since the 1st Cavalry Division had sent no aid men as it had promised to the 5th RCT. One of Jack's men died of shock; another bled to death from lack of attention. Jack received a Silver Star for the engagement.

I got patched up and came back to the regiment. My platoon became the regimental I&R [Intelligence and Reconnaissance] Platoon, thirty-five guys. We were really mobile and armed: ten jeeps, five .50-caliber MGs, two 57-millimeter recoilless rifles, three 3.5-inch rocket launchers, tommy guns, BARs [Browning automatic rifles]. But we hadn't been issued much tactical sense. We roared around the countryside shooting up retreating KPA units, but we got ambushed and shot up pretty badly. I had lost my second platoon and got shot in both legs. This time I went back to Japan for treatment. This was around 30 September, so I'd been in Korea about two months. Boy, it seemed a lifetime. When I returned to full duty in November, I volunteered to join the Special Action Group, a bunch of raiders. I figured it couldn't be much more dangerous than fighting in the 5th RCT—which was a *good* regiment! Nothing could have been much worse than the combat I'd already seen.

# 33

## By Faith I Fly

**AIR FORCE MUSEUM, FAIRBORN, OHIO, May 2000,**
**and HONOLULU, HAWAII, June 2001**

Dean Hess was alive! And living in Huber Heights, Ohio, a bedroom community of middle-class probity north of the city of Dayton. Why a retired Air Force colonel would live in Huber Heights was no puzzle: The main post of Wright-Patterson Air Force Base was twenty minutes away down Route 4. But Dean Hess? My informant had a high degree of reliability. Donald M. Bishop, a public information and cultural affairs officer for the Department of State, had spent an earlier life as an Air Force Academy graduate, Vietnam veteran, intelligence and base security officer, Korean expert, history professor at the Academy, and student of America's air wars in Asia. In the spring of 2000 the news reports of the No Gun-ri incident—in which a handful of panicked GIs had gunned down some harmless Korean refugees—had raised related questions about the bombing and strafing of refugee columns in the summer of 1950. Don sent me a cable from his post in Beijing and suggested I look up Dean Hess. My friends and colleagues—including my Korean graduate students—thought my enthusiasm for meeting Dean Hess inexplicable. They do not watch or remember classic war movies; any fool knows that Rock Hudson is Dean Hess.

DEAN HESS

**Maj. Dean Hess, USAF, completes his 100th mission, Korea, 1950**

When we met Dean Hess at the Air Force Museum in May 2000, he looked nothing like Rock Hudson, but he was very much alive and active at the age of eighty-one. He is compact, perhaps five feet and eight inches, thin, almost frail, wears glasses, but he moves and speaks with the confidence that befits a fighter pilot of the pre-jet era. He smiles with ease. Dean Hess flew P-47 Thunderbolts and P-51 Mustangs in Europe in World War II. In 1948 when the new U.S. Air Force faced a pilot shortage, Hess, a captain in the Air Force Reserve, returned to active duty and learned that his assignment was not flying at all but visiting universities and colleges to organize officer procurement programs. In the spring of 1950 he received orders to go overseas to Japan, where he stood watch as a radar intelligence officer and awaited another challenging assignment as a group information and education officer.

It takes little imagination to see a senior Air Force commander examining Hess's qualifications. Hmmm, one-hundred-plus missions, good combat flying record with the 511th Fighter Squadron and 405th Fighter-Bomber Group. Definite leadership qualities, mature and responsible, solid family man with a wife and children, seems good at working with people. But, my God, he's a reservist and not checked out on F-80s or our other new jets, and he was working on a Ph.D. in history at Ohio State when he volunteered to rejoin the Air Force. Here's the kicker: He's an ordained minister! He calls his plane *Per Fidem Volo.* What the hell does that mean? And he flies fighter-bombers? Well, I guess we need guys like Hess to do all these ground jobs, so that the regular officers like us can fly jets and prepare for a war with the Russians. That's why we're here in Japan to build up the air defenses and prepare our B-50s to drop nukes on Vladivostok.

Dean Hess told his story in his autobiography. *Battle Hymn,* a minor best-seller in 1956 and made into a Hollywood movie with Rock Hudson playing Dean Hess, a case of the monumental miscasting typical of movies in the 1950s. Hess and a friend, Clark St. John, revised the book in 1987 and arranged for its republication by a small, specialized press, Buckeye Aviation Book Company, in Reynoldsburg, Ohio. You have to want the book to find it, but it is a steady seller at the Air Force Museum's bookstore. Colonel Hess never lost his interest in historical study (B.A., Marietta College, 1941, and M.A., Ohio University, 1947), and we use our visit to the museum not just to meet Colonel Hess, but to get a sneak preview of the Korean War exhibit set to open in June 2000. As I suspected, the curators did not object to having Colonel Hess show us through the exhibit with his running expert commentary. The private tour group included Major Park Il-song and Lieutenant Commander Cho Duk-hyun, doctoral candidates at Ohio State and faculty members at the Korean military and naval academies. The son of a prominent Presbyterian pastor, Cho brings Colonel Hess a Korean-English Bible. In a sense, Dean Hess gave up his graduate studies so that Park and Cho could pursue degrees in the United States fifty years later and not at the State University of Moscow.

Dean Hess still has the heavy dark eyebrows that always gave his face a special intensity, but his hair has thinned and he now has a trace of a mustache. Unlike many of his 1950 peers, he did not use the war as an excuse to look like Kaiser Wilhelm. We had all read *Battle Hymn,* so Colonel Hess's remarks over coffee in the "Air Force deco" cafeteria are essentially reflections upon what his life has meant to him and just what is fact and fiction in the movie and the many newspaper and journal articles that have been written about his humanitarian contributions to building modern Korea through orphanages for Korean children.

The movie exaggerates my feelings of guilt about strafing refugees in the summer of 1950. We had faced similar problems in France and Germany in 1944 to 1945—enemy troops mixed in with civilians, difficult target identification, that sort of thing. I know I may have bombed a German day-care center by accident. We tried to be careful, but making fine distinctions when you're fighting a war is not possible. There was another Korean War movie, *One Minute to Zero,* that tells the story pretty well. It's true that I did strafe one refugee column in Korea by mistake—a spotter aircraft said he saw enemy troops—and I'm sure I killed one young girl. I certainly regretted her death, and I took even more care, but I had faced a similar ethical crisis before, and I had made up my mind that there were evils in the world worse than war. I cherish peace, but not at the cost of other human values. On the other hand, I didn't feel comfortable becoming a minister again after World War II.

"For the record, I wanted Gregory Peck to play me, but he was unavailable." Hess laughs easily.

Dean Hess learned to fly and perform the duties of a minister of the Christian Church in the late 1930s along the Ohio River. The callings were related since he could serve several churches in the small river villages by flying from one pasture to another. As the possibility of American intervention grew in 1941, the Reverend Hess spoke in favor of intervention against Nazism. He started to apply for a reserve commission in the Army Corps of Chaplains, but he thought he had no right to take a noncombat assignment when he was urging his parishioners to fight—and perhaps die—in a war against evil. He postponed his wedding to Mary Lorenz (who became Mrs. Dean Hess for forty-four years until her death in 1996) so he could enter the Army's aviation cadet program. Against the wishes and advice of the Ohio board of the Christian Church, Dean Hess went off to war.

When the war in Korea began, Dean Hess again volunteered for combat, but at least he was now a major, a proven close air support pilot, and a candidate for a career as an Air Force officer. He won a lottery with another major and had his group commander tell him that he would form a special group (a squadron with ground support elements), called Bout One, that would fly F-51s to a primitive strip at Taegu. Hess's pilots would try to help the South Korean army and the first elements of the U.S. 24th Infantry Division. Hess's instructions did not include using his American pilots in combat; instead they would help South Korean pilots learn to fly F-51s. Hess's men were all volunteers, most of them for the wrong reasons. Of his first ten pilots, seven would die in the next year, so courage was not an issue. Hess did not think many of his pilots had the temperament or skill to be instructors; he wondered how they would get along with the South Korean pilots, all of whom had flown in the wartime Japanese air forces. The Koreans had already flown combat missions with their converted trainers, the North American AT-6 and two types of observation aircraft. The ten Korean pilots assigned to Hess were the most experienced pilots in the South Korean Air Force (ROKAF). The senior pilot, Colonel Lee Gun-suk, had twenty kills in World War II. Unfortunately, Colonel Lee thought a Mustang

DEAN HESS

**Maj. Dean Hess meets President Syngman Rhee, Korea, July 1950**

should handle like a Zero, and he flew his aircraft into the ground during an attack on July 4, 1950, four days after Hess's arrival in Taegu. Lee's death persuaded Brigadier General Kim Chong-yul to order his pilots to listen to the Americans and learn to fly and fight, but to fly to fight another day.

Bout One's greatest success came on July 10, when Hess and his wingman answered a frantic call from an Air Force tactical air control party on the ground. A North Korean armored column was bearing down on Taejon. The American ground forces could not stop it. Hess immediately relayed the information by radio to the 5th Air Force operations center before he and his wingman dove into the attack with their rockets and machine guns. They stopped the column by destroying the leading and rear vehicles, and then the rest of the 5th Air Force arrived—F-80s, F-84s, and A-26s—and completed "the Pyongtaek massacre." The U.S. Air Force left more than 150 tanks, combat vehicles, and trucks burning and exploding on the road to Taejon. Such good days made building up the ROKAF—as well as Bout One—look superfluous.

Throughout the summer and autumn of 1950, Dean Hess's training group worked to create a new air force for South Korea. Hess had to appeal to Maj.

**Col. Dean Hess, USAF (Ret.) discusses Korean War exhibit, Air Force Museum with the author and Lt. Cmdr. Cho Duk-hyun, ROK Navy, May 2000**

Gen. Earl E. Partridge Jr., USAF, the 5th Air Force commander, to keep the training mission alive when his group was redesignated the 6146th Air Base Unit, an ignominious title for a group that was flying combat missions in F-51s with ROK markings. General Kim and Major Hess established a regular F-51 training base at Chinhae and ran their practice flights against North Korean targets along the Pusan Perimeter. American and Korean pilots flew sorties together.

The number of ROKAF pilots and aircraft in the battle continued to increase. Most of the sorties supported South Korean divisions, which lacked organic artillery and would tolerate "blue on blue" accidents that the Americans would not. Hess thought the Inchon landing would mark the real coming-of-age of the ROKAF, but he could not persuade any American air commander (Air Force or Marine) to give him space at liberated Kimpo airfield. Instead he found the overgrown field on Youi-do Island, a small strip that had served downtown Seoul during the Japanese years and American occupation. Without prompting, thousands of Korean commoners—all ages, both sexes—rallied at the edge of the field and then weeded the field by hand to support their air force. This act of popular commitment—coupled with the ardor of the ROKAF pilots and their American counterparts—persuaded General Partridge to give the ROKAF the support it deserved.

When the Chinese entered the war, the ROKAF displaced all the way to Cheju-do Island, and this movement produced Dean Hess's moment in history: Operation Kiddy Car. An Air Force chaplain came to Hess during the dark December of 1950 and alerted him that a thousand orphans, many seriously ill and malnourished, had no way out of Seoul and thus out of the clutches of the oncoming Chinese. Hess immediately recognized the ethical dimensions of the crisis and arranged with General Partridge for twelve C-54 USAF medevac transports to evacuate 806 orphans to Cheju-do. The ROKAF transports took 245 more children, along with Korean military personnel and their families. Hess persuaded Cheju-do authorities to turn an abandoned school into an orphanage. The orphans enjoyed high-level support from Mrs. Syngman Rhee and the dedicated attention of Mrs. Whang On-soon, the de facto mother of thousands of Korean orphans. Medical attention for the orphans came from the ROKAF medical staff of Colonel Kay Won-chul, M.D. They could not save two hundred of the original evacuees. Both Mrs. Whang and General Kay died in the year 2000, venerated heroes of the Korean people.

In 1951, however, no one knew where the orphanage leaders would find money for their continuing operation. Colonel Hess hoped his prayers would work. In a few months, favorable press coverage of Operation Kiddy Car produced a book contract and then a movie contract. Hess used the money to create a trust fund for the orphanage.

By the spring of 1951 Lieutenant Colonel Dean Hess had flown more than 250 missions in his F-51, *By Faith I Fly,* the name emblazoned on the aircraft in Korean, not Latin, for this war. He had laid the foundations of the modern Korean air force, and he had provided a link between the Air Force and the orphanage on Cheju-do, and thereafter to other American and Korean sponsors. Ordered home in May 1951, much against his wishes, Hess made two predeparture visits, one to the Cheju-do orphanage and the other to the ROKAF's first major operating base at Taegu. A grateful Air Force awarded him a Legion of Merit, but a more grateful Republic of Korea presented Hess with the Order of Military Merit, the first American officer to be so honored who was not a general. Colonel Hess returns regularly to Korea, where his orphans have turned into productive citizens and his ROKAF officers and their students into the nation's leading military and commercial pilots. One of his wingmen, Kim Too-man, became a general and Chief of Staff, ROKAF in 1970. Hess himself has received more honors from the Korean government. Do the citizens of Huber Heights know that a hero lives among them? Dean Hess would never claim this honor, but he has as much right to this recognition as any veteran of the Korean War.

# 34

## Two-Time Survivor

**PRAGUE, CZECH REPUBLIC**
**August 1997**

Once again Bob Phillips, a retired historian of the U.S. Air Force, age seventy-two, and I meet at the annual congress of the International Commission on Military History, a meeting where he and his wife, Marjorie, and my wife, Martha, have enjoyed each other's company for more than twenty years. Introduced by one of my own former graduate students, Joe Gross, also an Air Force historian when he and Bob worked for Systems Command, my wife and I have been friends with the Phillipses for twenty-five years. I admire Bob's book, *To Save Bastogne* (1983), the story of the 110th Infantry Regiment's gallant rear guard action in the early days of the Battle of the Bulge. Bob Phillips, just twenty years old in 1944, had been there. And he had been in the U.S. Army in the Korean War. He is smart, fit, and still active. He is modest about his two wars.

I went into the Army after graduating from high school in 1943 and went through training as a field medical specialist or medic, a very dangerous and stressful job. I finally got into the war as a replacement medic in the 2nd Battalion, 110th Infantry, 28th Infantry Division, the old "Bloody Bucket" Division, Pennsylvania National Guard. I joined the division in August 1944 in northern France. We crossed into Germany on 11 September. I lasted two weeks in combat after entering Germany. I was trying to stop the bleeding of a rifleman who had taken shell fragments in the legs in the fighting south of Aachen. This kid was thrashing around and hollering, so I had my hands full—and very bloody. Another shell landed nearby and made me a casualty, a shell fragment in the chest. I yelled at a GI to look at my chest and see if he could see any air bubbles in the blood when I took a deep breath. He said there weren't, so no sucking chest wound, and I may make it. He patched me up with the compress from my first aid pouch and I crawled over to the wall of the building for better protection. I finally got evacuated by stretcher jeep and didn't rejoin the division until 15 December. I ended up back in the regiment, and I participated in the fighting near Clervaux, where we were defending a hotel and a chateau against the 2nd Panzer Division—you know, the Hollywood version of the battle, *Castle Keep*. Well, it was certainly surrealistic enough, but we escaped with some of our wounded in a truck and ended up in Belgium north of Bastogne. We were then sent south to the French-Belgian border where our regiment was being reconstituted.

Bob Phillips survived the war as a company medic in the 110th Infantry and finally left Germany in July 1945 for redeployment to the Pacific. When the war ended in September he was discharged and went to the University of Oregon on the GI Bill. Attracted by soldiering as a career, he joined the Army ROTC and finished college as a Distinguished Military Graduate or a top candidate for a regular commission as a second lieutenant. He learned, however, that the shell at Aachen had done more than scar his chest; the burst had permanently damaged his eardrums, and he could not pass a physical examination for admission to the regular Army as an officer. He did still qualify for a reserve commission (infantry) and volunteered for active duty. Since the Army had no money to call him to active duty as a reserve officer, Bob Phillips returned to the service as a private first class and reported to

ROBERT PHILLIPS

**Cpl. Bob Phillips, USA, Tokyo, 1951**

Fort Riley, Kansas, to work as a troop trainer. His paperwork for a commission disappeared into the maw of the Army personnel bureaucracy. The year was 1950.

As a veteran, Phillips received orders to Korea as an infantry replacement (seven days' delay en route) in early July. An emergency airlift put him in Japan, where he drew field gear and an M-1 rifle, which he tried to zero with the ration of five rounds. He and his comrades took a troopship to Pusan, sent off to war with a band playing "I Want to Get You on a Slow Boat to China." Pusan in early August 1950 reeked of disaster. The city was full of stragglers, refugees, tons of scattered equipment and munitions, and confused Korean and American soldiers. Bob saw a train pull into the city, with the coaches jammed with ROK army wounded and the flat cars piled high with bloated corpses. Taking some rations and ammunition, he and his replacement group eventually reached the ravaged 21st Infantry Regiment, 24th Infantry Division. His group became Company I in the 3rd Battalion, a unit that had been more or less wiped out in earlier fighting. There was only one senior NCO.

> The weather was very hot, and we never had enough pure water. We looked for wells, streams, and rice paddies in that order, and of course we had stomach cramps and the shits all the time. We were constantly hungry, but rations never seemed to find us. We stole chickens, apples, vegetables, and peppers to eat. I began to wonder if I really wanted that commission after all, even though the war made it a moot point whether I would be on active duty.
>
> We got into our first big fight on September 8 in the hills south of Kyongju. We were fighting for some key hills, stopping a penetration, and the platoon commander, Lieutenant Thomas G. Hardaway (USMA, Class of 1949), ordered a charge up one of the hills. Most of our platoon were World War II vets, but I wondered about some of them. When Hardaway yelled, "We've got to get that hill and hold it," he was running through my squad position. I just jumped up and followed him. When we got to the top of the hill, I looked around to see where the others were positioned. There was no one behind me. The rest of the squad was still crouched in their holes and looking up at us. I motioned for them to come up, but nobody moved. I returned to their positions once to get more grenades, but though they gave me the grenades, they said they were supposed to hold where they were. B.S. Anyway, Lieutenant Hardaway and I got into a grenade fight along the crest with some North Koreans in some holes on the reverse slope. Hardaway would throw and I would hand him the grenades. Half of them didn't explode. The rifle ammo wasn't so hot either. At that point one guy came up the hill, having done nothing up to that point. Seeing one of our KATUSAs in a foxhole near Lieutenant Hardaway, the soldier yelled, "Gook, gook," and fired an entire clip of bullets into one of our South Koreans. When I yelled at him that he was killing a KATUSA, the shooter went nuts and, screaming, headed for the rear. We never

saw him again. Anyway, Hardaway jumped up once too often and got killed, a bullet in the chest, so I threw the rest of the grenades. Fortunately, somebody with a tactical sense had gotten some tanks to blast the reverse-slope NKPA positions, and killed many of the attacking force. Not all of them. When I crossed the crest, I found five North Koreans. I think they must all have been wounded, but at least one had a burp gun. I killed them all with my rifle.

When the 8th Army shifted to the offensive in mid-September, the 21st Infantry pushed north toward the 38th Parallel. Bob's platoon had the satisfaction of ambushing an entire NKPA platoon, but much of the rest of the campaign in South Korea was bloodless. Bob's company rescued a 1st Cavalry unit from the wreckage of an ambushed convoy and endured strafing by American jets. He almost got into a fight when he used a 1st Cavalry Division yellow scarf to clean his M-1, an act of desecration that enraged some nearby troopers. Occasional North Korean night infiltrator aircraft dropped bombs on the American columns, with almost no damage. Bob's company used some abandoned Russian trucks and marked them with glowing air panels, but the Air Force still strafed them. The company simply fired back as fast as it could until it drove off the "friendly" attackers. There seemed to be plenty of ammo, but food remained scarce. In late October the company received sleeping bags and some cold-weather clothing, but not much. Thoroughly chilled on October 31, the regiment had reached a point only ten miles south of Sinuiju on the Yalu River. The word came down to halt, then to fall back to the battalion trucks. The GIs knew something was up, but their concern did not stop them from scooping popped rice from the burning paddies along the road. They passed soldiers of 3 Battalion, Royal Australian Regiment, one of the toughest outfits in the 8th Army. The Aussies made plenty of caustic remarks about retreating, but no one seemed very worried.

I celebrated my twenty-sixth birthday somewhere on the Chongchon River on November 3. By now we all knew the Chinese had entered the war. The I Corps had circled the wagons after the 1st ROK Division and the 1st Cavalry Division got so badly shot up at Unsan. I remember fires everywhere, some bonfires, some abandoned equipment. The first fires had spread to the hills, so smoke enveloped us. I think the Chinese started fires, too, to conceal their troops. There were wrecked trucks everywhere since the convoys moved at night; Chinese air strikes seemed a real threat, but never materialized. Anyway, we milled around until the great "Home for Christmas" offensive, when the Chinese attacked again. We didn't get hit too hard and got out okay. When we had one fight with the Chinese, I was amazed to find them armed with M-1s. They even had complete cleaning kits in the butt wells, which we did not. When we started the bug-out, as a rear guard for 8th Army, it was a great road race—if slow—all the way to Seoul. We lost our Russian trucks to the

**Robert Phillips receives a Silver Star medal for heroic combat in Korea, 1950, Washington, D.C., 2000**

logistics guys, so we walked out, supplying ourselves from wrecked and abandoned trucks along the road. When no convoys passed us, the whole country seemed empty, just cold and barren and really spooky. We had orders to burn anything we thought useful to the Chinese, and we interpreted that broadly. I think the only people we had to fight were some Korean guerrillas.

Pyongyang was a burning mess when we went through it, but at least we didn't have to fight. The only unpleasantness was when more Air Force jets strafed us, but again no one was hurt. I always thought our experience suggested that Air Force claims of enemy casualties might be a little inflated. By the time we reached South Korea I had a roaring fever from an ear infection and terminal exhaustion, so the CO [commanding officer] had me tagged and sent to Japan in January 1951. Needless to say, that Christmas present was late, but really appreciated.

Hospitalized in Tokyo, Bob Phillips learned in January that he had been simultaneously called to active duty as an infantry lieutenant, and found unfit for further field service. Enduring more ear tests and examinations he flew as a medical evacuee to Fort Carson, Colorado, in administrative limbo but officially a corporal. More ear examinations followed. He had gone almost deaf in his left ear. A medical officer at Fort Carson thought he should never have been evacuated, but now should be either discharged or ordered to active duty as an officer. In 1952 the Department of the Army ruled that all reserve officers then serving as enlisted men should be called to active duty as officers, but Bob still could get no firm decision whether his deafness was disqualifying since the Surgeon General's office kept changing the criteria for deafness disability. (If all partially deaf soldiers had been discharged then and now, the ranks would thin rapidly.) Bob continued to serve out his regular enlistment contract, worked in a supply office, and received a promotion to sergeant. He passed some audiometer tests, failed others. Exhausted and disillusioned, he turned down another promotion and left the Army in April 1953 when his enlistment expired. He returned to Oregon to earn his master's degree in history and, using veterans' preference and his disability points as civil service leverage, he took a job as a civil service personnel administrator in Washington. His former regimental commander in the 21st Infantry, Major General Robert W. Stephens, arranged his appointment as a historian in the U.S. Army Center of Military History. After his retirement in 1986 he returned to Korea and liked what he saw, but he still thinks the Army of 1950 to 1951 was not the same Army that defeated the Wehrmacht.

In February 2001 a grateful U.S. Army awarded Robert F. Phillips, age seventy-six, the Silver Star medal for gallantry in action on September 8, 1950, near Kyongju, the Republic of Korea. The citation repeats the same story Bob told me four years ago except that it also mentions that his jacket had four bullet holes in it and his helmet sported a bullet crease. The awards ceremony, well attended by Bob's family and friends, took place at Fort Leslie J. McNair, and the commanding general of the Military District of Washington made the presentation. His remarks suggest that the genial general knew nothing about Bob Phillips's military record since he called him "a young private first class." On the day Bob Phillips won the Silver Star he was twenty-five years old and fighting in his second war, but he has no complaints. "I'm lucky I did what I did and made it home."

# 35

# Fighting for the Koreans

The Seoul Foreigners' Cemetery at Yanghwajin, a Han River ferry crossing between Seoul and Yongdong-po, has been surrounded by apartments and is bounded by a subway bridge and the Second Han River Bridge for motor traffic. It is one of four religious sites on a low, wooded ridge between the bridges; the others are the site where Yi dynasty soldiers executed French and Korean Catholics in 1839 and 1866, the Catholic Church of the Martyrs, and the ecumenical Protestant Seoul Union Church. The Foreigners' Cemetery took its first interment in 1890. Those who rest there have varied backgrounds, but the most noted tombstones mark the graves of Korea's great Protestant missionary families: Hulbert, Appenzeller, Underwood, Clark, Avison, Moore, Heron, Baird, Bell, Linton, Jensen, and Shaw. Below a hillside pocked by tombstones, cedars, and shrubs rest the remains of the Reverend William E. and Adeline H. Shaw, who came to Korea in 1921 as Methodist missionaries. Beside them is their son, William Hamilton Shaw, who died on September 22, 1950.

When I saw Bill Shaw's grave for the first time, I imagined him a Christian martyr held prisoner by the Communists and executed as the 1st Marine Division penetrated Seoul's outskirts. I got the killers right, but not Bill Shaw's death. He died in the uniform of the U.S. Navy and in combat. Like his friend and fellow Navy lieutenant, Horace G. Underwood, Bill Shaw came to Seoul as a liberator, interpreting for and guiding the 5th Marines, the veteran infantry regiment that fought its way into a maze of ridge lines, ridge spurs, draws, and hilltops known as An San and Yonhui Ridge to the inhabitants and Hill 296 and the three Hills 105 to Marines. Today the terrain is the site of a public park, an ROK army communications facility, the Yonsei University campus, Seoul Foreign School, and the homes of the affluent residents of Shinchon-dong and Yonhui-dong.

Bill Shaw's road to Seoul started in Pyongyang, where he was born in 1922. As the son of a missionary pastor and seminary teacher, Bill Shaw grew up in the mounting anxiety caused by Japanese repression of Korean Christianity. A graduate of Pyongyang Foreign School, Bill went to the United States to enter Ohio Wesleyan College in 1939, thus missing his parents' internment and re-

**Lt. (JG) William H. Shaw, USNR, 1945**

patriation in 1941 to 1942. His father was an Ohio Wesleyan graduate and former World War I Army chaplain. Bill did not join a social fraternity but won admiration for his debating skills. Omicron Delta Kappa, an elite honor society, elected him a member, an unusual honor for a non-Greek. He became student body president. Handsome, captain of the swimming team, and a charming social companion, he graduated in 1943 with a Phi Beta Kappa key and a new wife, Juanita Robinson, the daughter of a Methodist minister. He immediately entered the U.S. Navy, completed officer candidate school at Columbia University, and then became a PT boat officer, eager for duty in the Pacific war. His squadron instead ended up in the English Channel on routine patrol duties. Bill Shaw

STEPHEN SHAW

**The Shaw family in Seoul, Korea, 1949 (from left) the Rev. William F. Shaw, Juanita Robinson Shaw, Adline Hamilton Shaw, William H. Shaw, William R. Shaw**

volunteered for Japanese language school at Oklahoma A&M University in 1945, but the war ended before he finished the course.

At loose ends after VE Day, Shaw looked for a job and some way to return to Korea, although his parents were then occupied with missionary relief work in the Philippines. He worked in the Navy Document Center in Washington until released from active duty in August 1946. Needing work to support Juanita and two-year-old son William Robinson Shaw, Bill managed to become an instructor at the South Korean Coast Guard Academy at Chinhae as a civilian employee of the military government. There he found a friend, Bill Sherman, from the Japanese language school. Sherman, now a retired foreign service officer in the rank of ambassador, recalls that Shaw's Korean was very good, as was his Japanese. Of the three officers at Chinhae, only Shaw had wartime sea service. He made a great impression on the infant ROK navy (Hae Gun) with his nautical skill, enthusiasm, linguistic ability, good humor, and unrelenting demand for superior performance of duty. The midshipmen adored him.

When the Republic of Korea became a sovereign nation in 1948, Bill Shaw and Bill Sherman joined the Korean mission of the Economic Cooperation Administration (ECA), the U.S. foreign aid agency, in Seoul. The change in status meant they qualified for government housing and could bring their families from Chinhae to Seoul. The work was demanding but exciting since ECA officers had an active role in relief work, economic reform, combating the Communist rural guerrillas, and trying to inculcate American business practices. Bill Sherman and Horace G. Underwood recalled that Bill Shaw wanted more education and that he wanted to study Asian history and culture. Moved by the murder of Ethel Underwood at the hands of Communist terrorists, Bill told his father that he would become a missionary-professor. At twenty-eight, with a GI Bill income and a wife and two small sons, he arrived at Harvard University in the summer of 1949 and made an immediate impression with his intelligence, energy, real-world experience, language skills, sociability, and talent at mimicry. He impressed Edwin Reischauer and John King Fairbank. He also took an appointment as a student pastor. He was clear on his goal: He would return to Korea to teach at Yonhui University.

Bill Shaw went back to Korea, but not when and how he expected—and he never left. When the North Korean invasion began, he volunteered for active duty as an intelligence officer and immediately received orders to Commander Naval Forces Far East for staff service. He went to war to liberate his homeland. He settled his family with Juanita's parents in Ohio, then went to Washington for his plane. There he saw Bill Sherman, now a junior foreign service officer, and two other missionary sons, Dick Underwood and Charlie Bernheisel, both headed for Korea, too, as Army officers. Upon joining Joint Task Force 7 for the Inchon Landing, Bill discovered his friend Lieutenant (Senior Grade) Horace G. Underwood, USNR, also a World War II veteran and student of Korean and Japanese and at age thirty-three already a missionary-professor at Yonhui University. Bill's father was in the Army for his third war, this time as a civilian relief administrator in Pusan. Bill wrote his dad on September 14 that he was confident in his choice to go to war to liberate Korea and that he trusted God's will. He had joined the intelligence staff of the 1st Marine Division, where he impressed everyone with his knowledge and enthusiasm.

> I'm writing you both together because Mother can pass the letter on about as quickly as one can get to you from here, Daddy.
> During the past few days I have had some occasion to think about things other than work or immediate objectives, and when I have I certainly have

enjoyed the memories of our times together in Tokyo this past few weeks. First
with all three of us—then Mother and I holding the fort. Now Mother holds it
alone—and bravely too—for you surprised even me, Mother, by accepting it all
so well. I couldn't tell you anything, and the news will tell you so much before
you get this that it will help to know how brave you are. It was just plain swell
to have so much time with you, Mother, and it did help tremendously in those
last days of waiting, especially.

We are near home and will be nearer before you get this. There is nothing
else I can say, but it will all have been said for me when you read this. Horace
and I are at peak—never again will our word be given so often to so powerful
a group. Never again will so much depend on what we know and are able to
state and explain and describe. Believe me, we couldn't be in a more commanding position from the standpoint of *who* is doing the asking and what will
be done with the answers.

Today has dawned bright and clear—a beautiful day and near enough to
my stomping grounds that summer of 1947 that I have to pinch myself to real-
ize that I'm not on a midshipman cruise still.

Very soon the issue should be well under decision and I hope you'll notice
it down there, Daddy—the news from your front has been anything but
reassuring.

Well, it's in His hands now and I only pray that the loved ones will be fortified for the anxious waiting as in 1944—my own mind is calm and at ease for
I *know* I am right in being here and He has given the comfort necessary to
make being here comfortable.

A week after the Inchon Landing, Bill and Horace had pushed close to the
front as the 5th Marines crossed from Kimpo to the north bank of the Han-gang
and turned east toward the outskirts of Seoul. They interrogated POWs and
civilian Koreans as the 5th Marines advanced toward Seoul. When an attached
ROK Marine battalion ran into some nasty North Korean defenses on Yonhui
Ridge, the 5th Marines deployed three battalions on line to take An San and the
three Hills 105. Artillery and air strikes ravaged the ridge and Yonhui College.
Horace and Bill discussed which battalion they should accompany; they agreed
that Horace should go with the 2nd Battalion, whose objective was Yonhui Ridge,
while Bill would go with the 3rd Battalion, assigned to assault An San (Hill 296).
Bill found the 3rd Battalion encamped north of Hill 216 and joined the advance
party of Company I, commanded by Captain Robert A. McMullen. Bill shared a
poncho that night (September 21) with First Lieutenant Wallace L. Williamson,
a platoon commander.

Much to the surprise of the Marine planners, the 3rd Battalion, 5th Marines
took An San's peak within two hours against light resistance, while the two
down-slope battalions fought almost all day to destroy bunker after bunker of

Grave of Lt. William H. Shaw, USNR, KIA 22 September 1950, near Seoul, Korea

North Korean machine gunners as mortar and artillery shells walked up and down the Marine skirmish lines with deadly effect. The same mortars, hidden in the ridge folds to the east in the current site of Ewha Women's University, pinned the 3rd Battalion's leading company to An San's peak and steep western slope. The battalion commander sent out patrols to preempt any Communist counterattack on the Marines' open northern and eastern flanks and to trip any ambush that lay waiting for the 7th Marines, another regiment approaching Seoul to isolate it from the north. Bill Shaw accompanied one such patrol by Williamson's platoon. Its mission was to check out the village of Nokponi.

The Marine patrol walked into an ambush, at least a KPA platoon with several machine guns. Bill Shaw and the point man went down in the first blast of fire. The rest of the patrol dove for cover and returned fire, and no one really paid much attention to the still bodies in the dusty road. The firefight went on for two hours with neither side able to retreat or advance; only when the rest of Item Company came to the rescue did the battle shift toward the Americans. Marine artillery and machine guns quieted the Koreans enough for Lieutenant Williamson to call for volunteers to retrieve Lieutenant Shaw, who might be alive.

Lieutenant Williamson knew little about Bill except that he had lived in Korea, spoke Korean, came highly recommended from battalion headquarters, and feared for the lives of Korean civilians, but he had become a friend in their one long night together under the poncho. Six Marines agreed to go back to Nokponi for Bill Shaw. They were Sergeant Robert F. Blum, Sergeant Walter C. Brazill, Sergeant Arnold A. Lentz, PFC Edward L. Tressler, PFC R. C. Jenkins, and PFC Thomas S. Tischler. Williamson picked Lentz to lead the rescue team. Using a culvert for cover, Lentz led his patrol close to Shaw, who was unconscious but still breathing when the Marines rushed to his side. Shaw had several holes in his lower torso with exit wounds in his back. As the rescue party placed Shaw in a poncho, the Koreans opened fire on the Marines with a machine gun. Lentz remembers the blue-green tracers bouncing off the road. Sergeant Brazill went down with a mortal wound, and now the patrol had two men to evacuate. Some of the other rescuers had minor wounds in their legs from the ricochets off the road. The Korean fusillade also hit Bill Shaw in the head, but a Navy surgeon later told Bill's father that the body wounds would probably have been fatal from shock and internal bleeding. Back along the culvert and then back to the patrol's main body the rescuers struggled, covered by Marines' return fire that raked the village. That night another group recovered the dead point man. In the meantime, Bill Shaw's body went through the battalion aid station to the graves registration team and then to a temporary cemetery near Kimpo airport. There Bill Shaw's grief-stricken father, traveling from Pusan with the 8th Army, found his son's grave and arranged for his reburial in the Foreigners' Cemetery after Seoul fell on September 29.

Today Bill Shaw is memorialized with a monument in a children's park in Nokponi, an affluent Seoul suburb almost visible from the reconstructed sixteenth-century watchtower on An San. The Korean Methodist Church provided the memorial under the leadership of the late Dr. George Paik (Paik Nak-jun), venerable president of Yonsei University. The Reverend Shaw built a chapel as a memorial to his son in a seminary in Taejon. The United States gave Shaw's widow a posthumous Silver Star, and the Korean government gave her a Chongmu Distinguished Silver Medal with Gold Star, a Silver Star equivalent. A plaque in Harvard's Center for Asian Studies reminds other students of Shaw's commitment to Korean freedom. Bill Shaw's widow, Juanita, returned to Korea as a medical social worker and built the service at Severance Hospital, 1963 to 1968. His son, Bill, completed a doctorate in Asian studies at Harvard, taught in Korea, and became one of the Defense Department's principal Asian analysts and counterterrorism experts. But William H. Shaw's best memorial is the tens of thousands of Koreans who live in peace and prosperity within sight of the busy boulevard where he died fifty years ago.

# 36

# The Air War: Heroes

O f the 131 Medals of Honor awarded to American servicemen for heroism in the Korean War "above and beyond the call of duty," only four went to members of the U.S. Air Force. All four Air Force recipients were pilots who died in the actions that gave them historical immortality. This was not unusual since only thirty-seven Korean War heroes survived to receive their medals in person. The 70 percent posthumous rate for the Korean War still stands as the highest percentage of posthumous medals awarded. One pilot-winner was Major George A. Davis, a MiG-killer whose luck ran out in a dogfight in February 1952. Two medals, however, went to veteran pilots, both majors, who finished their ground attack missions by flying their crippled aircraft right into their targets, kamikazes of a sort. They were Major Louis J. Sebille and Major Charles J. Loring Jr.

I thought a comparative study by Sebille and Loring, whose acts of ultimate sacrifice occurred more than two years apart (August 5, 1950, and November 22, 1952), might reveal some interesting aspects of the air war and the wartime Air Force. Looking beyond the obvious sources, I wrote Colonel Thomas M. Crawford Jr., USAF (Ret.), former president of the Mosquito Association, the veterans of the 6147th Tactical Control Group. I knew Tom Crawford from a study I'd done for the Air Force on close air support, and next to the late Master Sergeant Bill Cleveland, Crawford was the historian of choice for Korean War air-ground

LT. COL. D.E. BITEMAN FOR THE 18TH FIGHTER WING

**Capt. Donald D. Bolt, USAAF, 1945**

operations. A first lieutenant flying a propeller-driven two-seat trainer, the North American T-6, Crawford had directed the strikes that ended Major Loring's life. As I suspected, Colonel Crawford knew someone who knew Major Sebille, in this case Lieutenant Colonel Duane E. "Bud" Biteman, USAF (Ret.), president of the 18th Fighter Wing Association. In our subsequent correspondence, Bud Biteman convinced me I should tell the story not of Majors Loring and Sebille, but of his friend, First Lieutenant Donald D. Bolt, USAF, whose medals were a posthumous Purple Heart and an Air Medal. Before his own death Don Bolt had written Lou Sebille's Medal of Honor nomination.

Unlike Sebille and Loring, Don Bolt had not flown combat missions in World War II, and also unlike them, Don Bolt was not a confident, aggressive flyer. He had barely gotten his wings in 1945, and the Army Air Forces released him in 1946. He returned to the University of Maryland to earn a degree in architectural engineering. Two years later he immediately responded to an Air Force appeal for reserve pilots to return to active duty, to fill seats emptied by the mass exodus of pilots whose obligated service had ended in 1948. Two other officers who answered the call with Don Bolt were Lou Sebille and Bud Biteman, and all three of them joined the 67th Fighter-Bomber Squadron (F-51s) at Clark Air Force Base in the Philippines. Sebille immediately impressed his fellow pilots with his flying skill, his aggressiveness toward his superior officers, and his thoroughness as a maintenance and safety officer.

Don Bolt impressed his new friend, Bud Biteman, as a fine officer, if not a great pilot. He was withdrawn, brainy, small (five feet five inches tall and perhaps 125 pounds), and given to quiet jobs such as serving as squadron public information officer. Even Bud Biteman, the squadron intelligence officer, admitted that because of his inexperience Don Bolt did not fly with confidence, but he valued Bolt's way with words and creative instincts with pictures. The Air Force shared Biteman's assessment. In an economy move, the Air Force offered Bolt and hundreds of other marginal pilots a new deal: accept grounding and remain in the Air Force as a specialist (no more flight pay), or leave active duty. Don Bolt took the loss of pilot status to remain in a squadron he loved, even if it did not love him. Lou Sebille, who never doubted his own skill in the air, got a promotion and became the commander of the 67th Fighter-Bomber Group in 1949. Sebille's squadron became the first in the 18th Wing to receive jet F-80Cs.

When the Korean War began, the Air Force suddenly needed Don Bolt back in the cockpit. It offered him and other groundlings immediate reinstatement as pilots if they would volunteer for combat in Korea. There is still some doubt about how much choice Bolt had, but none about the first volunteers' fates; in a few months thirteen of seventeen Far East Air Forces' "reborn" pilots were dead. Bolt joined his friends Bud Biteman and Harry H. Moreland, well-qualified F-51 pilots, in the newly formed 12th Fighter-Bomber Squadron, flying from a dirt strip near Taegu, in a desperate effort to halt the Korean People's Army with feeble air strikes. He arrived with 240 cans of altitude-cooled beer, which Biteman used to encourage better poststrike evaluations. After waiting for an aircraft and taking it for a very cautious test flight, Don Bolt started flying combat missions, completing eight or ten missions by September 1. He told Bud Biteman that the plane and its ordnance went more or less where he pointed them. In the meantime, Lou Sebille had crashed his grievously wounded body and crippled F-51 into a North Korean armored column, less than a week after entering the war.

Don Bolt's meager stock of skill ran out on September 1 during a mission against the North Koreans in the desperate battle for Pohang. His F-51 disabled by ground fire, Bolt managed to crash land his Mustang on a deserted airstrip, but his lead, Captain Jerry Mau, had not reported his peril. Bolt and Mau were on different radio frequencies when Bolt went in, but other flight members saw his peril and reported his situation and location. Badly shaken by his crash, Bolt was further unnerved by his wait in a no-man's-land before his rescue. His squadron commander mercifully excused him from flying because he also had a bad cold. Besides, Bud Biteman needed help with his intelligence reports and recommendations for awards. Bolt's wordsmithing and searching interviews produced a citation for Lou Sebille that finally convinced Far East Air Forces that his Medal of Honor nomination should go to Washington.

Don Bolt gradually recovered his courage to fly during September, but every mission took a toll on his nerves. Knowing that United Nations Command was winning the war helped. Bolt told Bud Biteman that he no longer felt like "an albatross among the eagles." On October 2 Bolt took his F-51 to Pyongyang on a routine interdiction mission. He took more routine ground fire in his engine, which began to smoke and lose coolant and power. Bolt managed to crash land the Mustang in a rice paddy. He sprinted toward some nearby trees, thought better of it, and waved to his circling flight leader, who saw a North Korean truck at the tree line and a queue of soldiers moving toward Bolt's aircraft. The pilot turned back the Koreans rather than kill them with his strafing since he feared they would kill Bolt in retaliation before he could be rescued. He called for more air support. Bolt watched the show from his wing. His flight leader thought he looked dejected.

For ten hours Don Bolt watched flight after flight of Air Force fighter-bombers drive back the North Koreans. Bolt huddled below a wing of his Mustang. All the air cover could not conquer one hard fact: No air-rescue helicopter had the range to pick up Bolt and return him to friendly lines eighty-five miles away. No closer air-rescue units yet occupied the western offshore islands, which later in the war plucked pilots out of North Korea. As darkness fell, Far East Air Forces called off the combat air patrols. The flight leader last saw Bolt still crouched next to his aircraft.

Despite rumors that Don Bolt's body had been recovered, he is still missing in action (presumed dead), for no one yet knows exactly what happened to him. Bud Biteman still remembers him as one of the bravest pilots he knew in Korea.

# 37

## The Boys of Winter

**COLUMBUS, OHIO**
**April 1998**

They are the Boys of Winter, and every April they assemble to drink beer, eat bratwurst sandwiches, and talk about how they fought their way out of the Chosin Reservoir in December 1950 and gained historical immortality. At the moment, simple mortality is quite enough since most of them admit that on those dark, frozen nights so long ago they doubted that they would see the sun again, let alone another forty-eight years. They are amused that "that place" was not the "Chosin" Reservoir, but the Changjin Reservoir (in Korean) or the Chosen Reservoir (in Japanese). They see no merit to accepting the culturally correct spellings of the 1990s, since they were there and the Asian geographers were not. The Boys of Winter meet at VFW Post No. 495 in an unfashionable part of Columbus, "the Bottoms," a floodplain of the Scioto River. "The Bottoms" attracted working-class families who found cheap housing there in return for being flooded out. The Boys of Winter more likely than not actually grew up on "the Hilltop," a neighborhood on higher ground to the west only slightly upscale but still infused by a community spirit that grows at West High School, St. Mary Magdalene Roman Catholic Church and Bishop Ready High School, and the United States Marine Corps. Too young to join the service in World War II, the

JACK KELLY

**Pvt. Jack Kelly, USMCR, 1950**

Boys of Winter joined the Marine Corps Reserve in 1948 and 1949 while still in high school.

I am invited to meet with the Boys of Winter because I have written about the Marine Corps, but it is more important to them that I commanded Company L, 3rd Battalion, 25th Marines, which as Company C, 7th Infantry Battalion, Marine Corps Reserve, was their old outfit in 1950. It is probably even more important that I was a friend of CWO-2 Richard L. Holycross, USMCR, an old buddy of theirs who also survived the reservoir as a Marine rifleman. Dick would no doubt be here if he could, but in September 1967, serving as the mortar platoon commander of the 3rd Battalion, 26th Marines, Dick died in action near Con Thien fighting a regiment of North Vietnamese regulars. He did not have to be there, and he already had one Purple Heart, but he was Dick Holycross and he could not imagine a war in which Marines were fighting and he was not. He is buried a few miles west of VFW Post 495, but we all feel he is with us still, fighting the Chinese with the 7th Marines around Yudam-ni.

The organizer of the annual reunion is Jack Kelly, a spare, energetic West High classmate of Dick Holycross, and a veteran of Company E, 2nd Battalion, 7th Marines. Like his comrades, Jack wanted to be a Marine, at least part-time, and the recruiters assured him that if he joined Company C he would not be drafted into the Army. Anything would be preferable to a Hilltopper than being a "doggie." The Marines also played lots of basketball and softball, the recruiters promised.

When we were called to active duty in 1950, I realized how poorly prepared for war we were. I had been to one summer camp in 1949 and most of the weekly drills, but I had only fired a Browning light machine gun a couple of times and fam-fired the .45-caliber pistol with no great success. Of course, I became a rifleman replacement, but at least I got to shoot my M-1 during the four weeks of training we had at Camp Pendleton before we shipped out for

Korea. Today's Marines—including some prominent generals—don't believe that some of us hadn't been to boot camp, but it wasn't a requirement in the Marine reserves. I can think of fifteen members of our Company C reunion group who never went to boot camp—and that doesn't count the guys who got killed. Three of the five KIAs from old Company C hadn't been to boot camp. Of the others, I think ten or twelve of us got Purple Hearts.

Jack remembers joining Company E, 2nd Battalion, 7th Marines in early November 1950, just in time for the march into the mountains on the road to the reservoir. Except for the cold and the uncertainty about where the Chinese were and how many there were, he does not remember anything very special until the night of November 27–28, 1950.

We had had some fighting on the 27th, then gone into defensive positions early. We all expected an attack, but it was hard to stay alert. We were lucky that our officers and NCOs were combat veterans. When the Chinese attacked, we had a helluva fight on our hands on Hill 1282. On that first night Easy Company held the line, but it was touch and go. I can't remember the exact figures, but I think we had twenty-two killed or missing in action and at least twice that many or more wounded, not to count the guys with frostbite, which was about everybody. We lost our skipper, Walter Phillips, also Lieutenant Ball, the XO [Executive Officer], and all the other officers wounded. John Yancey was a lieutenant in our company and got his second Navy Cross that night with his face all shot up. He got his first Navy Cross as a sergeant in World War II. Easy Company Marines got a Medal of Honor and four Navy Crosses that night. We almost ran out of ammo and grenades all night long. Sometimes it seemed that the side who didn't run out of ammo would win—and the Chinese kept coming. We had maybe 30 or 40 guys out of 160 still fighting when dawn came.

**Jack Kelly, 2001**

A trip to the rear for ammunition took Jack Kelly out of the battle. While struggling back to the company with many bandoliers of bullets and a case of grenades, Jack walked into a Chinese grenade that knocked out most of his teeth, deafened him, and resulted in a serious concussion. The head injury eventually brought about his medical "retirement" in 1951 and his return to Columbus.

> My face hurt like hell, my mouth wasn't good for much, and I kept black-
> ing out. The next day I was hospitalized, and for the rest of the campaign
> I walked along with the convoy as a truck guard or rode when I blacked out.
> We walked until we were exhausted, then we rode until we froze up, and then
> we walked again to get warm. With my mouth ruined, I couldn't eat any hard
> food, which was everything we had. I put frozen chocolate patties in my mouth
> and sucked on them until they melted. And drank some water. That was it.
> With my concussion I couldn't be of much help, so I was evacuated finally by
> train when we reached the railroad to Hungnam, so I made most of the march
> out. I remember the first solid food I ate in a field hospital, fruit cocktail and
> some bacon. I immediately threw up.

Jack Kelly thinks about how naive he and his young Marine buddies had been when they joined the 1st Marine Division: "We thought the war was over and that we would help with the mopping up and go home. We made silly remarks about all the Asiatics, calling them 'gooks' or 'slants' or worse. Well, the Chinese sure showed us the meaning of discipline and raw guts. We heard all sorts of stories about them being drunk or doped up, but I think they were simple peasant soldiers who just wanted to wipe us out at whatever cost. That first night's battle at the reservoir was beyond my imagination. I am still amazed I survived."

WILLIAM J. JOHNSON

**PFC William J. Johnson, USMCR, Korea, 1951**

A bearded, pudgy, cherub, William "Jay" Johnson lives in Amanda, Ohio, and drives to Columbus for the annual reunion. Like Jack Kelly, he went to Camp Pendleton as a mobilized Marine reserve with scant prewar training (one trip to the rifle range, one summer camp, no boot

camp) and shipped to Korea with the
2nd Replacement Draft, which
landed at Wonsan on November
10–11, and then took a train north
to Hungnam to join the 1st Marine
Division. "I'll always remember that
train ride since we huddled together
in open coal cars on this old, slow
Jap train. I got cold then and didn't
feel close to normal for two months.
I still feel the effects of frostbite in
my hands and feet." Jay became a
rifleman in Company E, 2nd Battalion, 5th Marines and joined the company just before the 5th Marines
followed the 7th Marines up the
western shore of the reservoir. On
the evening of November 27, 1950,
the company held the center sector
of Northwest Ridge, west of Yudam-

**William J. Johnson, 2000**

ni. The temperature fell to zero degrees Fahrenheit before wind chill, and the
wind roared in from the north all night. So, too, did the infantrymen of the 89th
Division, Chinese People's Volunteers Force.

Jay Johnson's company stopped a major Chinese assault down a draw between
his company and Company H, 5th Marines. Since the Chinese could not take
Easy Company's part of Northwest Ridge, they tried to ram through the intervening draw and fell by the hundreds to machine-gun fire and artillery. Jay Johnson remembers small things, not the tactical situation:

> I remember how thirsty we got. I didn't know how easy it was to get heat
> exhaustion in a winter battle. That was supposed to be a desert problem. Of
> course, we couldn't heat our rations and couldn't eat them frozen. I think
> I lived on candy for about a week . . . maybe some crackers, too. I vividly
> remember one real problem with our M-1s. They didn't freeze much or we
> could get them to work pretty quickly, but we forgot to save our clips. You
> know—Ping!—and it's gone into the snow. Well, we started to run short of
> ammo, and we got some loose ammo taken from machine-gun belts. No clips.
> Well, the M-1 was a great rifle, but it isn't designed for single-shot loading.
> That sort of evened the firepower odds with the Chinese—which we didn't
> need. I sure was glad to see clipped ammo again—air-dropped, I suppose—
> and I held on to empty clips after that.

MRS. O.L. SCHODORF

**PFC Otto L. Schodorf, Jr., USMCR, Korea, 1951**

Johnson has no doubt that Marine artillery and air support saved the regiment and made the withdrawal to Hagaru-ri possible. "I remember all the planes we had in support. At one time I counted thirty-two Corsairs above us, waiting to make a run on the Chinese. I don't know how much damage they did, but we sure liked to see those napalm tanks bounce and explode in the hills. Watching all that jellied gasoline burn made you even feel a little warmer." Jay also remembers seeing the Royal Marines of 41 Independent Commando, Task Force Drysdale, who had fought their way into the Marine perimeter at Hagaru-ri. "Gee, we looked, felt, and smelled bad, and these guys were shaving and cleaning their gear! I was really impressed. Even though they'd had a tough fight, they looked ready for more, certainly better than we did. It was sort of like watching some British war movie. We all felt better with them on our side, even though there couldn't have been more than 150 of them." Jay Johnson marched south with the 5th Marines all the way to the sea.

Across the table Otto L. Schodorf Jr. follows Johnson's story with emphatic nods. Their memories fuse in a discussion of the perils of crossing a narrow walkway across the gap blown in the road by the Chinese at the power station at Funchilin Pass. The gap was twenty-nine feet across; the drop to the valley floor below was several hundred feet. Johnson and Schodorf cannot agree whether it was worse to cross the walkway in the dark with a flashlight, when you could not see the drop, or during the day, when you could. Both agree that the tightrope walk was a terrifying experience. Schodorf, still a big man with a mane of white hair and bristling black eyebrows, is one of the few Boys of Winter who has returned to Korea, and he agrees that the Koreans have used their second chance well. We disagree about whether the country smells the same in the 1990s as it did in the 1950s, but finally agree that the mix of garlic and smoke does make Korea smell different. Otto is honest about his war:

I was a replacement BAR-man in Company F, 2nd Battalion. 1st Marines, so we were holding Koto-ri on the road up to the reservoir. We had a tight perimeter of the whole battalion, plus some Army troops, when the Chinese attacked on 28 November. We drove them off with very few casualties on our side, and we kept getting more troops coming north to the point where we almost had too many troops for the position. We didn't really have much heavy fighting, but we couldn't get out of the perimeter either. Then the rest of the division fought its way south to us, and we all marched out together. My biggest problem was making my BAR shoot more than one shot at a time. The sonofabitch who had it before me didn't clean it right, so the gas ports were clogged with carbon and the rounds wouldn't eject. I tore that gun apart several times, but it never did work right.

Other than my problems with my weapon and being cold, I remember the flow of refugees and wondering how many of them had frozen to death or

how many of them were really Chinks. On the way out of Koto-ri, as we went down the road to the sea, the column was ambushed. The fighting was taking place well ahead of us. It should be remembered that the road was solid with Marines and vehicles. Somewhere ahead the Chinese tried to stop us. I recall that the column stopped for well over an hour, then finally got moving again. Maybe two miles farther along we came upon one burning truck in the center of the road and seven or eight trucks off the road, some on one side and some on the other side. I'd seen a few dead Marines, around at Koto-ri but not this many. These men were still in the cabs, bullet holes in the windshields, in various stages of attempting to get out of the trucks. I counted about ten dead Marines. Needless to say, there must have been a number of

**The late Otto L. Schodorf, Jr., Columbus, Ohio 2000**

angry Marines, because the numerous dead Chinks I saw were very, very dead. In fact, it appeared that a steamroller had rolled over their heads. Some Marines in the trucks had gotten burned. God, they were awful to look at, just charred flesh with bones sticking out. I sure hope they were dead before they burned.

We have a good chat, but somehow the bratwurst sandwiches have lost their charm.

# 38

## Medal of Honor Winner

**SERGEANT CORNELIUS H. CHARLTON BRIDGE,**
**BLUESTONE RIVER, and THE WEST VIRGINIA TURNPIKE**
**1979–1998**

For almost twenty years my family has driven over Charlton Bridge on the freeway between Beckley and Princeton, West Virginia, on the way to my wife's home near Peterstown. I can no longer remember when I became curious about Cornelius Charlton's identity, but I did, and I learned he had won a Medal of Honor, posthumously, in the Korean War. And I learned a great deal more.

Like many Medal of Honor winners and generations of African American soldiers, Cornelius Charlton did not aspire to military glory, just the chance to be a good soldier and serve his country. One of the seventeen children of Clara E. Thompson and Henry Cornelius Vanderbilt ("Van") Charlton, he was born July 24, 1929, in East Gulf, West Virginia, and grew up in nearby Coalwood. His family, however, fled the coalfields of Raleigh County and moved to the Bronx in 1944, seeking better jobs. Cornelius became an ardent Boy Scout and graduated from James Monroe High School with good grades. He joined the U.S. Army in 1946 at age seventeen, six feet tall and two hundred pounds, quiet, steady, "a good boy" to his parents, and a buddy to his fellow scouts. He didn't need a home in the Army, because he had one, but he did need more training and opportunity than the Bronx offered a black man.

Cornelius Charlton proved to be an exemplary soldier in the peacetime Army. He flourished in assignments in all-black engineer units in Germany and the United States. He reenlisted in 1950, already a sergeant, and went overseas to Okinawa to join another all-black service unit. He arrived in Korea, where he remained a supply administrator—busy, safe, and bored. He asked for reassignment to an infantry unit, a request his CO regarded as slightly mad. Nevertheless, the request meandered through channels until some disinterested personnel officer approved the change of occupational specialty. In March 1951 Charlton received orders to the 24th Infantry Regiment, U.S. 25th Infantry Division, one of the last, largest, and most troubled segregated units in the U.S. Army and close to its abolition as an all-black unit—or any unit at all.

If he joined Company C, 1st Battalion, 24th Infantry to be a credit to his race or to redeem the soiled reputation of his new regiment, Sergeant Charlton confided his motives to no one. He went about the business of being a squad leader with his usual methodical care and patient good humor. His company commander, a white officer, wondered what disgrace he was hiding by volunteering for the infantry. Of course, there was none. The CO soon admired his leadership skills so highly that he made him platoon sergeant of the 3rd Platoon and discussed the possibility of a battlefield commission with Charlton. In the heavy fighting in April and May 1951, east of Seoul, Charlton performed his duties with skill and energy, one of the stalwarts of Company C who held the unit together through more bad times of weak leadership, low morale, mediocre combat performance, and stiffening Chinese resistance.

After another battalion of the 24th Infantry failed to take and hold a hill near Chipo-ri, south of Chorwon, Company C and the rest of the 1st Battalion took its turn in the "meat grinder," a fortified ridge defended by machine-gun bunkers, reverse slope infantry positions, and ample Chinese mortar fire. The objective was identified as Hill 534. Charlton had no illusions about the attack; he told another West Virginian in a supporting artillery battery that Company C had a tough mission. He did not mention his own fate.

On the hot, clear morning of 2 June 1951, the 3rd Platoon started up a steep transverse spur of Hill 543 near Chipo-ri and immediately shrank back under a hail of mortar shells, hand grenades, and small arms fire from a series of well-concealed bunkers hidden among the rocks near the hill's crest. Many of the 2nd Platoon soldiers went to ground among the survivors of the 1st Platoon, which was providing some supporting fire, but Second Lieutenant Moir E. Eames and Sergeant Cornelius Charlton attacked the bunkers with less than a squad by working their way slowly up the hill among the protecting rocks. Under fire the entire way, the group shrank, discouraged and wounded by the shower of grenades. Eames ordered three assaults, but only he and Charlton went forward, and only Charlton destroyed two bunkers with carbine fire and grenades before being driven off the crest by machine-gun fire and grenades from several Chinese reverse slope bunkers. On the third assault, Eames fell from grenade fragments, but Charlton rallied four or five of his soldiers and went forward to the crest again, only to be driven back by more grenades. This time a fragment hit him in the chest, and he was bleeding heavily when he returned to the 1st Platoon position on the forward slope.

Left in command of the platoon by Lieutenant Eames, Charlton organized another assault over the crest against the reverse slope defenses. The 1st Platoon commander, Second Lieutenant Roland F. Michelson Jr., told Charlton to go to the rear for medical attention, but

**Sgt. Cornelius H. Charlton, USA, Korea, 1951**

Charlton refused. Instead he collected more grenades and, armed with a captured Chinese submachine gun, he struggled back to the crest, followed by the reluctant warriors from his own platoon, perhaps twelve in number. Charlton spread his group, already reduced by wounds and straggling to half its original number, in positions along the crest where the soldiers could fire on the Chinese bunkers. He himself advanced alone on the key bunker, a machine-gun position, and managed to crawl close enough to hurl grenades into the bunker. He then charged the bunker, firing the burp gun, and killed the remaining Chinese, but in the battle more grenades landed around him. He went down with a second chest wound. His soldiers came forward to shoot at the fleeing Chinese, who had abandoned the position and could be seen running down the ridgeline. Medics came forward to try frantically to stem Charlton's bleeding and halt the effects of shock, but Cornelius Charlton, already unconscious, died quietly next to the bunker he had just destroyed.

On 12 March 1952, slim, handsome Secretary of the Army Frank C. Pace presented Mrs. Charlton with the Medal of Honor so dearly bought by the life of her son, Cornelius. Eight of his other brothers and sisters had already died, four in

THE AUTHOR

**Gravesite of Sgt. Cornelius H. Charlton, USA, Medal of Honor, KIA, Korea, 1951, Beckley, West Virginia**

infancy, so death was no stranger to the Charltons. Public acclaim was a new experience and came with the Medal. When the southern section of the West Virginia Turnpike opened in 1954, the turnpike commission named the bridge over the Bluestone River for Charlton and brought his parents (at state expense) from the Bronx to cut the ribbon. The Army named a Governors Island, New York harbor, ferry for him (1952), and a barracks at 8th Army headquarters, Yongsan-ku, Seoul, also bears his name (1974). The Prince Hall Masonic Chapter provided a tree and plaque in his name for a grove of memorial trees in New York City's Van Cortlandt Park (1958).

The Charlton family, however, nursed a grievance through the years over the selection of Cornelius's gravesite. His mother and sisters believed that a racist Army did not want a black man buried in Arlington National Cemetery and refused to accept its responsibility when Cornelius's body came back from Korea in the summer of 1951. Of course, no one knew then that Charlton would be a Medal of Honor winner. His brother, Arthur, also a veteran, thought that the casualty assistance team simply did not make clear to his mother that Cornelius had the right to be buried in a national cemetery, including Arlington, where black soldiers had been buried since the Civil War. One still wonders, however, if the casualty assistance team worked very hard in succoring the trusting family of just another poor, black, dead GI. Cornelius Charlton was buried in a small, ill-kept, all-black cemetery near Bramwell, Mercer County, West Virginia, in a plot provided by his family. As the years passed, the family's sense of injustice grew apace with the weeds and bushes that soon choked the headstones in the abandoned cemetery. With no political leverage, the family did not pursue the possibility of reinterment.

In the 1980s, as the songs of Lee Greenwood drove the peace psalms of Joan Baez from the jukeboxes of West Virginia, the Medal of Honor Society contacted the state division of veterans affairs about the location of Sergeant Charlton's gravesite. The state passed the torch (or the buck) to John Shumate, Beckley, State Commander of the American Legion, who hired a genealogical sleuth to find Cornelius's grave, largely by calling Arthur Charlton. With the gravesite located in Bryant Memorial Park Cemetery on Route 120, American Legion Chapter 32 mobilized for action to move Cornelius's remains to the nearest federally funded veterans' cemetery, maintained by the Legion, in Beckley. With much fanfare and the full majesty of the State of West Virginia, the U.S. Army, and the American Legion, Sergeant Cornelius Charlton's earthly remains moved by cortege across "his" bridge and came to final rest in an honored place in the Beckley American Legion Post 32 Cemetery on March 10, 1990. His new headstone identified him as a recipient of the Medal of Honor, awarded in the name of the Congress of the United States of America. Among the eulogists were Secretary of State Ken Hechler, a World War II combat veteran and former congressman, and Arthur Charlton. Cornelius's sister, Fair May Popudopoules, sang a hymn at the gravesite. The family members present, at least fifteen in number, remained divided over Cornelius's race consciousness and victimization.

I doubt that Cornelius Herod Charlton would have been too concerned about all the excitement about his place of burial. He had done his duty as a platoon sergeant, Company C, 24th Infantry. He had closed with and destroyed the enemy and taken his scared and demoralized black soldiers up Hill 534 and taken the damn thing at whatever cost, because the Army expected him to.

# 39

## Marine

OXFORD, OHIO
April 20, 1997

W hen I was a university student, Frederick Francis Brower, then administrative secretary of Beta Theta Pi international fraternity, suggested I might want to be—as he had been—an officer of Marines since I was already a Beta. Fred was the first Marine officer I had ever met. Years later, after I have known thousands of Marine officers, Fred, at nearly seventy, still sets the standard. We are sitting in his new, spartan office in the home he and Mary Jane have kept a showpiece for nearly thirty years. There are no signs of war in the room, but there is Marine Corps memorabilia. Marines call such a place the "I love me" room, but it is usually an "I love the Corps" room. We talk about the Korean War.

After I graduated from Miami University, Oxford, Ohio, in early June 1950, I joined the 7th Basic School class at Quantico, a great group of new second lieutenants, all regulars from Annapolis or NROTC, plus some outstanding former NCOs just commissioned. Thirteen of my classmates became generals. When the war began, I was working at the rifle range as an instructor since our formal class work hadn't begun yet. Not much changed after June 25 except that someone had the main gate locked—a symbolic end to the peacetime pace at Quantico, but unnecessary. We certainly took our instruction in weapons and tactics seriously before we graduated in February 1951. The realities of war reached even Quantico. First of all, the winter of 1950–51 was cold in Virginia as well as Korea. We also got instructors who were new veterans, many of them wounded officers. We also had two big training accidents, so we even saw real casualties, dead and wounded. We felt well prepared when we shipped out as part of the 8th Replacement Draft.

My introduction to the war and the 1st Marine Division disappointed me. We landed in Kobe, then transshipped to Pusan on 1 May 1951, and joined the division near Hongchon five days later. We met the first Marines rotated home, mostly infantry survivors, and they looked awful—very unmilitary, long hair and mustaches, ragged uniforms, surly in looks and manner. We could hardly believe they were Marines, but of course they were and damned good ones. I imagine we looked strange to them, too. Well, I wanted to go to an infantry battalion since I was a basic infantry officer, but one of my friends and I ended up in the 1st Shore Party Battalion. The CO was a legend, Henry "Jim" Crowe, the old mustang who had won about every known medal but

**Marine Second Lieutenants at the front, October 1951, (left to right) Earl Roth, Fred Brower, and Troy T. Highsmith**

the Medal of Honor at Tarawa and Saipan as an infantry officer. He still had his big handlebar mustache. He sympathized with us, but he needed officers, too. I ended up commanding an engineer platoon of earthmovers and Korean laborers; we repaired roads. This was May 1951, and the division was back in the line fighting the Chinese. The roads certainly needed fixing, but I wanted to fight, not fill potholes and clear away mudslides. I also didn't like being responsible for all the Mickey Mouse money [U.S. Army military pay certificates] I used to pay the Koreans. I kept it in bundles under my canvas rack, and I had so much money that I had trouble sleeping on top of it.

Well, we had an inspection by the new CG, General Jerry [Gerald C.] Thomas, and he asked how I was getting along. I thought he looked old and not very general-like in World War II leggings and boondockers [low-topped boots issued at boot camp], worn utilities, and soft cap. Well, he was very smart, very tough, and vigorous, and we learned that he had started learning about war as a sergeant at Belleau Wood and Soissons in World War I. He knew his business. All our senior officers did, all very experienced World War II veterans, just as Thomas was. Well, he got me transferred to the 3rd Battalion, 7th Marines [3/7]. I was now a real combat Marine—or was about to be.

When I joined Company H, 3/7 on 5 June, the battalion was not engaged. I think it was in reserve near Yanggu. First, the battalion was in regimental reserve until 18 June, which probably explains why I'm still here. Then the company was in battalion reserve when we moved up to the line. I took over How Company's 1st Platoon—good Marines but too careless with their gear, even their weapons. Many still acted like the reservists they were; some had never been to boot camp and didn't know better. I cracked down—and they didn't like it. They shaped up, but only when I pushed them. The fact that I was a team shooter finally broke the ice. I brought one of my match revolvers to Korea, a K-38 "Combat Masterpiece," and carried it instead of a .45. One of the troops asked whether I could really shoot, so I convinced them at target practice. I guess the troops were impressed; they still tell Mary Jane about my shooting at reunions.

I commanded the 1st Platoon for three months, but somehow we always seemed to be on the fringes of the big fights. We went into position on the division's extreme left flank in mid-July, tied into an ROK regiment. I'd heard they were retreat-prone, so I set up my machine gun so it could cover the ROKs as well as the Chinese. Our regimental commander, Colonel [Herman Jr.] Nickerson, came up our hill to see the position. He and I sat on a rock above the Hwachon Reservoir and smoked a couple of his very fine cigars. He was sharp, a handsome guy, a real favorite. [A veteran of three wars, the late Herman Nickerson—"Herman the German" to his troops—retired as a lieutenant general and died in 2000.] We talked about the great view. He thought my MG was right where it ought to be.

My worst experience was self-inflicted. After the truce talks broke off in

August, we were moving by truck on a very bad road up the Soyang-gang, really bad terrain, floods everywhere, washouts, mudslides, and this move was at night, too! Somehow our truck driver, a new guy, got lost, and we ended up wandering around the mountains. We might have driven to Pyongyang! Well, we were lost a whole day before I got us oriented and started overland to our assembly area. After we found the battalion command group and the rest of How Company, we had to cross the Soyang-gang, which was a torrent. Some of the troops got washed away from our crossing line. We never did find one Marine. We also lost some weapons, and we had no rations. One kid had a big pack of dried Lipton soup, which we made in a helmet. I've loved Lipton soup ever since.

**Frederick J. Brower, 1995**

I had one big battle—my first and my last—the assault on Hill 702, part of Yoke Ridge, north of the "Punchbowl," on 31 August 1951. We were on Hill 680, just south of 702, also part of Yoke Ridge. The day before the attack, we got hit with a heavy mortar barrage, a bad omen. It turned out that the bad guys were North Koreans, who had been retrained and armed with new Russian weapons. Unlike the Chinese, they had lots of shells. We jumped off on the morning of 31 August, as planned, against "light resistance"—or so says the Marine official history—but then the "forward elements of 3/7 were hit by a concentration of mortar and artillery fire . . . . " Well, that was me, a forward element. I went down with multiple shrapnel wounds in my leg, and my left knee was really a mess. I didn't hurt too badly, but I sure as hell couldn't walk. I came off Hill 702 on a stretcher carried by four little, old Korean men of the Korean Service Corps. Every time a shell landed anywhere, they dropped me and *that* hurt! In fact, getting up and down those hills was the toughest part of my war.

Anyway, I went back to a Navy hospital somewhere south of the front for preliminary treatment and diagnosis. Some corpsman came in to see me and told me my leg had to be amputated. I couldn't believe it. I yelled at him, almost attacked him. Well, he had the wrong patient. The guy next to me lost his leg. I've been very cautious about hospitals ever since. After three or four days at this Navy "Mayo Clinic," I went to the hospital ship *Repose* for some real healing and fixing, first-class care in every way. I was back to the 7th Marines on 5 October. By that time our attacks had ended—very tough fighting—and the truce talks had started up. I took over the regimental 4.2-inch mortar platoon—my knee couldn't handle all the hill climbing in a rifle company—and ended my tour as the Regimental S-2A [assistant intelligence officer].

Fred Brower's knee never fully recovered from that mortar fragment on Hill 702, and in 1955 he left the Marine Corps as a captain with a disability retirement for wounds. He succeeded another Oxford and Miami legend, Ralph Fey, as Beta Theta Pi's secretary. He also started a very successful real estate, construction, and property management business, but in his heart, Fred Brower will always be that young lieutenant who went up Hill 702 at the head of How Company's 1st Platoon. I know exactly how he feels.

# 40

## The Mountain
## and the Warrior

HEARTBREAK RIDGE, KOREA, December 1994, and
NATIONAL MEMORIAL CEMETERY OF THE PACIFIC, OAHU,
HAWAIIAN ISLANDS, 2000 and 2001

Heartbreak Ridge and Private First Class Herbert K. Pililaau, Waianae, Oahu, Hawaii, were not meant for each other. The ridge is sharp, dangerous, barren, and swept by winds, summer and winter, that close one's eyes and slice the body. Herbert K. Pililaau lived at ease with man and nature, attuned to gentleness and the common affection for the people and the land that characterizes the Polynesian Hawaiians. His father may have had a distant European ancestor, but his mother, Abigail, was a true woman of the *kanaka maoli* ("The People"), the children of *tangora,* the Spirit of the Sea. She spoke no English. Herbert's mountains were green, shrouded in rain clouds, not cold and stripped of foliage like Heartbreak Ridge. Herbert, the ninth of fourteen children, grew up a village child in Waianae, a working-class suburb of Honolulu. He had no plans to be a soldier and certainly none to be a warrior.

In August 1951 the U.S. 2nd Infantry Division and two South Korean divisions attacked and finally captured a ridge complex in east central Korea that became "Bloody Ridge" to the American soldiers. In three weeks of fighting the Americans and Koreans endured twenty-seven hundred casualties to wrest

U.S. ARMY

**PFC Herbert K. Pililaau, U.S. Army, 1951**

the mountain from a determined North Korean force drawn from three different divisions. Looking north across the Sochon River, they could see nothing but more mountains. The nearest hill had nothing but an objective number assigned from the U.S. 2nd Division. It had two observable peaks—Hill 894 and Hill 931—to distinguish it from all the other mountains. It became known as Heartbreak Ridge.

Herbert Pililaau's journey to Heartbreak Ridge began with his graduation from Waipahu High School in 1948. Waipahu High did not cater to the upper-class *haoles;* Herbert's classmates were named Ruaa, Ramos, Pestana, Quizon, Oshira, Pang, and Olivares. Herbert Pililaau was a good student—quiet, disciplined, committed to self-improvement. His great love was music. He sang in the advanced chorus for three years, and his skill with his ukulele became the talk of Waianae. When he was not helping with the chores at home, running errands, or reading—another passion—Herbert entertained the neighbors with his Hawaiian interpretations of European operas, much to the delight of his classically inclined Japanese audience. Although he was almost six feet tall and athletic, Herbert played no sports in high school and generally went his own way, untouched by the surfboard life of Hawaiian teenagers. Determined to improve his family's economic security, he enrolled at Cannon Business School for courses in administration, secretarial skills, and accounting. Before he learned the results of his entrance examination for employment in the Honolulu city government, he received a draft notice. Thus the war in Korea reached out and took Herbert Pililaau.

Well-educated, physically fit, twenty years old, and unmarried, Herbert K. Pililaau had no refuge from war. His strong sense of duty and honor compelled him to serve, although his Christian convictions made it difficult for him to accept the idea of killing others. The possibility of his own death did not influence his thinking about joining the Army, although he did briefly consider applying for conscientious objector status. His patriotism and pride as a Hawaiian carried the internal argument, and Herbert became a soldier. His basic training at Fort Shafter did not turn him into a noisy soldier, loud about his warrior skills. Barracks life did not agree with Herbert, who loved privacy. His comrades bullied him until he scored highest in his training battalion in a series of physical endurance tests. Herbert excelled in field training, and he often carried the weapons of his struggling comrades on long marches. His natural selflessness endured and justified his mother's concern for his safety. She told her friends that she feared Herbert would be killed because he could not resist helping others.

Arriving in Korea in March 1951 as an infantry replacement, Private First Class Herbert Pililaau joined Company C, 23rd Infantry, U.S. 2nd Infantry Division, a regiment fresh from its triumph over four Chinese divisions in the battle of Chipyong-ni in February. He volunteered to become his squad's automatic rifleman, an unusual act much appreciated by his comrades since the Browning automatic rifle (BAR) weighed twice that of an M-1 and invariably drew enemy fire. In the fighting for Bloody Ridge, Herbert Pililaau proved dependable, durable, but too uncommunicative to be considered a natural leader in First Lieutenant Walter S. Lewis's 3rd Platoon, Charlie Company. Nevertheless, Herbert never shirked, never avoided unavoidable risks, and he kept his BAR firing.

During one dark night, September 17, 1951, PFC Herbert K. Pililaau forever abandoned obscurity at the cost of his life. When its attack on Hill 931 stalled in

**Gravesite, PFC Herbert K. Pililaau, Medal of Honor, KIA, 17 September 1951, Heartbreak Ridge, Korea**

the face of bitter North Korean resistance, Charlie Company, one of three companies committed to taking the sharp peak to its front, went to ground along a ridgeline than ran south from the main peak. The 3rd Platoon established a perimeter defense in advance of the rest of the company. Its position was anchored on a small hill, and Lewis arranged for defensive fires from artillery, mortars, and heavy machine guns to strengthen the fires of his three BARs and two Browning M1919A5 light machine guns. When the North Koreans started probing attacks at about 1400 on the afternoon of September 17, the platoon had little trouble holding its position. It did not know that it faced an entirely fresh North Korean force, the 13th Regiment of the Korean People's Army's crack 6th Division. When the main assault by two Korean battalions came that night, however, at around 2200, Lewis's platoon, despite heavy fire support and the advantage of a moonlit night, faced the peril of being overrun. Boxed in by enemy artillery fire, the 3rd Platoon ran short of ammunition and Lieutenant Lewis received permission to fall back as quickly as possible to the company's main position. Pililaau's squad had the dubious honor of holding the original position while the rest of the platoon started for the rear with haste. The withdrawal, harried by Korean artillery fire, might have become a rout, but Pililaau refused to leave his position, instead firing all the ammunition available for his BAR and then throwing grenades as fast as he could pull the pins. He fought on alone since his only companion, his squad leader, left the battle. No one knew whether Pililaau had already been wounded or not. Some of his comrades, however, saw the end of his first and last stand from the safety of their new position.

Facing one more North Korean assault without ammunition or grenades, Pililaau threw rocks at his assailants as they closed around him. He then pulled his bayonet and charged the Koreans, slashing with one hand and throwing punches with the other. He went down under a swarm of bayonet-wielding Koreans. When the 3rd Platoon retook the position the next day, it counted forty dead Koreans around Pililaau's punctured body. Lieutenant Lewis estimated that Pililaau had wounded many more with his BAR and grenades before he died. In May 1952 the Department of the Army announced that in the name of Congress, President Harry S. Truman had approved the posthumous award of the Medal of Honor to PFC Herbert K. Pililaau, U.S. 50001702, Army of the United States. A week after his death, the city of Honolulu wrote Pililaau a letter announcing he had passed the civil service examination and qualified for municipal employment.

Today the remains of Herbert K. Pililaau rest in Grave Number 127, Section P, National Memorial Cemetery of the Pacific, the site known to most of the world as "the Punchbowl." The cemetery is located at the Puowaina, or what the Hawaiians refer to as "The Hill of Sacrifice." Herbert came home for a hero's burial on February 26, 1952. He was not yet a Medal of Honor winner when he was interred in the presence of hundreds of his family and friends. It made no difference. To his family and neighbors Herbert K. Pililaau, friend of the elderly, happy singer, and ukelele player, had been a hero long before the U.S. Army found an heir worthy of King Kamehameha I in a slim, brown boy from Waianae.

# 41

## War Crimes and a
## Matter of Accountability

Colonel James M. Hanley, Judge Advocate Generals Corps, brought a reputation of heroism and honor to an assignment that would produce few heroes and little honor: the investigation and prosecution of war criminals. Jim Hanley possessed unusual qualifications for his position as Chief, War Crimes Division, Office of the Judge Advocate, Headquarters, U.S. 8th Army. His credentials as a lawyer were impressive: Juris Doctorate, University of Chicago, 1931, and then experience in private practice and public office, up to the position of assistant attorney general for the state of North Dakota by 1941.

Like his father before him, Jim Hanley did not define civic duty by legal matters alone. He obtained an Army Reserve commission in the 1930s, but as an infantry officer, not a judge advocate. Mobilized in 1941, he went on active duty as a captain. By 1943 he had reached the rank of lieutenant colonel as a training officer at the Infantry School at Fort Benning when he learned that he would command one of the battalions of a newly formed special unit, the 442nd Regimental Combat Team, in which one-third of the officers and almost all the enlisted men would be Japanese American (*Nisei*) volunteers for combat duty in the European theater. Until the famous "Go for Broke" regimental combat team returned to the United States in 1946, Jim Hanley commanded his battalion with distinction in Italy, France, and back again to Italy. The 442nd Regimental Combat Team set an all-Army record for decorations for valor and

Purple Hearts. It also dealt a deathblow to the assumption that Japanese Americans were disloyal and deserved the disgraceful internment and pauperization inflicted upon them by the United States in 1942.

Recalled to active duty, this time as a judge advocate, during the summer of 1950, Jim Hanley had the combat experience, talent for command, legal expertise, and sympathy for victims of any race that made him an ideal choice for his job. He would organize a coordinated investigation to document the numerous atrocities committed upon Americans, other foreign soldiers and civilians, and South Korean soldiers and civilians by the Korean People's Army and its southern partisan allies. That there was an atrocity problem was self-evident by October 1950. On July 4, General Douglas MacArthur announced that United Nations Command would adhere to the most recent version of the Geneva Convention (1949), although the United States had not yet ratified the agreement. MacArthur called for the KPA to do the same, especially as he had heard reports of several incidents in which the North Koreans had executed wounded South Koreans during the capture of Seoul. The next day the North Koreans captured seventy-two officers and men of Task Force Smith near Osan, and on July 11 the North Koreans made a radio broadcast from Seoul (featuring a captured Army captain) that announced their dedication to the principles of humane treatment of prisoners. The North Koreans protested too much, since the day before North Korean soldiers had captured and executed six GIs from the 21st Infantry in front of other Americans, watching from a helpless distance.

Episode after episode accumulated with dead bodies, wounded survivors, and escaping POWs giving irrefutable testimony to the torture and death of American and Korean POWs. The shifting fortunes of battle in September and October 1950 both worsened the atrocity problem and made it more obvious. The retreating North Koreans shot their captives rather than take them north; the advancing United Nations troops found more and more bodies, including almost five thousand civilians in mass graves at Taejon. The trail of slaughter went north past Pyongyang, but so did the number of numbed survivors who could testify to the atrocities. The GIs' testimony received verification from compliant, even enthusiastic, North Korean POWs, either remorseless revolutionaries who believed they would be executed anyway or survivalists who decided that confession might mean mercy.

Following instructions issued by General MacArthur, the judge advocates of all the United Nations Command field agencies collected evidence of North Korean atrocities, but the mounting evidence, uninvestigated incidents, and the anticipated end of the war and the subsequent trials of war criminals suggested to the Far East Command staff judge advocate, Colonel George W. Hickman, that a new agency was required. Colonel Hanley organized the War Crimes

HANLEY FAMILY

**Lt. Col. James M. Hanley, JAG, USA, on ferry to Koje-do, Korea 1951**

Division of twenty-seven officers, two civilians, and fifteen enlisted men (only half his authorized strength) and went into business in October 1950 in Seoul and, later, Pusan. The war crimes investigating teams took testimony in the field, conducted site visits (including exhumations), and reviewed interrogations and other intelligence documents and agent reports. The mother lode of atrocity information seemed to be the 120,000 North Korean POWs who huddled in the raw, overcrowded camps on Koje-do Island and the southwestern mainland in early 1951. Hanley's operatives infiltrated the POW groups and recruited informers; Koreans eager to sever their ties with the South Korean Labor (Communist) Party and the KPA proved willing converts and informers. In his Field Memorandum No.1, Colonel Hanley established his priorities: to gather evidence that would allow the prosecution of those who had killed or brutalized POWs; to identify those Koreans who had committed crimes against defenseless civilians; and to find out who had used POWs for propaganda purposes or impressed them into the North Korean armed forces. Hanley made no distinction between American and Korean victims.

Chinese intervention and the subsequent start of armistice negotiations in 1951 threw the whole war crimes question into a new political-strategic context. First, the Chinese took thousands of American and Korean POWs in their victorious First, Second, and Third Offensives, but they also turned hundreds of captives loose to testify to their humane treatment of prisoners. They showed a great partiality to members of "the working class" and "oppressed races," so few officers and no airmen suddenly returned to friendly lines, courtesy of the political directorate of the Chinese People's Volunteers Force. In September 1951 Colonel Hanley saw an 8th Army training directive and reports in *Stars and Stripes* implying that the Chinese were observing the Geneva Convention and made (comparatively) good warders, not exactly a positive morale message. Hanley already knew something about the miserable life of POWs in Chinese hands. During a trip to Tokyo, he discussed the issue with a staff judge advocate, who suggested that Hanley draft a statement that could be released by the FECOM (Far East Command) public information officer. Hanley agreed that such an official statement about Chinese brutality would squash any notion that the Chinese would treat POWs well and thus improve the Allied will to fight. By early November, Hanley had drafted a statement, which was approved by the PIO (FECOM Public Information Officer), presumably with General Matthew B. Ridgway's approval. Hanley found himself scheduled to give a news conference in Pusan on November 14.

The press release, later known internationally as "the Hanley Report," began its tumultuous life as a memorandum issued to four Korean newspaper stringers in Pusan and a release sent to the press offices in Seoul and Tokyo. Within twenty-four hours America's major newspapers—which also meant the White House and Congress—decided that Jim Hanley had just dropped a public relations bombshell that would slow or again disrupt the ongoing negotiations at Panmunjom. Hanley's major purpose was served in his "Report's" first four paragraphs: From the evidence collected by Hanley's office, it had been determined that the Chinese had killed 2,513 American POWs and about 250 other UNC prisoners since November 1950. North Koreans had killed "only" 147 American POWs in the same time period. Hanley, however, used the rest of the press release to identify the North Koreans as the real mass murderers of the Korean War, the executioners of at least twenty-five thousand South Koreans and at least ten thousand northern Korean "reactionaries." Hanley did not release any estimates on the number of Americans who might have died in the hands of the KPA, but subsequent disclosures suggested that the victims might number more than six thousand. Virtually every American serviceman then carried as "missing-in-action" seemed to fall into the victim category. Suddenly the Hanley Report looked as if it had exposed an Army cover-up—that all the families who had been informed that their soldiers were "missing in action" had been lied to, that their loved ones were all murdered POWs.

For President Harry S. Truman, the Hanley Report produced a deluge of letters demanding a strict accounting of all American POWs and missing in action (MIAs), which in turn produced lots of message traffic for the Department of the Army and General Ridgway. Ridgway—always slippery in bureaucratic battles—did not quite disown and condemn Hanley, but he did not exactly defend him either. He certainly implied that neither he nor his chief of staff had any prior knowledge of the Hanley Report. Colonel Hickman, using Hanley's own data, gave Ridgway a perfect answer: There might be claims that 6,202 Americans had become POWs and MIAs, but until the Communists provided a definitive POW list, no one could be sure who was or was not a POW. What General Ridgway knew for certain was that his command had recovered the bodies of 365 murdered American servicemen, 259 of whom had been identified. The official number of American MIAs believed captured was 3,545, and some of them had probably died in captivity. Most of the other MIAs were most assuredly dead (but body not recovered) or dead but unidentified. In theory, the number of United Nations atrocity deaths might run as high as six thousand, which would include POWs who had been untreated or mistreated wounded, or others who had died of disease and malnutrition. Ridgway admitted there had been no coordination with Washington on the Hanley Report, which had complicated the armistice negotiations, but not much. Hanley had just been overly enthusiastic about prosecuting war criminals and unaware of the larger implications of his concern about the misrepresentation of Chinese POW treatment.

Jim Hanley never lost his conviction that Communist war criminals—meaning the murderers of POWs and helpless civilians—should be held accountable in some fashion, but all the tides of expediency and political calculation were now running against him. His major source of information—the testimony of enemy POWs—disappeared as Korean and Chinese political organizers wrested control of the prison compounds from those POWs who allied themselves with South Korea and who sought release, not repatriation. Murder, intimidation, torture, and beatings became common in every Koje-do compound as 1952 dawned. Informants died or fell silent; some managed to escape into protective custody, which ended their work. Examination of POW confessions produced inevitable results: the fabrication of stories in return for favors, the misidentification of suspects, evidence of torture to extract confessions, multiple testimony that applied to only one incident, not several. Nevertheless, the War Crimes Division in 1952 had compiled a list of 936 POWs (two-thirds Koreans) who appeared triable for violent war crimes. It also had a witness list of almost 200 prisoners. The difficulty was finding evidence that corroborated the confessions; of 1,185 confessions Hanley's staff reviewed, only seventy-three could be supported with other evidence. Other judge advocates in the chain of command raised another issue: Under whose jurisdiction would the criminals be tried? For reasons political and legal, the U.S. Army did not want to return to the war crimes trials business. Yet it was unclear that the United Nations or some other international authority would take the crimes to court.

The issue of exchanging POWs as part of an armistice agreement buried the idea of trying the Communist war criminals held in the UNC prison compounds. Hanley's research and intelligence reports confirmed that the POWs in Communist hands were dying from malnutrition and assorted diseases that the Communists would not or could not treat. The Joint Chiefs of Staff advised that time was critical, that the Panmunjom negotiators should get a count of the POWs and draft a formula such as "all for all" or some other scheme that would get the United Nations Command POWs back as quickly as possible. Other advisors—civilian and military—

The late Col. James M. Hanley, JAG, USA, (Ret.) 1993, age 88

wanted to score a political-propaganda victory over the Communists by allowing the Korean and Chinese POWs to refuse repatriation, a concept about which the Geneva Convention (1949) was vague. While a detaining power had the obligation to return enemy POWs under its control, thus eliminating the German, Japanese, and Russian practice of holding POWs for slave laborers as a form of reparations, the convention did not give clear guidance on whether an individual prisoner had to accept repatriation when he believed his return would not be triumphal but fatal. President Truman sided with the no-forced-repatriation faction in his government in December 1951. He and his advisors also accepted the Joint Chiefs of Staff's recommendation that suspected war criminals should be repatriated, on the assumption that the Communists would otherwise hold back their own self-defined Allied "war criminals," principally air crewmen and intelligence agents.

As the negotiations dragged on through 1952, complicated by a series of Communist POW riots throughout the UNC camp system, the work of the War Crimes Division faded away. The division was transferred to the control of the Korea Communications Zone, the rear area logistical command that ran the POW camp system. By September 1952 its total staff numbered seven officers, thirteen enlisted men, and eight interpreters, or about half of its reduced authorized strength. Hanley left the division and Korea, returning to the United States to the staff judge advocate at Camp Atterbury, Indiana. He saw little hope that any sort of justice would come from his investigations. In fact, when he raised the issue of investigating war crimes committed by the South Korean army, the Korean National Police, paramilitary and special forces under ROK control, and civilian vigilantes, he found no command interest in the issue. The same disinterest characterized the prosecution of GIs for crimes against Koreans, although such prosecutions did occur. The War Crimes Division, supervised by two Army judge advocates who had no thirst for controversy, limped through its investigations—usually site visits and local interviews in South Korea—until it received a whole new source of testimony, the horror stories of the Allied POWs exchanged in April and in August–September 1953 with the final acceptance of the Armistice Agreement.

Before it finally shut down its offices in May 1954, the War Crimes Division verified many of Jim Hanley's charges of 1951 and abandoned others. At final count 3,746 American POWs returned home, but that left more than 8,000 still missing in action. The best count from sources Communist and Allied placed the number of Americans who had died in custody at around 2,600. How many Americans might have been murdered remained uncertain, but Hanley and his successors testified to Senator Joseph McCarthy's congressional investigations committee that they still believed the Communist had killed between 5,600 to 6,100 American POWs and ten times more Korean servicemen. Yet the case-by-case review—based on surviving POW interrogations—did not produce similar numbers. It made little difference. With the tacit approval of the Korean government, United Nations Command had issued a blanket amnesty in August 1953 to suspected war criminals, including those who refused repatriation, as part of the armistice process. The suspects returned to North Korea and China or chose to stay in South Korea or go to Taiwan or some other distant nation. American politicians, pundits, and psychological warfare enthusiasts argued back and forth on how to exploit the accumulated evidence of Communist war crimes, but they produced no meaningful plan except to train American servicemen to be tougher POWs. Certainly the criminals themselves had passed beyond the hands of justice, as Jim Hanley probably knew they would. His only consolation from the whole affair was that the Hanley Report had shocked the Chinese into improving living conditions at their Yalu River POW camps, or so the returned POWs testified. It was a small but real reward for Hanley's lonely crusade to hold the Communists responsible for their ill treatment not only of Americans, but the thousands of Koreans who had disappeared while in Communist hands.

# 42

## They Also Fought Who Flew and Seldom Fired

**HONOLULU, HAWAII**
**June 2001**

The Pacific Air Forces' conference on the Korean air war did not attract any American jet aces, the knights of the North American F-86E and F-86F Sabre interceptor. Two of the officers present, however, had an unparalleled opportunity to watch the aces of the aces, the top MiG killers of the U.S. Air Force. Lieutenant General William E. Brown Jr. USAF, and Lieutenant Colonel Dean E. Abbott, USAF, both now retired, had flown as the wingmen of aces. In Earl Brown's case, the ace was Captain Manuel J. "Pete" Fernandez Jr., USAF, the third highest scorer, with 14.5 kills. General Brown was still flying in the 334th Fighter Interceptor Squadron, 4th Fighter Interceptor Wing (FIW), when Major James Jabara, USAF, got his fifteenth kill and moved into second place in "the Great MiG Hunt." Dean Abbott flew wing for Captain Joseph M. McConnell Jr., USAF, the leading American ace of the Korean War, with sixteen kills, and he later flew wing for Major John Bolt, USMC, another ace, with six kills. Dean Abbott flew all his missions with the 39th Fighter Interceptor Squadron, 51st Fighter Interceptor Wing. Neither Earl Brown nor Dean Abbott ever shot down a MiG.

U.S. AIR FORCE

**F-86 Sabrejets on patrol in MiG Alley**

Having spent some time over the years with American fighter pilots, I can attest that they are a special breed—and they are keenly aware of it. Whatever their sterling qualities or awful shortcomings as human beings, they can do something denied all but a handful of mortals, careening around the sky at the speed of sound in a complex machine that sometimes seems to overwhelm even experienced pilots with its technology. I have sat in the simulator of a space shuttle and worked the heads-up display of a Marine F-18, and I cannot imagine the skill and nerves it takes to fly these craft, yet two of my best friends did so and flew them with confidence. The Korean War pilots became the first elite of the age of jet warfare, and those who won five or more aerial battles (American, Russians, and Chinese) against comparable jet fighter interceptors became the most exalted pilots of the 1950s. The American aces were certainly a small group, forty in number. Only one was a Navy officer, and one was a Marine. Thirty-nine of these pilots shot down almost half of the Communist aircraft lost in air-to-air combat (over 300 of an estimated 600 to 700 enemy aircraft, most of them MiG-15s). The fortieth ace, Navy Lieutenant Guy Bordelon, specialized in slaying North Korean bi-plane night intruders with a propeller-driven F4U Corsair especially equipped for night operations. One can tell that

Air Force pilots and historians think that Bordelon should have an asterisk attached to his ace status since his kills were not jets.

General Brown and Colonel Abbott did not discuss the special circumstances of the Great MiG Hunt of 1953, when both they and their "leads" made their combat reputations. In truth, there were great egos on the line and a fair amount of Air Force show business—fueled by media fascination with a new set of flying heroes who had "the right stuff." There is no discussion of "MiG madness," the mental condition that seized some F-86 pilots. Among the forty American aces, only eight Air Force officers shot down ten or more MiGs. All of them flew the E-Model or F-Model F-86, the improved fighters of 1952 to 1953. In accordance with the American system of forming flying teams, the F-86s went up in flights of two pairs, each pair including one "lead" and one wingman. Depending on the mission, the flights might mass or not. For a sortie into "MiG Alley" without other planes to escort, the F-86s usually deployed in two flights of eight aircraft. Even though they often faced three times as many MiGs, the F-86 squadrons preferred fighting in "fluid fours" with the "leads" doing the attacking and the wingmen guarding their rears, a term that has several usages in aerial combat. The "leads" won their positions by rank, experience, and flying skill as judged by their squadron commanders; of the eight triple and double aces, two were colonels, one was a lieutenant colonel, three were majors, and five were captains. Of the thirty-eight Air Force aces, there were only four lieutenants. One of them, First Lieutenant James F. Low (nine MiGs), earned himself an unflattering portrait as a glory hound in a novel and in the movie *The Hunters.* The Air Force way of war emphasized experience and teamwork.

The timing of the air war had even more impact than seniority and flying experience. The place where an officer ranked in a chronological "lineal list" of new aces provides the clue. The first officer to down five MiGs was then-Captain James Jabara, who made his fifth kill on May 20, 1951. He made one more kill before retiring from the sky for an unwelcome reassignment; when Jabara returned to the air battle by his own request in May 1953, he shot down nine more MiGs in two and a half months. His successor as the leading MiG killer in 1951 became Major George A. Davis, USAF, a wiry Texan, who became Ace No. 5 and scored a total of eleven kills before he was shot down and killed on February 10, 1952. All the other high scorers did their damage to the Communist MiG force in the war's waning days. Of the other pilots with ten or more MiG kills, Colonel Royal N. "The King" Baker became Ace No. 21 (November 1952); Captain Harold E. Fischer Jr., Ace No. 25 (January 1953); Captain Pete Fernandez, Ace No. 26 (February 1953); Captain Joseph McConnell, Ace No. 27 (February 1953); Colonel James K. Johnson, Ace No. 29 (March 1953); and Captain Ralph S. Parr, who had already flown 105 missions as an F-80 pilot in an earlier

**Capt. Joseph M. McConnell, Jr., USAF, leading Korean War ace (16 kills), Korea, 1953**

tour, Ace No. 33 (June 1953). At the time he was shot down on April 7, 1953, Fischer, who had also flown more than one hundred missions in F-80s, was the leading active ace, with eleven kills. (Fischer survived two years in Chinese captivity until released in 1955.) Fischer's imprisonment opened the competition between McConnell and Fernandez for Ace of Aces in the spring of 1953.

Brown and Abbott agree that McConnell and Fernandez were well matched. The wingmen say that their aces were among the best "stick men," or aircraft handlers, they saw in Korea. They were relaxed, extremely self-confident, and instinctive in their flying, honed by hours of practice. "We had many fine pilots in our squadron," Brown recalled "or they wouldn't have been assigned to either the 4th FIW or 51st FIW. We had the best fighter pilots in the Air Force." Abbott remembers that he learned quickly to stay close to McConnell, however difficult that was. The first discriminator between the aces and everyone else, Brown and Abbott agree, was their shooting ability. First, the F-Model F-86 had a superior radar-ranging gun sight, but McConnell and Fernandez improved their odds for a kill by closing to one thousand feet or less. They also maneuvered slightly port or starboard of their quarry in order to get more fuselage surface in their cone of fire, which was easy to understand but hard to do. "Joe could really shoot," Abbott remembers, "and he was always maneuvering with shooting in mind." The bold flying even had payoffs before the six .50-caliber guns in the Sabre's nose opened fire. At lower altitudes and with violent maneuvering, the MiG had a tendency to spin out of control or flame out. Far East Air Forces ruled that a MiG that crashed under such stress rated as a "kill."

"I still think that flying and shooting alone don't explain Pete's success as a MiG killer," Brown recalls. "He was not a flamboyant guy, but in the air he was a killer. He really wanted to mix it up with the MiGs. Pete was consistent in the air. His fourteen kills were spread over eight months; only May 1953 stands out as the exception since Pete shot down four MiGs in about eight days." Colonel Abbott remembers McConnell as exceptionally aggressive:

> I may be exaggerating, since I was the poor lieutenant who had to fly with Joe wherever he went. But Joe hated to miss a fight, and he never worried about the odds. One time we were flying with six other F-86s, and we got separated when a "train" of MiGs came roaring down on us from forty-five thousand feet. There must have been at least twenty of them. I called Joe on the radio and reported our tactical condition, which I thought justified a hasty retreat. Joe said that I shouldn't worry, that now we had all the MiGs to ourselves. That's the kind of attitude that allowed Joe to shoot down six MiGs in four days in May 1953.

Brown and Abbott agree that McConnell and Fernandez felt cheated when Lieutenant General Glenn O. Barcus, 5th Air Force commander, grounded both them in May 1953 so that the Air Force would have live "triple aces," not a dead hero like George Davis (who received the Medal of Honor) or a prisoner like Harold Fischer. McConnell was especially incensed, since he suspected that Jim Jabara would make a run on his record of sixteen kills. McConnell had honed his four-plane flight to a fighting edge; Marine Major John Bolt joined the flight and received his initiation to combat by flying eleven missions on McConnell's wing. He then flew second lead for Dog Flight, called "Hot Dog Flight" by the rest of the squadron. On the day (May 18) that McConnell made his last three kills, Abbott had returned to the place of honor as McConnell's wingman. "I had gotten the spirit, so sometimes when we made some tight breaks or turns, I got my aircraft in front of Joe's. He always reminded me that I would draw fire that way and to get the hell out of his shooting zone or he'd get me, too. I don't think he was kidding." Brown does not remember Fernandez as

U.S. AIR FORCE

**Capt. Manuel J. "Pete" Fernandez, Jr., USAF, third highest ace (14.5 kills), Korean War, Korea, 1953**

quite so colorful. "Pete had plenty of personality and pride, but he was not a prima donna. For the time, the nose art and decorations on his F-86 were subdued." The same could not be said of Joe McConnell, whose "Beautious [*sic*] Butch" (two different aircraft) was as flashy as its pilot. McConnell also survived a dramatic air-sea rescue in April 1953 when he ditched Beautious Butch I, full of cannon holes, in the West Sea.

General Brown and Colonel Abbott now know that in the spring of 1953 the Chinese and Russians tried to overwhelm the F-86 force with literally hundreds of relatively untried pilots. In the "Big Month" of May, the Sabre pilots shot down fifty-six MiGs at the cost of only one F-86. The next month, the F-86s sent the number of downed MiGs up to seventy-seven, with no friendly F-86 losses, largely because a change in the wing of the F-Model Sabre and some engine improvements now allowed the Sabres to initiate attacks at higher altitudes. The Korean rainy season and the armistice brought an end to the massacre. If the Communists thought they could seize last-minute advantage—other than some deadly on-the-job-training—from the air war, they were disappointed.

# 43

## Missing in Action

**COLUMBUS, OHIO**
**October 1998**

The night attack of the 134th Regiment, 45th Division, Chinese People's Volunteers Force rolled up Hill 598 (Triangle Hill) and almost swamped two companies of the 3rd Battalion, 17th Infantry, U.S. 7th Infantry Division. In the fifth day of battle for Triangle Hill, the Chinese seemed determined to take the ridge, which dominated the main road into Kumhwa, the battered town that anchored the United Nations' hold on a corner of the "Iron Triangle." The night of October 19–20, 1952, capped the seesaw struggle for Triangle Hill, so steep and broken that no more than two or three companies of Chinese and American soldiers at a time could destroy each other in the trenches and bunkers along the ridge. One after another the companies disappeared in the furnace of artillery and small arms fire. Most of the fighting went on in a darkness ripped only by the flashes of gunfire.

Even though it held Triangle Hill, the 3rd Battalion, 17th Infantry faced collapse when dawn came on October 20. Two days later the survivors of Companies I, K, and L stumbled from their bunkers. The battalion had lost 15 men killed in action, 112 wounded in action, and a disturbing 63 missing in action (MIA), which meant that sixty-three American soldiers had somehow disappeared, unseen by any living comrade. Company K alone had lost 76 of 150 soldiers on that one awful night. Since another American battalion occupied the hill, the problem was not just uncollected or unidentified bodies. The soldiers were simply gone. One of them was Sergeant Marvin L. Rodman, U.S. 55 200 683, a squad leader in Company K's 3rd Platoon.

Back in Salem, Indiana, Elsie and Jesse Rodman soon learned that their twenty-two-year-old son, Marvin, had entered a sort of military administrative purgatory called "missing in action" on October 20, 1952. The Army reported simply that Marvin could not be found or accounted for by his buddies. That—officially—is all the Army could say. However, Sergeant Ken Holstine told a reporter that he had heard from another soldier that Rodman had been wounded in the right shoulder and left leg and evacuated during the battle. Holstine could not remember the soldier's name, he later wrote the Rodmans, but he thought the man was from Salem, too. Holstine certainly had not seen Marvin, an inference the reporter had made. Another friend, Sergeant Bob Williamson, thought Marvin was "sure a good kid," but did not know any details of his disappearance. Holstine and Williamson heard a rumor that someone had seen Marvin in a hospital in Japan. The Rodmans continued to write the Army demanding a full accounting of their son's loss. They wrote their congressman and hired an attorney.

The Army did its best to respond to the Rodman's firm but shrill letters. The commander of the 17th Infantry conducted his own inquiry and found the shadowy Salem soldier, Sergeant Willis R. Price, but Price denied he had seen Marvin evacuated or knew anything about his disappearance. Price last saw Rodman in a foxhole on the forward slope, blasting away with his M-1 at the advancing Chinese. Both Chinese and American shells were falling on Company K at the peak of the battle. The survivors of Company K scrambled through the rocks for a last stand in the trenches. No one had seen Rodman leave his foxhole. Due to the fact that forty thousand shells fell on or around Triangle Hill in six days of fighting, no one did much extra moving or looking beyond shooting and cowering.

The Army tried to reduce the Rodmans' expectations that Marvin might be a prisoner. Chinese POWs from the battle told their interrogators that their leaders wanted no Chinese captured; they may have been told not to take American prisoners. Someone thought that the 187th Regimental Combat Team (Airborne) had killed Chinese POWs and the 134th Regiment had taken its revenge on Triangle Hill. No one knew for certain. In 1953 when the Chinese returned the surviving American POWs, no soldier from the 17th Infantry's Triangle Hill battalions appeared in the exchanges at Panmunjom. The Rodmans also learned that some of the regiment's wounded had died in their ambulances, caught by a Chinese artillery barrage on the road to Kumhwa.

Even the armistice brought no new clues of Rodman's fate. As well as not receiving any information from the POWS, search parties found nothing after being given seventy-two hours to recover remains and abandoned equipment from the new Demilitarized Zone. Since the Chinese had finally captured Triangle Hill from the ROK 2nd Division on October 30, 1952, any search took place in their zone. Surviving records could not place any United Nations recovery team on the north slope of Triangle Hill, a maze of sharp cliffs, draws choked with rubble and refuse, and ruined field fortifications. The Chinese and North Koreans never produced any remains in the exchanges conducted by the Military Armistice Commission at Panmunjom. In December 1953, the Department of the Army ruled Sergeant Rodman a "presumptive death," and his parents received his death settlement and benefits, established by the Missing Persons Act (1942). He became one of the eight-thousand-plus American MIAs now added to the known American deaths, thus becoming a statistic, not an administrative problem. (The MIAs fall into two categories: six thousand combat MIAs, twenty-seven hundred POW MIAs.) He now rested in the bosom of the body counters, one of 27,731 Army combat deaths in Korea.

The Rodmans continued their private search for Marvin. They now accepted the fact that he was dead, but they refused to believe that no one knew how Marvin died or where his remains might be. As Elsie and Jesse aged, another son inherited the family crusade for closure. More letters came to the 8th Army History Office at Yongsan. At the suggestion of Herman Katz, a command historian who never found a document he did not like or personal case he did not investigate, the family placed appeals for information in the 7th Infantry Division Association newsletter. Two years later (1977) the Rodmans received the first of several letters from Gerald F. Lane, a former artillery lieutenant and forward observer who had manned an outpost on Triangle Hill.

Lane could offer the Rodmans little hope that they would ever know just what happened to Marvin. The Chinese had deluged the hill with heavy artillery. No doubt many dead GIs had simply been blown apart beyond recovery and recognition. The terrain itself favored disappearance. He himself had been injured when he slipped over the edge of a cliff. Marvin might have fallen off a cliff, wounded or not, and disappeared in the chaos of a night battle. Lane did not think the Chinese would have taken Marvin prisoner, since the GIs had all heard that the 134th Infantry intended to avenge what the Chinese believed were

American atrocities. Although Lane, the Rodmans, and the Rodmans' lawyer continued to correspond, no one learned any more information nor did anyone else respond to the Rodmans' repeated pleas for help. The family now wanted some assurance that Marvin's name appeared in the memory books and plaques on the United Nations memorials in Korea. Rodman inquiries continued until 1987, and were subsequently taken over by his Indiana high school classmates and friends. Then the letters—at least those to the 8th Army—stopped.

Had Marvin Rodman survived the Korean War, he probably would have returned to his respected and profitable civilian occupation of mortician and funeral director.

# 44

# The Navy's War on
# Germs in Korea

The Communists charged that the United States conducted germ warfare during the Korean War. The medical officers of United Nations Command did in fact conduct a war on microbes, but not on people. One Navy doctor, Lieutenant Gerald A. Martin, M.D., MC, USN, played a key role in the battle against epidemic enteric fevers until his death in an aircraft accident on September 27, 1951. Martin and other Navy medical and medical service personnel created and manned one of the most unusual vessels in Naval Forces Far East, USS *LSI(L) 1091,* a converted landing ship that became a floating laboratory. The crew and the vessel became Fleet Mobile Epidemic Disease Control Unit No. One (FMEDCU ONE), commanded by Commander Joseph M. Coppoletta, M.D., MC, USN.

Before Dr. Martin joined FMEDCU ONE in late March 1951, the laboratory ship had not contributed much to the United Nations Command's war on disease. Used to process Korean refugees in Pusan harbor through the bleak, defeat-plagued winter of 1950 to 1951, Coppoletta's ship finally received a significant mission in March 1951. Headquarters U.S. Naval Forces Far East assigned FMEDCU ONE to an intelligence mission, organized by Brig. Gen. Crawford F. Sams, M.D., MC, U.S. Army, the Asian theater preventive disease officer. In a high-risk commando mission, Sams went ashore with a Korean American special operations team to investigate agent reports of bubonic plague near Wonsan.

MRS. G. A. MARTIN

**Lt. Gerald A. Martin, MD, MC, USN examining dysentery cultures aboard the *LSI(L) 1091*, Korea, 1951**

Unable to penetrate the Communist security system, Sams had to be satisfied with questioning an agent who had seen the disease victims. Had his team found a diseased Korean, the "specimen" would have gone to FMEDCU ONE for examination. Sams concluded that the disease was real enough (probably a virulent form of hemorrhagic fever, a smallpox variant), but not a threat to the immunized soldiers and civilians under United Nations control.

The research mission of FMEDCU ONE started with a plan drafted by the Armed Forces Epidemiological Board, a group of civilian and military experts for the identification and control of epidemic diseases. Heartened by its success in developing preventive medicine programs and respiratory disease treatment during World War II, the board, chaired by Dr. Colin M. MacLeod, created a special commission to study epidemic enteric (gastrointestinal) diseases and to devise more effective preventive medicine programs and treatments for disabling diarrhea and dysentery. The board declared war on that traditional bane of the all armies, "the runs." Dr. MacLeod and fellow board member Dr. Thomas Francis Jr. organized the Commission on Enteric Infections at the 1948 meeting of the American Public Health Association. They recruited three key people for the commission: Dr. James Watt, a noted epidemiologist at the Louisiana State University Medical School, New Orleans; Dr. Albert V. Hardy, laboratory director of the Florida State Board of Health; and Col. Richard P. Mason, M.D., MC, USA. In its first studies the commission concluded that basic research on the shigella and salmonella bacteria, the principal culprits in diarrheal epidemics, did not exist.

The threat of epidemics of many kinds in Korea made it an ideal site for both good research and good preventive medicine. Assigned as the commanding officer, 406th Medical General Laboratory, Tokyo, Colonel Mason recruited FMEDCU ONE as one of his two principal field investigative units. After the Sams mission, Colonel Mason took over operational control of FMEDCU ONE. He widened its research mission to include the administration of experimental drugs in five different combinations that the commission believed might arrest and cure epidemic diarrhea. A veteran of the Sams mission, Lieutenant Martin joined the unit as Mason's action officer.

In addition to his impressive qualifications as a doctor, Jerry Martin brought special qualifications to his assignment as the principal medical officer of FMEDCU ONE. Born and raised in Korea, Martin was the son of a Canadian

*LSI(L) 1091* **tied up in Koje-do harbor, Korea, 1951, as diagnostic laboratory for treating POWs and refugees**

medical missionary, Dr. Stanley H. Martin, who had been a staff physician at Severance Hospital, Seoul, until 1940. Jerry Martin had retained his affection for afflicted Asians during his long medical education in the United States at the Medical College of Virginia, Baltimore's University Hospital, and the National Naval Medical Center. He still spoke fluent Korean. His sister, Ruth, was a missionary nurse, and his family had close ties with the Protestant missionary community through the Kilbourne and Moore families. Designated codirector, Joint Dysentery Study Group, Martin accompanied FMEDCU ONE to Koje-do in March 1951. Martin and his team immediately started a stool-collection and analysis program and provided the medical personnel of the 60th General Depot, the camp administrator, with a variety of drugs for their patients.

Over the next six months all the key leaders of the Commission on Enteric Infections visited Koje-do and reported that Martin and the FMEDCU ONE staff had done an exceptional job in their research assignment and equally well as serving as emergency treatment teams. Martin's own contribution had been exceptional for reasons above and beyond his high medical competence; his fluency in Korean won the cooperation of the POWs and the Korean camp personnel, and he enlisted the cooperation of the American civilian staff at Koje-do, the psychological warfare agents of Far East Command's Civilian Information and Education Division, many of whom were Protestant missionaries and family friends like the Reverend Harold Voelkel and the Reverend Edwin W. Kilbourne, Martin's brother-in-law. Martin also proved instrumental in the organization and staffing of a medical clinic to provide care for the Korean refugees on Koje-do, many of whom had become employees of the United Nations Civil Assistance Command. The Korean doctors and nurses themselves were refugees from Severance Hospital in Seoul, a missionary and teaching hospital of international renown. The Korean refugee community on Koje-do also included North Korean intelligence agents who served as liaison officers between the political directorate of the North Korean army and the political officers inside the wire who were leading a life-and-death struggle for the hearts and minds of the North Korean POWs. No doubt Pyongyang knew of Martin's successful medical work, for its agents tried to disrupt his efforts and condemned the work of FMEDCU ONE as heinous research worthy of Unit 731, the Japanese germ warfare agency in World War II.

Although FMEDCU ONE found its research efforts limited by the POW violence that grew at Koje-do in late 1951 and became a war in 1952, its findings confirmed the parasitic nature of diarrhea bacteria that made them immune to normal field sanitation measures. Only inoculation and prompt medical treatment would curb an epidemic. The research provided valuable clues of differ-

MRS. G. A. MARTIN

**Dr. Jerry Martin shares a happy moment with Dr. Chong Song-po and the Severance Hospital Clinic nurses, Koje-do, Korea, May 1951**

ent varieties of diarrhea and amoebic dysentery. The Navy floating laboratory developed the capability of processing three to four hundred stool samples a day, an unpleasant but essential part of its diagnostic work. The clinic to treat Korean camp personnel flourished and provided a more cooperative set of patients for drug experimentation, mostly with new antibiotics. FMEDCU ONE became a principal agency for training medical personnel to deal with enteric diseases.

Dr. Jerry Martin did not live to see his pioneering work come to fruition. Taking laboratory findings and sample cultures to Tokyo, he died when the Air Force C-46 in which he was traveling crashed into a mountain in bad weather. Awarded a posthumous Legion of Merit, Martin received additional recognition when his clinic for Koreans on Koje-do was named the Gerald A. Martin Memorial Health Center. Korean POWs carved the granite memorial that leads to the clinic's open door.

The unanticipated success of Dr. Martin's war on epidemic diarrhea and dysentery among Korean Communist prisoners of war set off a flurry of additional charges by the Communists that United Nations Command was conducting germ warfare experiments on helpless Korean captives. South Koreans believed that Communist agents sabotaged Martin's aircraft because of his reputation for good works. The truth is that Martin and his colleagues kept the prisoners alive and well, thus encouraging many of them to refuse repatriation in 1953.

# 45

## The Marine Colonel
## Becomes a War Criminal

While making a routine reconnaissance flight over the frontlines on July 8, 1952, Colonel Frank H. Schwable's luck deserted him, and it never returned. As the new chief of staff of the 1st Marine Aircraft Wing, Frank Schwable could look back on a Marine Corps career as a fighter pilot that had made him a strong candidate to become a general officer and one of the future architects of Marine aviation policy. The son of a respected Marine colonel who had marched to Peking in 1900, Schwable grew up in the Corps and graduated from the U.S. Naval Academy in 1929. After obligatory attendance at The Basic School, Schwable started his training to be a naval aviator and earned his "wings of gold" in May 1931. By the time the United States entered World War II, Schwable had already flown combat missions in Nicaragua and served with distinction in both flying squadrons and important nonflying staff positions in the naval aviation establishment. Thirty-three years old when the Japanese struck Pearl Harbor, Frank Schwable belonged to the cohort of seasoned prewar officers (most promoted to major and lieutenant colonel in 1940 and 1941) who created the World War II aircraft wings of the Fleet Marine Force.

His service in the Pacific war against Japan established Frank Schwable's reputation as a Marine aviator, a leader in the air and an extraordinarily energetic and intelligent planner on the ground. He was far more than a simple fighter pilot, but he won his future with his hand on the stick of a specially equipped

F4U Corsair. Frank Schwable was a pioneer in night combat operations. He commanded the first Marine night fighter group and then deployed to the Pacific as the commanding officer, Marine Night Fighter Squadron 531. For his night combat heroics in 1943 to 1944 and his subsequent service as a high-level staff officer in the Solomons, Schwable won four Distinguished Flying Crosses and two Legions of Merit before his return to the United States in November 1944. His career continued to fly high and fast. He commanded a Marine Aircraft Group and attended the National War College, but he further enhanced his reputation as a key planner in the Division of Aviation (1950–1952). In his prior assignment (1948–1950) he served in the Joint Plans and Operations Division, Joint Staff, Commander in Chief Pacific, an assignment in which he helped plan for a number of Asian and World War II contingencies, some of which involved the possible use of nuclear weapons.

When Major General Clayton C. Jerome went to Korea to take command of the 1st Marine Aircraft Wing, by choice he took Frank Schwable with him as chief of staff. The assignment could only be viewed as Schwable's preselection for brigadier general. He assumed his new post on May 1, 1950. Just two months later, his nightmare began with a routine flight to orient himself to the U.S. 8th Army's positions and to get his obligatory four-hours-a-month flight time. Flying an SNB twin-engine Beechcraft with Major Roy H. Bley, Schwable strayed briefly over enemy lines and drew a barrage of small arms fire. One bullet cut the plane's main fuel line, and its engines immediately quit. With no obvious place to land, Schwable and Bley bailed out, but Schwable first learned that Bley had been wounded in the thigh and required help to get out of the cockpit, which Schwable provided. The aviators left the plane at a minimum altitude for parachuting. Within fifteen minutes of reaching the ground, they met a very large and aggressive patrol of the Chinese army and became prisoners of war.

With his capture Frank Schwable entered some very elite company, but not a group one would volunteer to join. He was one of four colonels of the American armed forces captured in Korea—or at least captured and eventually released—and he was second in seniority only to Major General William F. Dean, the captive commander of the U.S. 24th Infantry Division. Like the three Air Force colonels who became POWs, Schwable was a pilot, and thus, seniority aside, part of a POW population that the Russians, Chinese, and North Koreans prized for its intelligence and propaganda potential. From his personal effects and material taken from the Beechcraft's wreckage, the Communists knew exactly who Schwable was and how he might be useful to them. What they did not know—but Schwable could not know of their ignorance—was Schwable's familiarity with the extant American contingency plans. Fortunately, Chinese intelligence officers apparently did not read the *New York Times,* for the newspaper published a short announcement of Schwable's capture that listed his previous assignments. For the first two months of his captivity, Schwable faced no unanticipated problems, since his interrogators pressed him for operational intelligence, questions he could duck by asserting that he was a Marine and a pilot and did not know anything about Army and Air Force plans and operations. What Schwable did not yet know was that he was viewed as a war criminal who had become an important part of America's alleged bacteriological warfare campaign against the innocent Korean and Chinese people.

The question of prisoner-of-war experiences in the Korean War—enmeshed in the issues of war crimes and missing-in-action accountability—still generates great passion and statistical uncertainties. The general experience for American POWs was not happy, especially for the common soldiers captured by the Communists in 1950 and early 1951. Only about half of the Americans captured before March 1951 survived captivity, and just how many died from battlefield executions and on "death marches" will always be uncertain. Of the 7,179 Americans who almost certainly were captured, 2,730 died in captivity. In raw numbers, POW accounting is largely an Army problem. The Army claimed 5,961 of the POWs and 2,638 of those who died in captivity. By comparison, the other American branches of service did not lose many POWs, and most of them were eventually repatriated.

|                    | Air Force | Marines | Navy |
|--------------------|-----------|---------|------|
| Presumed POW       | 263       | 225     | 40   |
| Repatriated by 1955 | 235      | 200     | 31   |

The services other than the Army concluded that misbehavior in the Communist POW camps was also an Army problem, and the twenty-one Americans who refused repatriation were all soldiers.

The issue of bacteriological warfare, however, presented another problem— the confessions of American airmen that they had participated in an immoral, illegal campaign of spreading epidemic diseases that surely qualified under international law as a crime against humanity, thus making them war criminals. Again the extant statistics on these confessions makes the issue appear to be a service-specific problem; thirty-eight of the forty-one confessors were Air Force officers. Frank Schwable and Roy Bley, however, were two of the three non-Air Force confessors, and their cases gave the Marine Corps, whose other POWs had exemplary records as captives, a problem of public perception and internal morale, at least from the perspective of General Lemuel C. Shepherd Jr., the Commandant of the Marine Corps in 1953 to 1956.

By 1952 intelligence and political officers of the Chinese army and air forces—with some coaching and observing by Soviet specialists—had developed a consistent system for handling captive American airmen whom they intended to exploit for intelligence and propaganda purposes. Initial treatment was "lenient," but within four to six weeks of processing and evaluation, the captives began almost constant interrogation, characterized by imprisonment in solitary confinement, minimal rations, little or no medical care, poor sanitary conditions, sleep deprivation, and constant intimidation, all designed to put the captive on the slippery slope to hopelessness and degradation. Frank Schwable and Roy Bley underwent the same treatment as their more numerous Air Force fellow victims.

After the exchange of POWs in 1953, followed by the tardy release of fifteen more Air Force personnel in 1955, an extensive study by an American joint intelligence investigating team examined the whole issue of bacteriological warfare confessions. The analysts reported that the Communists interrogated ninety-five Air Force officers about germ warfare. The interrogators apparently decided that sixty-five officers were vulnerable and/or useful for further exploitation, and this group received the maximum pressure to confess, which included death threats, the prospect of life imprisonment as a war criminal, and a wide range of psychological and physical assaults. From this group of sixty-five Air Force officers, the Communists extracted thirty-two confessions in the form of signed statements, radio recordings, and filmed confessions. The Communists did not give enlisted POWs the same attention; they interrogated only seventeen of thirty-six enlisted air crewmen and received only six confessions for their trouble. When the analysts examined twenty-nine different types of coercion endured by confessors and nonconfessors alike, they found no obvious way to predict who would eventually confess and who would not, but it was also obvious that the senior officers received the most pressure and endured longer before confessing. Air Force Colonel Walker M. "Honest John" Mahurin did not confess for 284 days, and Colonel Andrew J. Evans Jr. lasted ninety-seven days; both men confessed when they became convinced that they would not otherwise be repatriated and that no one would believe their confessions anyway. Frank Schwable resisted for about four months, but nevertheless remained uncertain about the point at which he became a pawn in the propaganda war, although the time is probably early December 1952. Major Bley may have resisted a little longer, but not much since the Communists published both their confessions in January 1953.

Although he did not know where he was, for almost a year Frank Schwable lived in a thin-walled mud hut attached to a Korean house somewhere in the vicinity of the Communist camp complex at Pyoktong and Yongdok on the Yalu

River. When he could reach it in time, his "head" was a nearby woods. He had no chance to exercise or talk to anyone. He sat and sat and sat, and his back and legs became painful. He endured cold to the point of frostbite. "[I]n the wintertime the sun goes down early, and in a valley like that it goes down much earlier, and I would just sit there and watch the water drip, drip, drip. Pretty soon it would be drip-drip-drip, and pretty soon it would quit dripping, and it was freezing and so was I. Oh, I used to dread that." Schwable's food came at five in the morning and four in the afternoon. He had nothing to do, nothing to read. His only amusement was carving a corncob pipe with a nail.

**Colonel Frank H. Schwable, USMC**

U.S. MARINE CORPS

The only change in his routine was the interrogations, and almost unconsciously he became more cooperative. Schwable gave the Chinese samples of his signature; he provided some confirmation of data he believed harmless; he gave personal information that seemed innocent, but then came back to haunt him as his confessions simply fed his sense of guilt and degradation. Always an active person, the enforced solitude and endless hours drove him to the brink of madness. Much of his anxiety was the fear that the Chinese would eventually torture him and pry from him information about American war plans. Confessing to bacteriological warfare—he said the 1st Marine Aircraft Wing carried out "experiments"—seemed the lesser of the many evils he faced. In early 1953 the Communists released his "confession," later accompanied by a radio tape and crude motion picture film. Schwable later insisted—and experts agreed—that his written confession was not his prose, but a Chinese version inserted in a longer document that Schwable had written about himself and the war. Although other POWs later testified that Schwable's confession was a serious psychological blow, the embattled colonel did not believe he had crossed the line into treason, collaboration, and criminal behavior. The Chinese told him they had convicted him of war crimes as the price of his exchange.

As part of Operation Big Switch in September 1953, Frank Schwable returned to a Marine Corps that was unhappy with his conduct and embarrassed by its uncertainty about how to handle his case. The Corps embraced a heroic group of POW resisters who had indeed banded together to make life miserable for their Chinese captors. Two of these Marines, Lieutenant Colonel William G. Thrash and Warrant Officer Felix J. McCool, endured their second captivity, having been captured by the Japanese in World War II. Seven Marines had been questioned about germ warfare and not confessed. After the postrelief interrogations and interviews were completed in 1954, the Marine Corps had a new group of POW heroes: John N. McLaughlin, Gerald Fink, John R. Flynn, John T. Cain, Walter Harris, and others. Frank Schwable was not one of the group.

Frank Schwable returned to the United States to enter a military purgatory from which he never escaped. Schwable could tell from his friends and non-admirers that he had fallen from grace; old comrades and commanders seemed distant, and other senior officers simply shunned him. Only his family and a handful of friends—most of them former Marines or civilians—provided sympathetic support. Schwable received no assignment, but simply followed instructions from Headquarters to prepare for a court of inquiry into his germ warfare confession. He received no clues about what General Shepherd thought of his dilemma, and he tended to blame two of Shepherd's confidants—Major General Merrill B. Twining and Colonel Victor H. Krulak—for the apparent animus toward him at Headquarters. He received broad hints that he should retire, even before a court of inquiry, but he remained determined to finish a full thirty years of commissioned service, the legal limit for a colonel.

When the Naval Court of Inquiry in the Case of Colonel Frank H. Schwable, USMC, completed its investigation—a quasi-legal proceeding in which Schwable had military and civilian counsel—its formal findings were simply that the Communists had tortured the bacteriological warfare confession from the colonel and that he should not be subject to prosecution for the confession. On the surface, the findings, approved by the Commandant and the Secretary of the Navy, would appear to restore Schwable's reputation. Such was not the case. General Shepherd had already decided that prosecuting Schwable would simply continue the unfavorable publicity the colonel had attracted and that the case for a prosecution—based on Article 104 of the Uniform Code of Military Justice for aiding and abetting the enemy—might not be successful. From a legal point of view the postrelease interrogations had compromised Schwable's right to avoid self-incrimination. Except for Schwable's voluntary confessions about his behavior, the only evidence was Schwable's printed confession and media appearances, with no accompanying testimony, one way or another, about the degree of voluntarism involved. Much of the information provided the enemy was manifestly false, so just what aid he had provided was arguable. Moreover, the Court of Inquiry had established a pattern of deprivation that it had ruled torture, and there was not yet an overriding, legally binding definition of just how much abuse a serviceman could endure and still be held responsible for his actions. Then there was the issue of Schwable's knowledge of top-secret war plans. If he could not argue through counsel that his actions had been designed to protect real classified information, then his rights as a defendant were additionally compromised. Schwable's actions might be interpreted as true heroism, especially if the Chinese showed any awareness of his role as a war planner. General Shepherd concluded that the sooner the Schwable case went away, the better.

The Commandant also wanted Frank Schwable to disappear or at least move to the twilight zone populated by field grade officers who have received their last promotion and will never hold a key position again. In the aftermath of the Court of Inquiry's findings and the review of its work, in April 1954, Shepherd directed his chief of staff, Major General Gerald C. Thomas, to write and sign a letter ("By direction") that Schwable was never to command again. On the other hand, Schwable received another Legion of Merit award for his precapture service with the 1st Marine Aircraft Wing, and he soon received assignments to a pleasant duty station, Norfolk, Virginia, to serve as the Marine flight safety officer for the Atlantic Coast aviation units. He continued to fly and draw flight pay, and when he retired by law in 1959 he received a "tombstone promotion" to brigadier general, which he rated for his World War II decorations. But until the end of his life in 1988, Frank Schwable knew that his career as a Marine aviator had died in a place called No Name Valley in North Korea in the winter of 1952 to 1953.

# 46

## The Christian General
## at Panmunjom

The new U.S. Army representative on the United Nations Command negotiating team at Panmunjom probably did not impress the Chinese one way or the other, although they undoubtedly had a file on him. In December 1951 Major General William Kelly Harrison Jr. came to Korea to become deputy commander of the U.S. 8th Army, and the following month he replaced Major General Harry I. Hodes, U.S. Army, on the armistice negotiating team. As with most of the Army general officer assignments that followed the appearance of Matthew B. Ridgway and James Van Fleet in the Korean theater, Harrison's reputation rested upon his performance in the war against Germany and his relationship with the Europeanists who ran the Army. Bill Harrison was not only "Old Army," but "Old America." His great-grandfather was President William Henry Harrison, who made sure that the Ohio Valley belonged to Old Virginia, whatever Congress named the new states. Bill Harrison's grandfather commanded cavalry for the Confederacy, but his father graduated from the Naval Academy (1889) and served as a Navy administrator, which meant that Bill could attend the best preparatory schools in the District of Columbia. To honor his saber-wielding grandfather, Bill Harrison graduated from West Point in 1917, which made him a classmate of J. Lawton Collins, Mark W. Clark, and Matthew B. Ridgway.

Slight, trim, energetic, and very bright, Bill Harrison spent much of his next twenty years as a cavalry troop officer. His regiments read like the honor roll of the Old Army: 1st Cavalry, the Cavalry School, 7th Cavalry, 26th Cavalry (Philippine Scouts), 2nd Cavalry, 9th Cavalry, and 6th Cavalry. Bill Harrison, however, gave the Army a great deal more than "fours right into line" and stable inspections. He studied Romance languages abroad and then taught Spanish and French at West Point with his classmate, Matt Ridgway. He did so well at the prestigious two-year course at the Army Command and General Staff School that he remained there as an instructor. As war loomed in 1939 he arrived at the War Department for assignments in the War Plans Division, specializing in strategic planning, where he worked with Dwight D. Eisenhower and Wayne Clark. As a brigadier general he escaped Washington to serve as the assistant division commander of two divisions and was deployed to Europe in 1944 as the assistant commander of the U.S. 30th Infantry Division ("Old Hickory"), built on the Tennessee National Guard. Saddled with a division commander who specialized in talking rather than fighting, Bill Harrison proved to be the moral and professional foundation upon which the 30th Division built an enviable reputation for combat prowess, particularly fighting two Panzer Divisions to a standstill in the Mortain-Falaise campaign. Harrison ended the war as a major general and the commander of the U.S. 2nd Infantry Division, another prestigious assignment. He then showed his versatility by working three years in Japan as the chief of General MacArthur's reparations staff.

After eighteen months of commanding a training division in the United States, Harrison received surprise orders to report to the U.S. 8th Army, because General Ridgway and General Van Fleet thought he would be perfect as either a Corps commander or deputy Army commander, assignments that ensured a promotion to lieutenant general (1952). Wayne Clark was no less pleased to have Harrison in the theater when he replaced Ridgway in early 1952. Bill Harrison— Distinguished Service Cross, Distinguished Service Medal, Purple Heart—was disciplined, cadet-perfect in appearance even at the age of fifty-seven, and flexibly intelligent. He not only replaced Hodes, but when the chief delegate, Vice Admiral C. Turner Joy, USN, insisted he be replaced for ill-health and terminal frustration, all the generals who counted—which reached back to Omar Bradley and Joe Collins at the Pentagon—agreed that Bill Harrison was just the man to take over the onerous task of facing the Chinese and North Koreans in the tents at Panmunjom. Harrison took the job with complete lack of faith in the American negotiating position: "The only good way to have an armistice is to initiate discussions when the enemy is really defeated."

There was a dimension to Bill Harrison's life that discomfited his friends and enemies alike: He was an unabashed practicing Christian, who could read the Bible and pray in public without embarrassment. Raised an Episcopalian, he had become a Southern Baptist because he believed his family's church had lost its enthusiasm for evangelism. Harrison had been a founding member of the Officers' Christian Union (1943), which pledged itself to support missionary work in the wartime army. In Japan he had organized the Christian Japanese and foreign missionaries to support occupation policies. He continued his work while he was chief of the Army-Air Force Troop Information and Education Division (1949–1950). As the commanding general at Fort Dix, New Jersey, he strengthened his ties with the many missionary organizations that made New York City their home. Bill Harrison was not, however, the sort of Christian who expected to convert everyone around him, and he could even joke about his religiosity. He told a press conference in Korea that his assignment as chief of the UNC delegation would probably mean that he would be reading his Bible and praying more than usual. The international press corps he dealt with—which had driven Turner Joy to distraction—was impressed that he did not smoke, drink, or swear and that he talked about the negotiations with candor and brevity but did not pretend there was news when there was none. No one questioned his integrity and selflessness. Even the Chinese delegation, giants of intelligence compared to their North Korean counterparts, found Harrison worth respect for his toughness and directness.

As Army representative, Harrison had already impressed the UNC staff officers and interpreter-translators, and they welcomed his advancement to chief delegate. He laid out new ground rules: Dress down (no ties) for the Communists; deal with the press only in large groups; don't argue and don't get mad; break off plenary sessions and subcommittee meetings when the Communists become outrageous; and concede nothing that is not already established by the State Defense Committee in Washington that hammered out UNC positions. Harrison thought the United Nations had already made too many compromises, and he did not want his negotiators giving away even more by mistake. Harrison did not expect any dramatic changes in the negotiations based on the fighting, unless the Communists committed more troops and the Russian air force and navy entered the war, which seemed unlikely. It was equally unlikely that United Nations Command would initiate expanded operations: an amphibious envelopment at Wonsan or Pyongyang, bombing targets in Manchuria and Russia, and placing a naval blockade on China and Russia. Harrison's principal fear was that Washington and the United Nations allies would have a falling-out on armistice terms or that Syngman Rhee would reject any peace that did not unify Korea on his terms. By the autumn of 1952, after Rhee had engineered a constitutional change that ensured his reelection as president, relations with the Rhee government had become Van Fleet's and Clark's biggest challenge. The Communists seemed content to wait for the American-South Korean alliance to commit suicide. Their weapon to divide the Americans and South Koreans was

Lt. Gen. William K. Harrison, USA, and Gen. Mark W. Clark, USA, meet at the base near Munsan-ni to sign the Korean Armistice Agreement, July 1953

the major unresolved armistice issue, the provisions for the repatriation of the prisoners of war.

The American position, which Harrison accepted, and the South Korean position were essentially the same, but with different views on how it should be implemented: No POW should be forced against his will to return to the state that had put him in uniform and sent him off to war. It was inconceivable that Americans and their U.N. allies in Communist hands would choose not to return home. (The negotiators had limited knowledge of allied war criminals and turncoats.) The South Koreans in Communist hands were a huge problem, but no one had a good answer except to take back whomever the Communists sent south. In their first list of POWs the Communists claimed to hold only 7,142 South Korean soldiers, but the ROK army headquarters estimated that it had eighty-eight thousand soldiers missing in action. The Chinese and Koreans in UNC prison camps had gone to war with one another, divided into die-hard repatriates and die-hard nonrepatriates who preyed on the majority of the prisoners as potential converts or victims. Riots and terrorism became a common phenomenon in the spring of 1952 and continued to war's end. President Rhee feared that UNC would tire of the embarrassing task of crushing prison riots and send all the Koreans in its custody back to North Korea, even South Koreans or North Korean refugees who for various reasons had ended up in UNC prison camps. United Nations Command and the Rhee administration actually agreed that about two-thirds of the Koreans in the camps would refuse repatriation, an estimate that proved relatively accurate. The Communist position was simple: Send everyone back. The Chinese were aware that India had taken the lead in the United Nations in proposing exchange schemes that included nonrepatriation, but that India was a puppet of the Chinese as far as Syngman Rhee was concerned. For the Chinese 1952 would be the Year of Patience and Inscrutability . . . and some serious fighting in October and November.

Bill Harrison showed his mettle even before replacing Admiral Joy, walking out of a subcommittee meeting after fifteen seconds in April 1952. Six months later—after prior coordination—Harrison walked out of a plenary session with his negotiators and announced that the talks had reached an impasse. In fact, the timing was determined by the fighting and the prospect of an American presidential election, the likely winner being General Dwight D. Eisenhower. The Chinese watched the course of the election with some concern; they thought Eisenhower and his old friend Wayne Clark could not resist more bombing and amphibious operations, the same instruments they used to destroy the Third Reich. The Communists even hardened their position on the POWs, rejecting the "neutral nations" proposal from the United Nations. If the Communists had accepted it, it would have added even more stress to the U.S.-ROK relationship.

General Harrison realized that much of the theater at Panmunjom was designed to impress the media representatives and, through them, public opinion. He took the offensive against the Communists. When either of the two senior North Korean generals became particularly insulting, he directed First Lieutenant Richard F. Underwood, U.S. Army, one of the three Korean interpreters, to reply in his best street Korean. He told the Koreans that their language identified them as "common criminals or persons who through ignorance and stupidity are unable to speak logically or convincingly." The Chinese delegates, the shrewd and powerful generals Deng Hua and Xie Fang, found these exchanges amusing since they had no special regard for Nam Il and Lee Sang-jo, their Korean counterparts. The Chinese adhered to higher standards; their principal interpreter was a Harvard-educated Ph.D. (in economics), while the North Korean interpreter was a turncoat Seoul high school teacher who was later executed for poor performance. Harrison instructed his own translating team—Horace G. and Richard Underwood, Army Warrant Officer Kenneth Wu, and ROK Lieutenant Colonel Lee Soo-yong—to be proper and specific, but not to accept Communist insults. If nothing else, his leadership won the lasting affection of his senior staff and interpreting team.

The turning point in the negotiations came with the death of Stalin in March 1953 and a very quick decision by a fractious committee of would-be successors to end Russia's support to the Korean War. Mao Zedong, however, was not yet ready to quit, nor was Zhou Enlai, the real brains behind the negotiations. The Chinese produced the ultimate and final act of "talking and fighting" before agreeing to an armistice that included the POW nonrepatriation option. In April the Communists agreed to an exchange of sick and wounded prisoners and started a series of major offensives against the 8th Army's most vulnerable outposts. The Chinese offensive swept eastward until four Chinese armies defeated the ROK II Corps in the Battle of the Kumsong salient. The political situation worsened when Syngman Rhee's military police arranged the release of twenty-seven thousand anti-Communist "detainees." Both Dwight D. Eisenhower and Mao Zedong did not take kindly to this bit of Korean unilateralism. In the Americans' case, the President, soothed by Secretary of State John Foster Dulles, agreed that a bilateral mutual security treaty and one-billion-dollar military and economic assistance program were preferable to continuing the war. Bill Harrison's last act at Panmunjom was to supervise the drafting of final armistice terms and preparing for the exchange of signatures and documents.

Bill Harrison remained on active duty until he reached mandatory retirement for age in rank in 1957 after forty years of commissioned service. Before his death in 1987 at the age of ninety-two, he devoted his life to evangelism. He believed that the war in Korea had been only a part of a global struggle between two irreconcilable systems of faith, and he knew which one would ultimately triumph.

# Appendix 1:
# A Reading Guide
# to the Korean War

The cultural and political context for the war, as well as information about specific people and events in Korean history, may be found in:

Nahm, Andrew C., *Korea: A History of the Korean People: Tradition and Transformation* (1988).

Pratt, Keith, and Richard Rutt, *Korea: A Historical and Cultural Dictionary* (1999).

The most useful references for specific information on the Korean War are:

Brune, Lester H., ed., *The Korean War: Handbook of the Literature and Research* (1996).

Hoare, James E., and Susan Pares, eds., *Conflict in Korea: An Encyclopedia* (1999).

Matray, James I., ed., *Historical Dictionary of the Korean War* (1991).

Tucker, Spencer, ed., *Encyclopedia of the Korean War,* 3 vols. (2000).

The history of the Korean War from the perspective of the major national belligerents, fusing political and geostrategic considerations with military operations, may be found in:

Academy of Military Sciences, People's Liberation Army, People's Republic of China, *Zhonggua Renmin Zhiyuanjun Kangmei Yuanchao Zhan Shi* [The History of the Chinese People's Volunteers Force in the War to Resist America and Assist Korea] (1988).

Condit, Doris, *History of the Office of the Secretary of Defense: The Test of War, 1950–1953* (1988).

Farrar-Hockley, Anthony, *The British Part in the Korean War,* 2 vols. (1990 and 1995).

Schnabel, James E., and Robert J. Watson, *History of the Joint Chiefs of Staff: The Joint Chiefs of Staff and National Policy: 1950–1953: The Korean War,* 2 vols. (1998).

The Staff of the War History Department, Korea Institute of Military History, Ministry of National Defense, Republic of Korea, *The Korean War,* 3 vols. (1997–1999).

All four of the American military services (Army, Air Force, Navy, and Marine Corps) have published histories of the Korean War written by their own staff historians. They are described in Brune, *The Korean War,* cited above. Of the commercial histories of the war written for a popular audience, all of which should be used with care, the best are:

Kim Chom-gon, *The Korean War, 1950–1953* (1980).

Halliday, Jon, and Bruce Cumings, *Korea: The Unknown War* (1988).

Hickey, Michael, *The Korean War* (1999).

MacDonald, Callum A., *Korea: The War before Vietnam* (1986).

Rees, David, *Korea: The Limited War* (1964).

For students of the war who want more detail on ground military operations, the best lines of departure are:

Appleman, Roy, *Disaster in Korea: The Chinese Confront MacArthur* (1989) and *Ridgway Duels for Korea* (1990).

Blair, Clay, *The Forgotten War: America in Korea, 1950–1953* (1987).

Hastings, Max, *The Korean War* (1987).

General histories of the war as an episode in the Cold War and in regional rivalries in Asia, written for an academic-professional audience are:

Foot, Rosemary, *The Wrong War: American Policy and the Dimensions of the Korean Conflict, 1950–1953* (1985).

Stueck, William, *The Korean War: An International History* (1995).
Thornton, Richard C., *Odd Man Out: Truman, Stalin, Mao, and the Origins of the Korean War* (2000).

The recent availability of Russian and Chinese sources, though still limited, has allowed the publication of books written from the perspective of Stalin, Kim Il-sung, and Mao Zedong:

Chen Jian, *China's Road to the Korean War: The Making of the Sino-American Confrontation* (1994).
Dae-Sook Suh, *Kim Il-sung* (1988).
Goncharov, Sergei N., John W. Lewis, and Xue Litai, *Uncertain Partners: Stalin, Mao, and the Korean War* (1993).
Shu Gang Zhang, *Mao's Military Romanticism: China and the Korean War, 1950–1953* (1995).
Li Xiaobing, Allan R. Millett, and Bin Yu, *Mao's Generals Remember Korea* (2001).

Korean political history and the role of the United States and the Soviet Union in polarizing the Korean Nationalist liberation movements is essential in understanding the war and can be investigated in:

Cumings, Bruce, *The Origins of the Korean War,* Volume I, *Liberation and the Emergency of Separate Regimes, 1945–1947* (1981) and Volume II, *The Roaring of the Cataract, 1947–1950* (1990).
Matray, James I., *The Reluctant Crusade: American Foreign Policy in Korea, 1941–1950* (1985).
Merrill, John, *Korea: The Peninsular Origins of the War* (1989).

The literature on the armistice negotiations, extensive in Korean, Chinese, and English and written by participants and scholars, can be sampled in:

Bailey, Sydney D., *The Korean Armistice* (1992).
Foot, Rosemary, *A Substitute for Victory: The Politics of Peacemaking at the Korean Armistice Talks* (1990).

The documentary films available to television audiences outside Russia, China, and North Korea almost always focus on the American military experience in Korea and seldom do justice to all the belligerents. Although one could hardly call them "balanced," the following documentaries do at least provide competitive visions and interpretations of the war that run counter to the American-centric view of the war:

*Korea: The Unknown War,* written by Jon Halliday with Bruce Cumings for Thames Television (1988), Philip Whitehead, executive producer, and WGBH/PBS (1990), Austin Hoyt and Peter McGee, executive producers.

*The Korean War,* produced by Dennis M. Hedlund, Pearle Lee, and Ahn Dae-won (1992), Korean Broadcasting Company/White Star.

*Korea: War at the 38th Parallel,* the Sterling Group and Turner Broadcasting (1985), A BBC/THE Production, written by Max Hastings and produced by John Bau and John Bird.

# Appendix 2:
# Selected Statistics,
# Korean War

## CASUALTIES: WAR-RELATED

South Korea: 187,712 military KIA; 30,000+ est. still MIA; 429,000 (est.) WIA (ROK, 2000); 500,000 to 1,000,000 civilians dead from all causes and missing (est.)

North Korea: 1.5 million military and civilians KIA or MIA

China: 152,400 military KIA and MIA; 238,000 WIA (Chinese) 600,000 to 800,000 (deaths from all causes, MIA, Western estimates)

United States: 33,741 military (KIA, MIA); 2,827 died in the war zone of other causes; 103,284 WIA; 36,568 total deaths in theater

All other UNC military contingents: 3,063 KIA or MIA (no national contingent had more than 700 KIA except Turkey, 721); 11,817 WIA

## MILITARY SERVICE, U.S., 1950–1953

| | |
|---|---|
| 2.8 million | U.S. Army |
| 1.28 million | U.S. Air Force |
| 1.1 million | U.S. Navy |
| 424,000 | U.S. Marine Corps |

Although service percentages vary, about 40 percent of Korean War-era servicemen served in the war zone (Korea, Japan, North Asian waters).

## AIR WAR (UNITED NATIONS COMMAND)

Far East Air Forces (Japan): 5th Air Force (Korea), 13th Air Force (Philippines and Guam), 20th Air Force (Japan); USN carrier aviation (Task Force 77); 1st Marine Aircraft Wing; Royal Navy carrier aviation; Australian and South African Squadrons

|                    |                       |
|--------------------|-----------------------|
| Total Sorties:     | 1 million+            |
| Counterair:        | 185,000 (est.)        |
| Strategic bombing: | 994 (defined by USAF) |
| Interdiction:      | 340,454               |
| Close air support: | 123,413               |
| Cargo:             | 67,000                |
| Misc.:             | 27,000 (est.)         |

All UNC air losses: 2,000 aircraft, about half to enemy action; 147 lost in air-to-air combat (78 F-86s), 816 to ground fire, 78 unknown; U.S. Air Force KIA or MIA 379, but 1,200 deaths from all causes

Total sorties by ROKAF/UNC air units: 44,873, interdiction and close air support

ROKAF: 27 pilots, 4 other officers, 26 enlisted, 2 civilians KIA; 117 aircraft lost; sorties flown 8,495. Strength 1953: 11,461

## PRISONERS OF WAR/DETAINEES

### United Nations Command

ROK: 60,000 estimated POWs, of which 8,321 repatriated; 327 refused repatriation; MIAs either died as POWs or slave laborers or dragooned into the NKPA

United States: 7,190 declared POWs (identified by name by the Communists), but as many as another 3,000 may have been in enemy custody and were eventually carried as MIA. Died in captivity: 2,730. Repatriated: 3,746. Refused repatriation: 21; 93 percent of POWs were U.S. Army

### All Other United Nations

A small number remain unaccounted for (est. 300-plus), and there are no totals for the number of soldiers who died in captivity. The total of repatriates was

1,379, and one (UK) refused repatriation. The largest number of repatriated servicemen were British soldiers (977), the next largest, Turks (243).

## Communist Forces

North Koreans and South Koreans identified as soldiers, guerrillas, and their
     families: 75,823, of which about 60,000 are identified as members of
     the NKPA. These are figures based on U.N. statistics in 1953, and do
     not include those who died in captivity (estimated in the thousands)
     and those released by the ROKA in 1953, which numbered around
     27,000. The figure of 75,823 represents those repatriated. Of the 7,900
     Koreans held as nonrepatriates, 7,604 eventually remained in South
     Korea.

Chinese: All military personnel, 6,670 returned to the PRC, but 14,704 re-
     mained in UNC control and most of these settled on Taiwan; 440 Chi-
     nese servicemen changed their minds and later requested return to
     the PRC.

Action against U.S. servicemen: After debriefing, military investigators deter-
     mined that 565 cases required further study, but of this group 373
     cases produced no actionable judicial or administrative procedures. Of
     the remaining 192 cases, the Army convicted six and separated 61; the
     Marine Corps reprimanded one and put two members on special
     assignment; the Air Force retired three and separated seven members.

## COST (U.S. ONLY)

$17.2 billion (U.S. Army)

    $11.7 billion    supplies shipped to FECOM
    $ 1.5 billion    contracted transportation
    $ 1.7 billion    for CONUS and FECOM installations
    $ 2.2 billion    personnel pay

$35 billion (+/-) estimated for all U.S. armed forces

# Appendix 3:
# Korean War Chronology

| | |
|---|---|
| c. 2000 B.C. | Kingdom of Chosun ("land of the morning calm") established. |
| July 1844 | Treaty establishing commercial relations between Kingdom of Korea and United States signed. |
| Aug. 1866 | Crew of U.S. schooner *General Sherman* massacred by Korean soldiers. |
| June 1870 | U.S. punitive attacks on Korean fortresses on Kanghwa Island; more than 250 Koreans killed. |
| 1876 | Treaty of Kanghwa between Korea and Japan. |
| May 1882 | Treaty of Chemulpo between Korea and U.S.A. |
| 1904–1905 | Russo-Japanese War; U.S. President Theodore Roosevelt brokers Treaty of Portsmouth (Sept. 1905) ending that war; Russia agrees to Japan's exercising a free hand in Korea. |
| Nov. 1905 | Japanese coerce Korean king to allow his nation to become a protectorate of Japan. |
| 1908 | Root-Takahira agreement recognizes Japan's primacy in Korea and southern Manchuria. |
| 1910 | Japan annexes Korea. |
| Dec. 1918 | Korean residents in United States petition President Wilson "to aid the Koreans in their aspirations for self-determination" |

|              | as a moral obligation resulting from unabrogated Treaty of Chemulpo. |
|--------------|---|
| Mar.–Apr. 1919 | "Mansei Revolution"; Korean patriotic demonstrations put down by Japanese occupation forces. |
| April 1919   | Provisional government-in-exile established in Shanghai. |
| Dec. 1, 1943 | Cairo Conference Declaration states that "in due course Korea shall become free and independent"; Korean Nationalists object to "in due course" qualifying phrase. |
| Aug. 15, 1945 | Premier Stalin approves President Harry Truman's General Order Number One, providing for temporary division of Korea at 38th Parallel of latitude into two temporary zones of military occupation, Soviet and United States. |
| Sept. 2, 1945 | Japanese sign unconditional surrender documents in Tokyo Bay. |
| Sept. 7, 1945 | U.S. occupation troops land at Inchon. |
| Dec. 1945    | U.S. and Soviet Union in Moscow draw up agreement providing for five-year trusteeship for Korea; large-scale demonstrations by resentful Korean patriots. |
| 1947         | Activation of "Peace Preservation Officers' Training Schools," nucleus of North Korean Army. |
| Sept.        | U.S. State Department agrees that South Korea should be left to its fate. |
| Sept. 17     | U.S. refers issue of reunification and independence of Korea to U.N. |
| Sept. 29     | U.S. Joint Chiefs of Staff agree that South Korea is of too little strategic value to justify stationing of 45,000 U.S. occupation troops. |
| Nov. 14      | Over Soviet objections, General Assembly of U.N. approves American-sponsored resolution calling for one government for all of Korea, and providing for a U.N. Temporary Commission on Korea (UNTCOK) to supervise national elections to lead to independence and unification. |
| Jan. 24, 1948 | Refusal of Soviet occupation commander in North Korea to permit entry of UNTCOK into his jurisdiction prevents Korea-wide elections. |
| Feb.         | Joint Chiefs of Staff recommend pulling out all American troops, even though this move will probably result in "eventual domination of Korea by the USSR"; (North) Korean People's Army formally activated. |

| | |
|---|---|
| April 2 | U.S. National Security Council Paper NSC-8 agrees that U.S. should help build up Korean economy and armed forces, but beyond that, South Koreans would have to maintain their own security against Communist north; paper approved by President Truman as basis for U.S. Korea policy. |
| April 3 | Opening of Cheju-do Rebellion, lasting into winter of 1949–1950. |
| May 10 | With Soviets refusing to admit United Nations commissioners to North Korea, U.N.-sponsored elections in southern Korea return representatives to National Assembly, which elects Syngman Rhee first president of a new republic. |
| Aug. 15 | Republic of Korea (ROK) formally inaugurated. |
| Sept. 9 | Establishment of Democratic People's Republic of Korea (DPRK). |
| Oct. | Yosu-Sunchon Communist-led uprising suppressed by ROK forces; war spreads to Chiri-san Mountains. |
| Dec. | Arrival of small but high-level Soviet military mission in Pyongyang. |
| Dec. 31 | Soviets announce that their forces have been withdrawn from North Korea. |
| Jan. 1949 | General MacArthur informs Joint Chiefs of Staff that ROK armed forces could not turn back an invasion from the north, that U.S. should not commit troops in case of such an invasion, and that U.S. should remove all of its combat forces as soon as possible. |
| May 2 | U.S.-Korean Military Advisory Group (KMAG) activated. |
| June 27 | U.S. State Department concludes that U.S. should respond to invasion from north by submitting matter to U.N. |
| June 29 | Last U.S. combat troops leave ROK. |
| Oct. 10 | Activation of South Korean Air Force. |
| Jan. 12, 1950 | U.S. Secretary of State Dean Acheson identifies America's defense perimeter in Asia in National Press Club speech; those omitted states would have to rely upon their own resources until U.N. could mobilize against an aggressor; this would include Korea. |
| Jan. 19 | U.S. House of Representatives defeats Korean aid bill for 1949–1950. |
| Jan.–March | MacArthur's G-2 staff evaluates reports of impending invasion of ROK from north but does not believe that an invasion is imminent. |

Feb. 14          The Commanding Officer of Korean Military Advisory Group
                 concedes that DPRK would give ROK "a bloody nose," that
                 southern civil population would accede to new regime, and
                 that ROK "would be gobbled up to be added to the rest of Red
                 Asia."

May 30           ROK-wide elections produce a majority of National Assembly
                 representatives not affiliated with Rhee government.

June 1           Intelligence Section of USAF Far East Air Forces (FEAF)
                 concludes that "South Korea will fall before a North Korean
                 invasion."

June 19          Central Intelligence Agency (CIA) determines that North
                 Korea could seize and hold at least upper reaches of South
                 Korea, including Seoul, without Chinese or Soviet military
                 units.

June 25          Korean People's Army invades Republic of Korea; U.N. Secu-
                 rity Council calls for cease-fire in Korea and withdrawal of
                 North Korean forces.

June 27          U.N. Security Council adopts U.S. resolution taking note of
                 North Korea's refusal to heed June 25 resolution and calls
                 upon members to assist Republic of Korea. President Truman
                 orders U.S. air and sea forces to support Korea and orders U.S.
                 7th Fleet to "neutralize" Formosa Strait; General Church's
                 survey group arrives at Suwon to assess ROKA operations.

June 28          KPA seizes Seoul.

June 29          British naval task force arrives in Korean waters.

June 30          President Truman commits U.S. ground forces to Korea. Aus-
                 tralian air squadron joins in U.S. forces.

July 4           President Truman declares a blockade of entire Korean
                 coastline.

July 5           U.S. Task Force Smith makes first contact with North Korean
                 forces near Osan.

July 7           U.N. Command for Korean War established. General Mac-
                 Arthur appointed Supreme Commander.

July 20          Taejon falls; 24th Infantry Division retreats south; French
                 navy commences Korean operations.

July 30          Naktong River defense established; Canadian destroyers enter
                 Sasebo to proceed to theater.

July 31          Chinju falls; General Walker announces, "There will be no
                 more retreating."

| | |
|---|---|
| Aug. 1 | Russia ends boycotting of U.N. Security Council as Jacob Malik assumes council presidency. |
| Aug. 4 | Soviet delegate Malik calls Korean fighting an "internal civil war" and demands withdrawal of "all foreign troops from Korea." |
| Aug. 5–19 | First battle of Naktong bulge. |
| Aug. 6–8 | General MacArthur meets top planners to discuss Inchon Landing. |
| Aug. 10 | U.S. suggests in U.N. General Assembly that goal of U.N. in Korea should be unification of country. |
| Aug. 17 | U.S. Marine brigade scores U.N.'s first offensive victory at No Name Ridge, halting North Korean forces. |
| Aug. 24 | British brigade arrives at Pusan. |
| Aug. 27 | Pusan Perimeter forces engage in heaviest fighting of war. |
| Sept. 1–5 | KPA begins Second Naktong Offensive; enemy offensive tries to destroy Pusan Perimeter. |
| Sept. 15 | Inchon Landing. |
| Sept. 16 | 8th U.S. Army launches offensive from Pusan Perimeter. |
| Sept. 19 | Enemy forces at Pusan Perimeter begin collapsing; Philippine force enters theater. |
| Sept. 22 | Walker's forces break out of Pusan Perimeter. |
| Sept. 25 | KPA in full retreat; U.N. pursuit begins. |
| Sept. 26 | U.S. I Corps forces moving north link up near Osan with allied amphibious forces. |
| Sept. 27 | Australian infantry battalion enters theater. |
| Sept. 28 | U.N. forces take back Seoul. |
| Sept. 30 | General MacArthur calls upon aggressors to surrender; Communist China's Foreign Minister Zhou Enlai warns: "The Chinese people will not supinely tolerate seeing their neighbors being savagely invaded by the imperialists." |
| Oct. 1 | General MacArthur authorizes ROK forces to cross 38th Parallel in pursuit of retreating KPA; 3rd ROK Division crosses parallel on east coast. |
| Oct. 2 | Zhou Enlai implies to Indian Ambassador in Beijing that Communist China will intervene in war if UNC enters North Korea. |
| Oct. 7 | U.N. General Assembly authorizes U.N. forces to pursue enemy across 38th Parallel and to unify Korea. |
| Oct. 7–9 | 1st U.S. Cavalry Division crosses 38th Parallel. |

| Oct. 10 | Wonsan captured by 3rd ROK Division; Communist China repeats threats of warning intervention in Korean War. |
|---|---|
| Oct. 15 | Truman and MacArthur confer at Wake Island. |
| Oct. 16 | First divisions of Chinese People's Volunteers Force (CPVF) secretly enter Korea from Manchuria. |
| Oct. 17 | Turkish brigade enters theater. |
| Oct. 19 | 1st ROK Division takes Pyongyang. |
| Oct. 26 | 6th Division of II ROK Corps reaches Yalu; first CPVF prisoners captured by ROK forces; U.S. X Corps lands at Wonsan; CPVF attacks ROK advance regiment along Yalu. |
| Oct. 27–31 | Chinese First Offensive commences. |
| Oct. 27 | 7th Regiment of 6th ROK Division badly mauled by strong Chinese attack near Yalu. |
| Oct. 29 | U.S. 7th Infantry Division lands at Iwon. |
| Oct. 30 | Elements of 24th U.S. Infantry Division reach within thirty-five miles of Yalu on west coast. |
| Oct. 31 | Chinese attack U.S. 1st Cavalry Division at Unsan. |
| Nov. 1 | First enemy MiG-15s appear along Yalu to counter U.N. air forces. |
| Nov. 2 | CPVF attacks other U.S. I Corps units. |
| Nov. 5 | General MacArthur informs U.N. that Chinese Communists are operating in Korea. South African fighter squadron arrives in Japan. |
| Nov. 6 | MacArthur warns U.S. Joint Chiefs of Staff that movement of Chinese forces across Yalu "threatens the ultimate destruction of my command." |
| Nov. 7 | Thai battalion disembarks at Pusan; advance party of Canadian brigade lands at Pusan. |
| Nov. 10–26 | U.S. X Corps advances toward Yalu in east, 8th U.S. Army in west. |
| Nov. 13 | Greek air transport detachment arrives in theater. |
| Nov. 20 | Indian field ambulance unit arrives in Korea. |
| Nov. 23 | Netherlands infantry battalion arrives in Korea. |
| Nov. 24 | U.S. 7th Infantry Division reaches at Hyesanjin; 8th U.S. Army continues advance toward Yalu; MacArthur's "final offensive" begins. |
| Nov. 25 | Chinese Second Offensive begins; ROK II Corps at Tokchon is smashed by CCF drive. |
| Nov. 26 | Twenty thousand CPVF attack 8th U.S. Army north of Chongchon River. |

| | |
|---|---|
| Nov. 26–27 | Chinese offensive in full swing on both fronts; in west 8th U.S. Army suffers deep penetration around Tokchon, and in east 1st Marine Division cut off at Changjin Reservoir. |
| Nov. 27 | 24th, 25th, and 2nd U.S. Divisions retreat to south of Chonchon River; CPVF attack 1st U.S. Marine Division on west side of Changjin Reservoir and a regimental combat team of 7th U.S. Division on east side. |
| Nov. 29 | French battalion lands at Pusan. |
| Dec. 4 | U.N. forces in full retreat; Pyongyang recaptured by Communists. |
| Dec. 4–6 | Chinampo evacuated. |
| Dec. 9 | Greek forces land at Pusan. |
| Dec. 10 | 1st U.S. Marine Division breaks out of Changjin Reservoir and begins march to join rest of X Corps at Hungnam. |
| Dec. 11 | 1st Marine and 7th U.S. Divisions converge toward Hungnam beachhead. |
| Dec. 15 | 1st U.S. Marine Division evacuates Hungnam, heads for Pusan; evacuation from Wonsan completed; U.N. forces form defensive line along 38th Parallel. |
| Dec. 23 | General Walker killed in accident; General Matthew B. Ridgway succeeds him on the 26th. |
| Dec. 24 | U.S. X Corps completes evacuation of Hungnam. |
| Dec. 31 | New Zealand Field Artillery Regiment enters war. |
| Dec. 31 | CCF Third Offensive begins. |
| Jan. 3–4, 1951 | U.N. forces abandon Seoul and withdraw to general line along Pyongtaek-Wonju-Samchok. |
| Jan. 7 | 8th U.S. Army initiates strong reconnaissance patrols northward. |
| Jan. 15 | Operation Wolfhound, a reconnaissance in force by a reinforced regimental combat team, reestablishes contact with enemy near Osan; enemy offensive halted. |
| Jan. 31 | Belgian and Luxembourg forces arrive in Korea. |
| Feb. 1 | U.N. resolves to end Korean conflict by negotiation. |
| Feb. 5 | Operation Roundup, a general advance by U.S. X Corps, begins on eastern flank. |
| Feb. 10 | U.N. forces retake Inchon and Kimpo. |
| Feb. 11–17 | Chinese Fourth Offensive begins with main effort in U.S. X Corps sector; advance halted at Wonju; 2nd U.S. Division heavily engaged; 23rd U.S. RCT with French battalion blunts attacks of five CCF divisions at Chipyong-ni. |

| | |
|---|---|
| Feb. 21 | Operation Killer, a general advance by U.S. IX and X Corps, begins. |
| Feb. 28 | Last enemy resistance south of Han River collapses. |
| March 7 | Operation Ripper begins in central and eastern zones with advance across Han by U.S. IX and X Corps. |
| March 14–15 | Seoul retaken by ROK and U.N. troops. |
| March 31 | U.N. advance reaches 38th Parallel. |
| April 5 | Operation Rugged, general advance to Kansas Line, begins. |
| April 11 | General MacArthur relieved from U.N. Command and General Ridgway appointed in his place. |
| April 14 | General Van Fleet succeeds to command 8th U.S. Army; all U.N. forces on Kansas Line. |
| April 19 | U.S. I and IX Corps on Utah Line. |
| April 22–28 | First phase of CCF Fifth Offensive begins. |
| April 30 | U.N. forces, after withdrawing to new defense line, halt CCF offensive north of Seoul and north of Han River. |
| May 7 | Ethiopian battalion enters theater. |
| May 16–23 | Second and final effort of CCF Fifth Offensive begins; U.N. forces halt CCF at Soyang River. |
| May 23 | CCF offensive halted; U.N. forces resume advance north. |
| May 30 | U.S. 8th Army recaptures Kansas Line. |
| June 1 | Operation Piledriver begins with elements of U.S. I and IX Corps advancing toward Wyoming Line. |
| June 13 | U.N. forces capture Chorwon and Kumhwa in Iron Triangle. |
| June 15 | Columbian battalion enters war. |
| June 23 | Jacob Malik, Deputy Foreign Commissar of Soviet Union, proposes cease-fire talks. |
| June 30 | General Ridgway announces U.N.'s readiness to discuss armistice. |
| July 10 | Negotiations between U.N. forces and Communists first opened at Kaesong. |
| July 27 | Negotiators at Kaesong agree on agenda. |
| July 28 | Formation of 1st British Commonwealth Division. |
| Aug. 1–Oct. 31 | U.N. launches limited attempts to straighten lines at Bloody Ridge and Heartbreak Ridge. |
| Aug. 5 | U.N. Command breaks off truce talks because of violations of neutral area. |
| Aug. 10 | Truce talks resumed. |
| Aug. 23 | Communists suspend negotiation, alleging "bombing" of their delegation at Kaesong. |

| | |
|---|---|
| Aug. 31 | 1st U.S. Marine Division opens assault at Punchbowl. |
| Sept. 2 | 2nd U.S. Infantry Division opens fire against Heartbreak and Bloody Ridges. |
| Sept. 18 | U.S. 1st Marine Division advances to Soyang River, north of Punchbowl. |
| Oct. 12 | U.S. IX Corps advances to Jamestown Line. |
| Oct. 15 | 2nd U.S. Division gains Heartbreak Ridge. |
| Nov. 12 | Ridgway orders Van Fleet to confine operations to active defense. |
| Nov. 27 | Truce talks resume at Panmunjom; stalemate dominates fighting fronts while talks continue. |
| Dec. 18 | Prisoner-of-war lists exchanged. |
| Jan. 1952 | Artillery and air pressure against Communist positions continues throughout the month. |
| April 2 | Screening of Communist POW's begins; Koje-do riots break out. |
| May 7 | Prisoners at Koje-do seize General Dodd and hold him hostage. |
| May 7 | General Mark Clark arrives in Tokyo to succeed General Ridgway as Supreme Commander of U.N. forces. |
| May 12 | General Haydon Boatner begins to quell disturbances on Koje-do. |
| June 6 | Stalemate along battlefront except on Old Baldy, White Horse, and several other outpost hills, while truce talks deadlocked on POW repatriation question. |
| Nov. 17 | Indian proposal on POWs in U.N. stirs peace plan. |
| Dec. 2 | General Dwight Eisenhower, President-elect, inspects Korean military situation. |
| Dec. 15 | Beijing radio announces Communist China's rejection of Indian compromise plan. |
| Dec. | Breakout attempt by prisoners at Pongam-do suppressed. |
| Feb. 1953 | General Van Fleet retires; General Maxwell D. Taylor assumes command of 8th U.S. Army. |
| March 5 | Death of Josef Stalin; struggle for power in Kremlin. |
| March 30 | Zhou Enlai indicates Communists will accept Indian U.N. proposal of November 17, 1952; resumption of truce talks at Panmunjom. |
| April 6 | First meeting of liaison groups held at Panmunjom after General Clark's proposal. |

April 11             Agreement reached on exchange of sick and wounded prison-
                     ers, to begin April 20.
April 16–18          Battle for Porkchop Hill.
April 20             Operation "Little Switch" begins at Panmunjom.
April 26             Armistice negotiations resumed after a recess of six and a half
                     months.
April 27             Resumption of plenary sessions at Panmunjom.
May                  Savage fighting along stalemated line while details of truce
                     ironed out at Panmunjom.
May 25               New proposals for ending prisoner deadlock offered at Pan-
                     munjom, but ROK observer boycotts meetings; ROK begins
                     campaign to block cease-fire.
May 28               Chinese attack five outposts of U.S. 25th Division.
June 9               ROK National Assembly unanimously rejects truce terms.
June 10              Chinese open assault against ROK II Corps near Kumsong.
June 15–30           Chinese attacks in U.S. I Corps sector take outpost position.
June 18              President Syngman Rhee releases approximately 27,000 anti-
                     Communist prisoners of war.
June 20              Communists accuse U.N. Command of complicity in freeing
                     of prisoners and suspend talks.
June 23              President Rhee reiterates opposition to truce terms.
June 25              Assistant Secretary of State Walter Robertson begins "Little
                     Truce Talks" with President Rhee to secure ROK acceptance
                     of armistice; CPVF launches massive attacks against ROK
                     divisions.
July 8               Communists agree to resumption of armistice talks; General
                     Clark's proposal to proceed with final arrangements without
                     ROK participation.
July 11              Assistant Secretary of State Robertson and President Rhee
                     announce agreement; President Rhee will no longer oppose
                     truce terms.
July 13              Final Chinese offensive begins in U.S. IX and ROK II Corps
                     sectors.
July 19              Negotiators at Panmunjom reach agreement on all points.
July 20              New Main Line of Resistance established by U.S. IX Corps
                     and ROK II Corps along south bank of Kumsong River.
July 27              Armistice signed, ending three years of war.
Aug. 5               Operation Big Switch begins at Panmunjom.
Dec. 23              Operation Big Switch concludes; 75,823 Communist soldiers
                     exchanged for 12,773 UNC personnel.

Jan. 1954        Neutral Nations Repatriation Committee completes screening on nonrepatriate POWs; 359 UNC personnel refuse repatriation; 22,604 Chinese and Koreans choose to remain in UNC or NNPC custody until settled elsewhere.

April 26        Geneva Conference on Asia political problems convenes; no agreement on political formula to unify Korea.

# Glossary

## ABBREVIATIONS AND MILITARY TERMS

**B-29:** A four-engine propeller-driven U.S. Air Force bomber used in the war with Japan and in the Korean War. Named the Superfortress and built by Boeing Aircraft.

**BAR:** Browning automatic rifle, an American automatic weapon firing 30.06-caliber bullets from a twenty-round magazine. Introduced in World War I and then widely used in World War II and the Korean War, even by the Chinese army. Fired from a barrel-end bipod.

**C-54:** U.S. Air Force four-engine transport used to carry supplies and personnel.

**CB:** Commander of the Bath, a British Royal order for distinguished and long military service.

**CBE:** Commander British Empire, a Royal honor for distinguished public service.

**DMZ:** Demilitarized Zone created by the Korean War Armistice, July 1953. Separates North and South Korea, but is definitely not demilitarized, as both sides patrol and garrison all but a narrow zone less than a mile wide in some places.

**DSO:** Distinguished Service Order, a British Commonwealth decoration for military leadership.

F4U:  A single-engine, propeller-driven fighter-bomber used by the U.S. Navy and Marine Corps for ground attack missions. Made by Chance-Vought and known for its gull-shaped wings.

F-51:  The Mustang, gas-piston engine, propeller-driven, single-seat fighter-bomber built by North American Aircraft and used as a long-range escort fighter in World War II. Flown by many Allied air forces in Korea, including the USAF, the South Korean Air Force, the South African Air Force, and the Royal Australian Air Force.

F-80:  The first all-purpose operational U.S. Air Force jet fighter, but converted to ground support role rather than escort duties during the Korean War. Built by Lockheed Aviation.

F-86:  U.S. Air Force jet air superiority fighter flown during the Korean War against Russian jets. Made by North American and noted for its durability and ease of handling. Flown by a single pilot.

FECOM:  Far East Command, the United States theater military headquarters in Tokyo, headed by Generals Douglas MacArthur, Matthew B. Ridgway, and Mark W. Clark during the Korean War. Commanded all American forces of all services in the war zone and managed logistical operations in Japan.

GOC:  General Officer Commanding, a British term for a general commanding a division, corps, or field army.

KATUSA:  Korean Augmentation U.S. Army or Korean nationals assigned to U.S. Army units to make up for shortages in infantry. Usually poorly trained and weak in combat motivation, in part because of language problems, strange food, and American antipathy to Asians.

KIA:  Killed in action, a casualty category in U.S. armed forces for service personnel witnessed as dead by comrades or body recovered and identifiable.

KMAG:  Korean Military Advisory Group, an organization of U.S. Army officers and men assigned to advise and train the South Korean army. Numbered about 500 before 1950, four times that number afterwards.

KPA:  Korean People's Army or *In Min Gun,* the armed forces of the Democratic People's Republic of Korea (Pyongyang) and commanded by Kim Il-sung.

M-1:  U.S. service rifle, 30.06 caliber, firing eight rounds from clip as a semi-automatic shoulder-held weapon. Designed by John Garand and introduced in World War II. Issued to South Korean army and most United Nations units.

M-2:  U.S. carbine or short-barreled rifle carried by officers, NCOs, and some team members of crew-served weapons. Fired as a fully automatic weapon with thirty-round magazine. Favored for close actions at night and self-protection. Not dependable in cold weather and poor stopping power from small .30-caliber bullet.

MiG-15: Russian single-engine jet fighter designed to counter USAF bombers. Designed by the Mikoyan and Gurevich Aircraft Design Bureau in the USSR, using a British Rolls-Royce engine. Known for speed, maneuverability, and firepower, but unstable in complicated flight actions and at low altitudes, and not durable under fire. Its .37-millimeter cannon was devastating against slow-flying aircraft, but too slow for aerial combat.

MASH: U.S. Army Mobile Army Surgical Hospital, widely used to provide sophisticated emergency surgical services near the fighting front where it could be reached by vehicles and helicopters. Provided advanced trauma treatment that saved many UNC and enemy lives.

MC: Military Cross, a British Commonwealth decoration for officers and other ranks for specific acts of heroism in combat.

MIA: Missing in action, a casualty category of the U.S. armed forces that means a body has not been recovered or cannot be identified.

Mortar: High-angle of indirect fire weapon of a large barrel, a base-plate, and a bipod. The shell is dropped in at the muzzle and activated by a firing pin at the base of the barrel. The shell fuses in flight. Sizes ranged from 60-mm to 4.2-inches. Widely used by all combat forces in Korea.

NATO: North Atlantic Treaty Organization, created in 1949. The military component of NATO included three theater commands (European Command, Channel Command, and Atlantic Command). In common 1950s usage, NATO meant the Allied air, ground, and naval forces stationed in Great Britain and Europe.

NNSC: Neutral Nations Supervisory Commission, originally a four-nation (Switzerland, Sweden, Poland, and Czechoslovakia) organization established by the armistice of 1953 to investigate alleged violations of the treaty, working from secure camps near the Demilitarized Zone. Only the Swiss and Swedes remain, housed in the Joint Security Area of Panmunjom.

OCS: Officer Candidate School. School run by military services to train, educate, and screen officer candidates before commissioning.

PFC: Private First Class, a trained but relatively young and inexperienced member of the U.S. Army and U.S. Marine Corps. Pay grade E-2 in 1950.

PLA: The army of the People's Republic of China, known as the People's Liberation Army to preserve its heritage as the armed force of the Communist Revolution in China.

PLAAF: The air force of the People's Republic of China or the PLA's AF. Formed in 1949 but not recognized as a service until 1951 when Chinese pilots in MiG-15s appeared in battle in squadrons.

POW: Prisoner of war held after surrender or capture by belligerent "detaining power" that assumes certain responsibilities for the prisoner's safety and health until he/she is exchanged or released by agreement or escape. A POW is obligated to give name, birth date, rank, and service in order to facilitate identification as a POW and pressure the detaining power to provide adequate care and security and to be accountable for same.

ROK: Republic of Korea (South Korea), established in 1948 under a United Nations mandate and supervised elections.

ROKA: South Korean army.

ROKAF: South Korean air force.

S-3/G-3: A staff officer (battalion and above) who specializes in operational planning and the conduct of operations.

UNC: United Nations Command, the Allied headquarters established in July 1950, to fight the Korean War and headed by the U.S. Army general also assigned to command FECOM. Still exists in Seoul, ROK.

USMA: U.S. Military Academy, West Point, New York, which provides a college education and basic training and socialization for career Army officers.

USNR: U.S. Naval Reserve, a reserve component of officers and naval ratings that can be mobilized for war.

WIA: U.S. casualty category, wounded in action, meaning a wound severe enough to require evacuation and treatment at a battalion medical station.

WO: Warrant officer, a category of rank and function in the U.S. armed forces that implies technical specialization and limited leadership responsibilities. In the British Commonwealth service the higher ranks of sergeants are also designated as warrant officers, recognizing leadership responsibilities.

XXIV Corps: U.S. 24th Corps, the three-division Korean occupation force that landed in September 1945 to repatriate the Japanese in Korea and to support the U.S. military government.

## NON-ENGLISH WORDS AND TERMS

*Arirang:* Korean folk song title about departing lovers, used as a magazine title today as well as in titles that arouse intense Korean nationalism.

*chaebol:* Korean corporation that is usually family-owned and managed and noted for the wide variety of goods it produces and services it provides, beyond (often) good economic sense.

Cheju-do: A large Korean island in the Straits of Tsushima known for its beauty, seafood, female pearl divers, citrus fruit, and rebellious population. The Cheju-do (Island) Rebellion of April 1948 started the Korean War.

*chige:* Korean word for a wooden A-frame backpack used by farmers and rural and urban laborers for loads that often reach 100–200 pounds. Common load carrier in Korean War.

*hakpyong:* Korean word, literally "student-soldier" but used to designate university students required to take military training during the Japanese imperial epoch. Many *hakpyong* became officers in the ROKA.

*hangul:* The Korean phonetic alphabet and written language developed in the fifteenth century by a committee of linguistic notables appointed by the revered King Sejong, who wanted a non-Chinese written language. It is not the spoken Korean language *(hanguk mal)* but many Europeans use the terms interchangeably.

*haoles:* Hawaiian word for European-origin Americans, mostly used to designate Mainlanders.

*kamsa hamnida:* Korean "Thank you."

*mugunghwa:* The Korean national flower, known as "the Rose of Sharon" in the West. It is a very hardy *hibiscus syriacus* that grows as a flowering bush of unusual durability. The blossoms are most often red, pink, or white. The *mugunghwa* is the symbol of Korean independence.

*myon:* A Korean territorial government unit roughly analogous to an American county.

*Renmin Zhiyuanjun:* The Chinese term (rendered in *pinyin*) for the Chinese expeditionary force drawn from the PLA and sent to Korea. Crude UNC translations were "Chinese Communist Forces" or "Chinese People's Volunteers." A more precise translation is Chinese *(zhi)* People's *(Renmin)* Volunteer(s) *(yuan* or representative) Army or Force(s) *(jun)*. To simplify pronoun agreement in English, I prefer Chinese People's Volunteers Force, but Army would be as good.

*yangban:* The traditional Korean land-holding rural males noted by their flowing robes; high, black horsehair hats; and hair in braided topknots. Often affluent landlords who dominated rice-growing and all forms of agriculture. Noted for their resistance to modernization, a bastion of Buddhist and Confucian values and traditional Korean culture.

Yosu-Sunchon: Two cities near the south-central coast of the ROK (Chollanam-do or South Cholla Province) and the site of a military mutiny and Communist uprising in October 1948, a military action that spread the Cheju-do insurgency to mainland Korea.

# Notes

## PART 1. THE KOREANS

### Chapter 1. The Koreans

*Sources:* Ahn Yong Choon, *The Seed Must Die: A Story of Christian Love in Action in Occupied Korea* (London: InterVarsity Fellowship, 1967); "Education," Report of the Military Governor, USAMGIK, "History of the United States Army Military Government in Korea, 1945–1946," Historical Archives, U.S. 8th Army History Office, Yongsan, Seoul, ROK; Cornelius Osgood, *The Koreans and Their Culture* (New York: Ronald Press, 1951), p. 323; Yonsei University, *Chilli wa chayu ui kisudul: Yonse ui ch'osok 15-in* [Standard Bearers of Truth and Freedom: Fifteen Yonsei Foundation Stories] (Seoul, ROK: Yonsei University Press, 1982).

### Chapter 2. Mr. Lee

*Sources:* Interviews with Lee Chang-sik, Dec. 1994, home of Dr. and Mrs. Horace G. Underwood, Yonsei University, Seoul, ROK; John W. Riley Jr. and Wilbur Schramm, *The Reds Take a City: The Communist Occupation of Seoul, with Eyewitness Accounts* (New Brunswick, N.J.: Rutgers University Press, 1951.)

### Chapter 3. A Korean in Ohio
*Sources:* Interview with Bryan Choi, Oct. 13, 1996, and subsequent correspondence with the author; "Monument Got Expert Help," *Dayton Daily News,* Aug. 30, 1995, B1–2; "Choi's Dream Finds Local Fulfillment," *Dayton Business Reporter,* March 1994, A–6.

### Chapter 4. The President as Refugee
*Sources:* Interview with Dr. Chang Sang, Ewha Women's University, Seoul, ROK, Aug. 18, 1998; Melanie Billings-Yun, "A Remarkable Woman: Ewha's Sang Chang," *arirang* (fall 1997), pp. 7–17; Dr. Chang to the author, with comments, Sept. 14, 2001.

### Chapter 5. The Rescuers
*Sources:* File 350.208, "Rescue of Airmen," U.S. 8th Army Historical Files, Yongsan, Seoul, ROK; special historical report, FEAF Bomber Command, Nov. 20, 1950; FEAF, periodical operational report, July 13, 1950, with attached msgs., provided by Maj. R. P. White, USAF, AF/CHO.

### Chapter 6. In Search of Lost Honor
*Sources:* John Hong Case, File 200.100, U.S. 8th Army Historical Reference Files, Yongsan, Seoul, ROK; interview including dossiers, "Hong's Return Saved Korea, Assisted the Strategies of the UN Forces, and Saved Hundreds of Thousands [of] Lives" (n.d.), and "The Hong Tragedy Records in the Korean War," 2000; Hong to author, Dec. 19, 2001, and Jan. 18, 2002, with comments; Dr. Richard Gorell interview, Sept. 7, 2001.

### Chapter 7. A Korean University Professor and General
*Sources:* Interview with Maj. Gen. Kim Ung-soo, May 7, 2000, Chevy Chase, Md.; correspondence with the author, Sept.–Oct. 2001; Maj. Gen. Kim Ung-soo to the author, Jan. 27, 2002, with a personal summary of service and comments.

### Chapter 8. Soldiers of the Korean People's Army
*Sources:* Dr. Kim—ATIS Interrogation Report No. 1725, Oct. 9, 1950, copy in Korean War reference files, Korean Institute of Military History, Korean War Memorial, Seoul, ROK; Sergeant "Park"—Special P-W Report, Periodic Intelligence Report No. 148, U.S. 2nd Infantry Division (G-2), copy in the Lt. Gen. Edward M. Almond Papers, U.S. Army Military History Institute, Carlisle Barracks, Penn.; Ju Young-bok, "I Was in the Invading Army in Korea," *Korean Survey* 7 (Oct. 1958), pp. 3–4, 11; Kevin Mahoney, *Formidable Enemies: The*

*North Korean and Chinese Soldier in the Korean War* (Novato, Calif.: Presidio, 2001).

### Chapter 9. Founders of an Industrial Empire
*Sources:* Donald Kirk, *Korean Dynasty: Hyundai and Chung Ju Yung* (Armonk, N.Y.: M. E. Sharpe, 1994); Richard Saccone, "Chung Ju Yung," in *Koreans to Remember* (Elizabeth, N.J.: Hollym, 1993), pp. 129–33; Shin Jae-hook, "Steel Yourself," *Far Eastern Economic Review* (May 18, 1995), pp. 89–92; Cho Tong-song, *Hanguk Chaebol Yongu* (Seoul: Maeil Kyongche Shinchwasa, 1994); Economist Intelligence Unit Country Report, *South Korea, North Korea,* Aug. 2001; Jon M. MacIntosh to author, Aug. 31, 2001, with comments.

### Chapter 10. The Teenage Guerrilla
*Sources:* The company of Lt. Col. Mark C. Monahan, USMC (Ret.), 1991–2000; Col. Ben S. Malcom, USA (Ret.), with Ron Martz, *White Tigers: My Secret War in North Korea* (Washington: Brassey's, 1996); Frederick Cleaver et al., "UN Partisan Warfare in Korea, 1951–1954," Operations Research Office, Johns Hopkins University, 1964.

### Chapter 11. The MiG Pilot
*Sources:* Interviews with Kenneth Rowe, PACAF Korean Air War Symposium, Honolulu, Hawaii, June 28 and 29, 2001; Kenneth Rowe to the author, Oct. 18 and Nov. 28, 2001; No Kum-sok, with J. Roger Osterholm, *A MiG-15 to Freedom: Memoir of the Wartime North Korean Defector Who First Delivered the Secret Fighter Jet to the Americans in 1953* (Jefferson, N.C.: McFarland and Co., 1996); Yefim Gordon and Valdimir Rigmant, *MiG-15* (Osceola, Wisc.: Motorbooks International, 1993); Hans-Henri Stapfer, *MiG-15, Aircraft No. 116* (Carrollton, Tex.: Squadron/Signal Publications, 1991).

### Chapter 12. The Student Becomes a Soldier and a Scholar
*Sources:* Interview with Brig. Gen. Lee Tong-hui, ROKA (Ret.), July 7, 2000, Seoul, ROK; Maj. Huh Nam-sung, "History of the Korean Military Academy," mss. history, 1980, synopsis provided by the author.

### Chapter 13. The Odd Couple Makes the Great Escape
*Sources:* Kim Chae-pil, "One Measure of Freedom," in Henry Chang, ed., *6 Insides from the Korean War* (Seoul: Dae-dong Moon Hwa Sa, 1958), pp. 143–219, with excerpts from accounts in the *Washington Post* and *Argosy* magazine and Millar-Kim correspondence, 1953–1954; 49th Fighter-Bomber Group operations reports, June and Sept. 1951, provided by the Air Force Historical

Research Center, Air University; Maj. Ward M. Millar, USAF, *Valley of the Shadow* (New York: D. McKay, 1955); Clay Blair Jr., *Beyond Courage* (New York: D. McKay, 1955); chapter 10, Joint Pub 3-50.3, *Joint Doctrine for Evasion and Recovery* (6 Sept. 1996), which recounts Millar's escape.

### Chapter 14. Sonny

*Sources:* Interview with MSgt. Sun K. Pang, USA (Ret.), July 8, 1996, Seoul, ROK; unpublished memoir, Sun K. Pang, 1996, author's possession; Mike Mooney, "From Korean Refugee to Army NCO," *Pacific Stars and Stripes,* Dec. 24, 1984, and supporting documents, File 230.000 (Sun K. Pang), U.S. 8th Army Historical Files, Yongsan, Seoul, ROK.

### Chapter 15. Birth of an Army and a General

*Sources:* Multiple interviews and conversations with Maj. Gen. Lim Sun-ha, ROKA (Ret.), and exchanged letters and documents, 1994–2001; interview with Lt. Col. James H. Hausman Jr., USA (Ret.), (1995) by the author and with John Toland, 1988 transcript in the Toland Papers, Franklin D. Roosevelt Library; interviews with Gen. Paik Sun-up, 1994 and 1995; Robert K. Sawyer et al., "History of the Korean Military Advisory Group," 4 vols., 1955–1958, copies in Records of the U.S. Army Pacific (Historical Files) RG 338; Gen. Lee Chi-op, with Lt. Col. Stephen M. Tharp, USA, *Call Me "Speedy Lee": Memoirs of a Korean War Soldier* (Seoul: Won Min Publishing, 2001); Kim Se-jin, *The Politics of Military Revolution in Korea* (Chapel Hill: University of North Carolina Press, 1971), pp. 36–63; Huh Nam-sung, "The Quest for a Bulwark of Anti-Communism: The Formation of the Republic of Korea Army Officer Corps and Its Political Socialization, 1945–1950," doctoral dissertation, The Ohio State University, 1987; Allan R. Millett, "Captain James H. Hausman and the Formation of the Korean Army, 1945–1950," *Armed Forces and Society* 23 (summer 1997), pp. 503–39.

### Chapter 16. The War Goes on for Some Koreans

*Sources:* "Korean War POW Escapes North" and "Five Former POWs Stayed Back in South Korea," *Seoul Herald,* Oct. 24, 1994, and July 1998.

### PART 2: THE ALLIES

### Chapter 17. Of War, Mines, and Pheasants

*Sources:* Storytelling by Colonel Dan Raschen, Coplow House, Shrivenham, Swindon, U.K., Sept. 1987 and Aug. 2001; Dan Raschen, *Send Port and Pyjamas!*

(London: Buckland Publications Ltd., 1987); Gen. Anthony Farrar-Hockley, *The British Part in the Korean War,* 2 vols. (London: Her Majesty's Stationery Office, 1990 and 1995); Ham Kwang-bok, "The Demilitarized Zone," *Koreana* 15 (summer 2001), pp. 18–29.

### Chapter 18. The Belgians

*Sources:* Interview, Aug. 19, 1998, Brussels, Belgium, and review of interview by Colonels de Buck and van Cauwelaert, 2000; Lt. Gen. Albert Crahay, *De Belgen in Korea* (Brussels: n.p., 1966; J.-P. Gahide, *La Belgique et le guerre de Corée, 1950–1955* (Brussels: Musée Royal de l'Armée, 1991).

### Chapter 19. Diggers

*Sources:* Interviews with Maj. Gen. Ronald Alwyn Grey, July 1995, Canberra, ACT, Australia, and subsequent correspondence with the author, 1999–2000; Robert O'Neill, *Australia in the Korean War, 1950–53,* 2 vols. (Canberra, ACT: Australian War Memorial, 1981 and 1985).

### Chapter 20. Commander, *Renmin Zhiyuanjun*

*Sources:* Peng Dehuai, *Memoirs of a Chinese Marshal: The Autobiographical Notes of Peng Dehuai (1898–1974),* translated by Zheng Longpu, English text edited by Sara Grimes (Beijing: Foreign Language Press, 1984); Xiaobing Li, Allan R. Millett, and Bin Yu, *Mao's Generals Remember Korea* (Lawrence: University Press of Kansas, 2001); Shu Guang Zhang, *Mao's Military Romanticism: China and the Korean War, 1950–1953* (Lawrence: University Press of Kansas, 1995); Chen Jian, *China's Road to the Korean War: The Making of the Sino-American Confrontation* (New York: Columbia University Press, 1994); Jürgen Domes, *Peng Te-huai: The Man and the Image* (London: C. Hurst, 1985); Ching Hsi-chen with Ting Lu-yen, ed., *Tsai P'eng-tsang shen-pi Ching-wei ts'an-no-te hyuyilu* [At the Side of Commander Peng: Memoirs of a Bodyguard] (Chengtu: Szechwan People's Publishing House, 1979).

### Chapter 21. A Doctor in Korea

*Sources:* Interviews with Col. Donald D. Beard, July 20–21, 2000, Canberra, Australia; Colonel Beard to the author, Aug. 8 and 13, 2001; Ben O'Dowd, *In Valiant Company: Diggers in Battle—Korea, 1950–51* (Queensland: University of Queensland Press, 2000); Jack Gallaway, *The Last Call of the Bugle: The Long Road to Kapyong* (Queensland: University of Queensland Press, 1994); Lt. Col. Bob Breen, *The Battle of Kapyong* (Georges Heights, NSW, Australia: Army Doctrine Centre, 1992).

**Chapter 22. The Thais**
*Sources:* Interviews, Thai generals Aug. 18, 1998, Bangkok, Thailand; Museum, Queen Sikirit's 21st Infantry Regiment (Airborne), Chon Buri, Thailand; *Thai-Korea War Veterans Association Bangkok Thailand* (Bangkok: Aroon Karn Phim, 1996).


**Chapter 23. Soldier of Orange**
*Sources:* Interview (taped) with Col. Leendert C. Schreuders, Royal Netherlands Army (Ret.), Jan. 16, 2000, conducted by John M. Stapleton Jr., Ohio State University Ph.D. candidate and Dutch linguist, tapes in the author's possession; Stapleton's additional notes; Col. Leendert C. Schreuders, Army Service (Korean War) Questionnaire, Jan. 2000, in the author's possession; Colonel Schreuders to the author, June 18, 2001, with comments; VOKS, "The Dutch Korean War Monument," 1996 copy provided by Colonel Schreuders; VOKS, "The Dutch Participation in the Korean War," n.d., provided by Colonel Schreuders; with appended list of casualties by name, excerpts from the history of the NDVN published in *VOX-V.O.K.S.,* newsletter of the VOKS, 1999–2000, provided by Colonel Schreuders; short history and inventory, records of the NDVN, Ministerie van Defensie, "Van Het Nederlands Detachment Verenigde Naties in Korea, 1950–1954," furnished by Col. Dr. Piet Kamphuis, Chief of Army History, RNA; War History Compilation Committee, MOD, ROK, "The Netherlands Forces in the Korean War," in *The History of the United Nations Forces in the Korean War,* 5 vols. (Seoul, ROK: Ministry of National Defense, ROK, 1972–1974) III, pp. 439–524.


**Chapter 24. Soldiers of the People's Republic of China**
*Sources:* Pa Chin [Li Pei-kan], *Living Amongst Heroes* (Peking: Foreign Languages Press, 1954); n.a. [PLA Political Department], *Racing Towards Victory: Stories from the Korean Front* (Beijing: Foreign Languages Press, 1954); n.a. [People's Literature Publishing House], *A Volunteer Soldier's Day: Recollections by Men of the Chinese People's Volunteers in the War to Resist U. S. Aggression and Aid Korea* (Beijing: Foreign Languages Press, 1961); Lloyd E. Ohlin and Richard P. Harris, interviewers and editors, "Wang Tsun-ming, Anti-Communist: An Autobiographical Account of Chinese Communist Thought Reform," in William C. Bradbury, Samuel M. Meyers, and Albert D. Biderman, eds., *Mass Behavior in Battle and Captivity: The Communist Soldier in the Korean War* (Chicago: University of Chicago Press, 1968), pp. 121–59; Pingchao Zhu, "The Korean War at the Dinner Table," and James Z. Gao, "Myth of the

Heroic Soldier and Images of the Enemy," in Philip West, Steven I. Levine, and Jackie Hiltz, eds., *America's Wars in Asia: A Cultural Approach to History and Memory* (Armonk, N.Y.: M.E. Sharpe, 1997), pp. 183–202; G-2, GHQ, FECOM *Order of Battle Information: Chinese Communist Army,* June 1951, File 320.013, Historical Reference Files, U.S. 8th Army History Office, Yongsan, Seoul, ROK; G-3, "Combat Notes and Enemy Tactics," memoranda and bulletins issued periodically from Aug. 1950, with coverage of the Chinese People's Volunteers Force commencing with Combat Information Bulletin No. 4 (Nov. 20, 1950) and extended in CIB No. 6 (Dec. 17, 1950) and CIB No. 11 (Feb. 1951), copies in File 800.069, U.S. 8th Army History Office, and the U.S. Army Military History Institute, Carlisle Barracks, Penn.: U.S. 8th Army, Enemy Tactics (EUSAK, Dec. 26, 1951), File 800.069, U.S. 8th Army History Office; AC/S, HQ, 2nd Infantry Division, U.S. 8th Army, "Chinese Tactics and Lessons Learned," Nov. 13, 1952, USAMHI; and Frank J. Harris, *Chinese Communist and North Korean Methods of Motivating Riflemen for Combat,* ORO (FECOM) Report T-44 (1953), copy USAMHI; Xu Fan, "The Chinese Forces and Their Casualties in the Korean War: Facts and Statistics," *Chinese Historians* 6 (fall 1993) pp. 45–58; Dr. Whu Zhi-li [Surgeon General, CPVF], "Medical Services of the Chinese People's Liberation Army," paper presented to U.S. Uniformed Services University of the Health Services, March 1989, copy given to the author by Col. R. J. T. Joy, M.D., USA (Ret.); Alexander L. George, *The Chinese Communist Army in Action: The Korean War and Its Aftermath* (New York: Columbia University Press, 1967); Zhang Da interview in John Pomfret, "Chinese Question Role in Korean War," *Washington Post* (Oct. 29, 2000).

## Chapter 25. The Russians: Allies of a Sort
*Sources:* Col. Victor Gavrilov, "The Role of the Soviet Union in the Korean War: A Retrospective," a paper presented at the Annual Conference of the International Council on Korean Studies, Washington, D.C., June 22–24, 2001; Mark A. O'Neill, "The Other Side of the Yalu: Soviet Pilots in the Korean War, Phase One, 1 Nov. 1950–12 April 1951," Ph.D. dissertation, Florida State University, 1996; Jon Halliday, "Air Operations in Korea: The Soviet Side of the Story," in William J. Williams, ed., *A Revolutionary War: Korea and the Transformation of the Postwar World,* proceedings of the U.S. Air Force Fifteenth Military History Symposium, 1992 (Chicago: Imprint Publications, 1993), pp. 149–70; Jon Halliday, "A Secret War," *Far Eastern Economic Review* (April 22, 1993), pp. 32–36; "Secrets of the Korean War," *U.S. News and World Report* (Aug. 9, 1993), pp. 335–70; Michael J. McCarthy, "Uncertain Enemies: Soviet Pilots in the Korean War," *Air Power History* 44 (spring 1997), pp. 32–45.

## PART 3: THE AMERICANS

### Chapter 26. A GI in Pyongyang

*Sources:* Richard F. Underwood, "Memories and Thoughts," unpublished autobiography, 1996–1999, Urbana, Illinois, copy in the author's possession; interviews with Richard and Horace G. Underwood, 1991–1999; Lillias H. Underwood, *Underwood of Korea: Being an Intimate Record of the Life and Work of the Rev. H. G. Underwood, D.D., LL.D., for Thirty-One Years a Missionary of the Presbyterian Board in Korea* (New York: Fleming H. Revell, 1918).

### Chapter 27. The Ambassador as Soldier

*Sources:* Interview, Ambassador James T. Laney, Seoul, ROK, July 1996, with the author and subsequent correspondence, 1998–2001, including "Biography: Ambassador James T. Laney;" Headquarters, U.S. Army Forces in Korea, "History of the United States Armed Forces in Korea," 1947 and 1948, copy in the Historical Reference Files, U.S. 8th Army History Office, Yongsan, Seoul, ROK; Sharon Merritt and Germaine Jerome, "Hooked on Korea: Reminiscing with Ambassador James T. Laney," *arirang* (winter 1994), pp. 13–19.

### Chapter 28. Advisors to the Korean Constabulary

*Sources:* Letters with enclosures from Robert G. Shackleton, July 1, 1996, April 11, 1997, and Sept. 9, 2001, to the author; letter with enclosures from Lt. Col. Ralph Bliss, USA (Ret.), to the author, Feb. 13, 1997; Robert K. Sawyer, "History of the Korean Military Advisory Group," 4 vols., Vol. I, 1954–1958, mss. copy in Records of the U.S. Army Pacific (Historical Files), RG 490; James H. Hausman Jr., "Yosu-Sunchon Rebellion," 1949, James H. Hausman Papers, Korea Institute, Harvard University, copy in the author's possession; "Revolt in Korea," *Life* (Nov. 8, 1948).

### Chapter 29. Early Casualties

*Sources:* Interview of Robert Alip, June 25, 2000, and subsequent correspondence; Brig. Gen. Uzal W. Ent, ANG (Ret.), *Fighting on the Brink: Defense of the Pusan Perimeter* (Paducah, Ky.: Turner Publishing, 1996).

### Chapter 30. A Korean from Hawaii

*Sources:* Interview with MSgt. Tae Soon Lee, USAF (Ret.), July 3, 1996, Honolulu, Hawaii; Michael Slater, *Hills of Sacrifice: The 5th RCT in Korea* (Paducah, Ky.: Turner Publishing, 2000).

## Chapter 31. Expatriate Veteran

*Sources:* Interview with MSgt. John McCarthy, USA (Ret.), Aug. 1996, Seoul, ROK; Brig. Gen. Uzal W. Ent, ANG (Ret.), *Fighting on the Brink: Defense of the Pusan Perimeter* (Paducah, Ky.: Turner Publishing, 1996).

## Chapter 32. The Making of a Special Forces Officer

*Sources:* Jessup interviews, Aug. 1995, and letter to author Aug. 2001; Michael Slater, *Hills of Sacrifice: The 5th RCT in Korea* (Paducah, Ky.: Turner Publishing, 2000).

## Chapter 33. *By Faith I Fly*

*Sources:* Interview with Colonel Dean E. Hess, USAF (Ret.), Air Force Museum, Dayton, Ohio, May 2000; Col. Dean E. Hess, remarks, PACAF Korean Air War Symposium, June 2001, Honolulu, Hawaii; Col. Dean E. Hess, *Battle Hymn* (Reynoldsburg, Ohio: Buckeye Aviation Book Company, 1987); Office of the Historian, Headquarters, ROKAF, translated by John C. Sullivan, historian, PACAF, *The Republic of Korea Air Force during the 25 June War* (Hickam AFB, May 2000 and Seoul, ROK, 2001); David R. McLaren, *Mustangs over Korea: The North American F-51 at War, 1950–1953* (Atglen, Pa.: Schiffer Military History, 1999).

## Chapter 34. Two-Time Survivor

*Sources:* Interview with Robert Phillips, Aug. 27, 1997; R. Phillips to the author, Oct. 23, 1998; Col. Harry J. Maihafer, USA (Ret.), *From the Hudson to the Yalu: West Point '49 in the Korean War* (College Station: Texas A&M University Press, 1993); Col. Harry J. Maihafer to the author, Dec. 1, 1998; Citation for the Silver Star Medal, PFC Robert F. Phillips, AUS, Oct. 10, 2000.

## Chapter 35. Fighting for the Koreans

*Sources:* "William H. Shaw," File 650.012, Historical Reference Files, U.S. 8th Army History Office, Yongsan, Seoul, ROK; Park Nyon-su, "Shaw Family . . ." *The Korean Times,* May 22, 1982; Rev. William Earl Shaw, ". . . and God Smiles," mss. memoir, 1960, copy from Mrs. Carole Cameron Shaw, with attached Shaw letters and Harvard University memorial; Ambassador William Sherman to author, Feb. 10, 1997; interviews with Dr. Horace G. Underwood, Seoul, ROK, 1996; Donald N. Clark, *Yanghwajin Seoul Foreigners' Cemetery, Korea: An Informal History, 1890–1984, with Notes on Other Foreign Cemeteries in Korea* (Seoul: Yongsan Library, 1984), pp. 42, 143–45; Annex P, Fifth Marines Special Action Report, Sept. 1950, Organizational Records, Marine

Corps Historical Center (MCHC), Washington Navy Yard, D.C.; roster, Company I, 3d Battalion, 5th Marines, Sept. 1950, MCHC; Sgt. Maj. Arnold Lentz to the author, Nov. 1, 1996; R. C. Jenkins to author, Dec. 15, 1996; Dr. Richard Smith, Professor of History (Emeritus) to the author, Feb. 2, 1999. Judge Stephen Shaw provided three excellent sources on his father: (1) the notes of Rev. William E. Shaw on his investigation of his son's death, Oct. 1950; (2) Richard T. Baker, "I'm Going to Be One of Them," *Motive* [Methodist Student Movement] (Nov. 1951), pp. 2–4; and (3) Dongkuk Lee, "The Shaw Family's Love for Korea," *Korean Naval Academy Magazine* (Oct. 2001).

## Chapter 36. The Air War: Heroes
*Source:* Lt. Col. D. E. Biteman, "A Brief Unofficial History of the 18th Fighter Wing," rev. ed., 1995; Lt. Col. D. E. Biteman to author, Jan. 31, 1996, and Oct. 21, 1998; Report No. 7, 18th Fighter Wing Association, Aug. 1995; Lt. Col. D.E. Biteman, "Courage, Valor, Heroism," n.d.; Lt. Col. D. E. Biteman, USAF (Ret.), to author, Oct. 21, 1998, and July 23, 2001; Jennie Ethell Chancey and William R. Forstchen, eds., *Hot Shots: An Oral History of the Air Force Combat Pilots of the Korean War* (New York: Morrow, 2000); David R. McLaren, *Mustangs over Korea: The North American F-51 at War, 1950–1953* (Atglen, Pa.: Schiffer Military History, 1999).

## Chapter 37. The Boys of Winter
*Sources:* Interviews with Jack Kelly, the late Otto Schodorff, Jr., and Jay Johnson, Columbus, Ohio, April 1, 1998, with subsequent Korean War Veterans Questionnaires, U.S. Army Military History Institute, completed by the subjects for the author, 1998, and re-interviews on April 1, 1999; Lynn Montross and Capt. Nicholas A. Canzona, USMC, *The Chosin Reservoir Campaign,* Vol. III, in *U.S. Marine Operations in Korea, 1950–1953* (Washington, D.C.: Historical Branch, G-3, HQMC, 1957).

## Chapter 38. Medal of Honor Winner
*Sources:* Sgt. Cornelius H. Charlton, USA, Medal of Honor File, Awards Case File, 1951–1952, U.S. 8th Army Command File, U.S. Army Command Records, RG 338, NARA; family information, Mrs. Shirley Davis (Bluefield, W.V.) and Arthur Charlton (Columbus, Ohio); correspondence and clipping files, case of Sgt. Cornelius H. Charlton, Division of Veterans Affairs, State of West Virginia, and John E. Shumate, Beckley, W.V.; *Seoul Word,* Feb. 24, 1994.

## Chapter 39. Marine
*Sources:* Interview with Fred Brower, Oxford, Ohio, April 20, 1997, and subsequent correspondence with the author; Allan R. Millett, *Drive North: U.S.*

*Marines at the Punchbowl* (Washington, D.C.: History and Museums Division, HQMC, 2001).

## Chapter 40. The Mountain and the Warrior

*Sources:* Exhibit, Hawaiian Medal of Honor Winners, Army Museum of Hawaii, Fort DeRussy, Waikiki, Oahu, Hawaii; Class of 1948, Yearbook, Waipuhu High School, Oahu, Hawaii, courtesy of Principal Patricia Pederson; Cobey Black, "Six Heroes to Be Saluted by Museum at DeRussy," *Honolulu Star-Bulletin,* Nov. 8, 1981; Mrs. Cobey Black to the author, July 7, 2000; Medal of Honor file, PFC Herbert K. Pililaau, with attached witness letters and endorsements, 1951–1952, Awards Case Files, U.S. 8th Army Command File, U.S. Army Command Records, RG-338; Harlan King, Bennet, Nebraska, Army Service (Korean War) Questionnaire, USAMHI, [Cpl., Company C, 23rd Infantry] 2001, author's possession; Command History Office, U.S. 8th Army, *Korean War Medal of Honor Recipients* (Seoul: FKHO, 1993), pp. 56–57; Edward F. Murphy, *Korean War Heroes* (Novato, Calif.: Presidio, 1992), pp. 193–94; Director G. E. Castagnetti, National Memorial Cemetery of the Pacific, Honolulu, Oahu, Hawaii, to the author, July 24, 1998; American Battle Monuments Commission, *Honolulu Memorial: National Cemetery of the Pacific, Honolulu, Hawaii* (Washington, D.C.: American Battle Monuments Commission (1985).

## Chapter 41. War Crimes and a Matter of Accountability

*Sources:* James M. Hanley, *A Matter of Honor: A Memoire* (New York: Vantage Press, 1995); Brig. Gen. Robert D. Upp, JAG, AUS (Ret.), to the author, April 18, 2001, with a copy of his "Historical Report: War Crimes Division," 1954; interview with William Thompson, former Technical Sergeant, Headquarters Company, 2nd Battalion, 442nd Regimental Combat Team, Honolulu, June 9, 1999; War Crimes Division, OJA, U.S. 8th Army, Command Report, Dec. 1950, copy in file 300.06, Reference Files, U.S. 8th Army Historical Office, Yongsan, Seoul, ROK; Col. Howard S. Levie, USA (Ret.), to the author, May 19, 1999; War Crimes Division, JAG Section, Korean Communications Zone, "Interim Historical Report . . . Cumulative to 30 June 1953," 1953, File 300.06, cited above; Military History Office War Crimes Division, JAG Section, Headquarters Korean Communications Zone, "Final Historical and Operational Report," 1954, with appendices of rosters of victims, witnesses, suspects, and cases, copy from War Crimes Branch, International Affairs Division, Records of the Office of the Judge Advocate General (Army), RG 153, NARA; Military History Office, AC/S (G-3), Headquarters U.S. Army Pacific, "The Handling of Prisoners of War during the Korean Conflict," June 1960, File 350.209, HO, U.S. 8th Army; CINCFE (Ridgway) to C/S, USA, Nov. 16 and 17, 1951, printed in Historical Office, Department of State, *Foreign Relations of the United States 1951,* Vol. VI, *Korea and*

*China* (Washington, D.C.: Government Printing Office, 1977–1985), 1143–46; *The New York Times,* Nov. 16, 17, and 24, 1951; File 471-B, "Prisoners of War" and "Missing Members of Armed Forces, Korean Emergency," memoranda and correspondence, Official Files, 1945–1953, Harry S. Truman Presidential Papers, Harry S. Truman Library, Independence, Missouri; Psychological Strategy Board, staff studies and memoranda, "Repatriation of Prisoners of War in Korea," 18 Oct. 1951, and "Chinese Communist Aggression, Barbarism and Criminal Activities, 10 Sept. 1953," both PSB File 383.6, Staff Member and Office Files, 1945–1953, Truman Presidential Papers; U.S. Army Security Center, Fort Meade, Maryland, "U.S. Prisoners of War in the Korean Operation," Nov. 1954, based on postrelease interviews and intelligence reports, copy in Reference Files, 40, U.S. 8th Army History Office; Chinese People's Committee on World Peace, *United Nations POWs in Korea* (Peking: CPCWP, 1953); Commission of International Association of Democratic Lawyers, *Report of War Crimes in Korea* (*Shanghai News,* April 10, 1952); Committee on Government Operations, U.S. Senate, 83rd Congress, 2nd Session, Report, "Korean War Atrocities," Report No. 848, Jan. 11, 1954 (Washington: GPO, 1954).

### Chapter 42. They Also Fought Who Flew and Seldom Fired

*Sources:* Testimony of Lt. Gen. William E. Brown Jr., USAF (Ret.), and Lt. Col. Dean E. Abbott, USAF (Ret.), June 28, 2001, PACAF Korean Air War Symposium; William T. Y'Blood, *MiG Alley: The Fight for Air Superiority* (Washington, D.C.: Office of Air Force History, 2000); Robert F. Dorr, Jon Lake, and Warren E. Thompson, *Korean War Aces* (London: Osprey, 1995); Larry Davis, *MiG Alley: Air to Air Combat over Korea* (Carrollton, Tex.: Squadron/Signal Publications, 1979); Larry Davis, *Walk Around: F-86 Sabre* (Carrollton, Tex.: Squadron/Signal Publications, 2000); John R. Bruning, *Crimson Sky: The Air Battle for Korea* (Dulles, Va.: Brassey's, 1999); Jennie Ethell Chancey and William R. Forstchen, eds. *Hot Shots: An Oral History of the Air Force Combat Pilots in the Korean War* (New York: Morrow, 2000); Thomas Hone, "Korea," in Benjamin Franklin Cooling III, ed., *Case Studies in the Achievement of Air Superiority* (Washington, D.C.: Office of Air Force History, 1994), pp. 453–504; film, "Great Planes, Series 1, Vol. 12, F-86 Saber Jet," Aeroco, Inc., 1986; Col. Flint O. DuPre, USAFR, *U.S. Air Force Biographical Dictionary* (New York: Franklin Watts, 1965).

### Chapter 43. Missing in Action

*Sources:* File, "Case of Sgt. Marvin L. Rodman, USA, MIA 20 Oct 52," File 350.201, Historical Reference Files, U.S. 8th Army History Office, Yongsan, Seoul, ROK; Summary of Rodman Case, Herman Katz, U.S. 8th Army Command Historian, April 11, 1979, Rodman File; Lt. Gen. Harold G. Moore, USA (Ret.), to the author, Oct. 1998; Walter G. Hermes, *Truce Tent and Fighting Front,* Vol. III in *U.S. Army in the Korean War* (Washington, D.C.: U.S. Army Center of Military History, 1966), pp. 283–318.

### Chapter 44. The Navy's War on Germs in Korea

*Sources:* Correspondence with Mrs. Gerald A. (Virginia) Martin, 1997–1999, and copies of Dr. Gerald Martin's military records; the Rev. Harold Voelkel to the friends of Dr. Gerald Martin, Oct. 2, 1951; Dr. Albert V. Hardy to Dr. James Watt, Chairman, Enteric Fever Commission, May 25, 1951, copy furnished by Mrs. Martin; FMEDCU ONE memo, "Gerald A. Martin Memorial Heath Center, Koje-do," Oct. 24, 1951; biographical file for Capt. Joseph M. Coppoletta, M.D., MC, USN, Naval Historical Center, Washington Navy Yard; Department of the Navy, U.S. Bureau of Medicine and Surgery, NAVMED P-5057, *The History of the Medical Department of the United States Navy, 1945–1955* (Washington: Dept. of the Navy, 1956); BUMED, "Military Medical Experience during the United Nations Police Action in Korea, June 1950 to 1 April 1951," Naval Historical Center; mss., "Epidemic Disease, Fleet Mobile Epidemic Disease Control Unit #1," 1951–1952, copy furnished by Mrs. Martin; correspondence with Dr. Richard P. Mason, MD, USA (Ret.), 1998, on FMEDCU ONE; and his Korean War Service Questionnaire (1997); Albert V. Hardy, Richard P. Mason, William W. Frye, Marion M. Brooke, and Donald J. Schliessmann, *Epidemic Enteric Infections among Prisoners of War in Korea* (Jacksonville: Florida State Board of Health, 1963); Albert E. Cowdrey, "'Germ Warfare' and the Public Health of the Korean Conflict," *Journal of the History of Medicine and Allied Sciences* 2 (April 1984), pp. 153–72. Note: An earlier version of this vignette appeared in the U.S. Naval Institute *Proceedings* (March 2001) and is reprinted with permission of the U.S. Naval Institute.

### Chapter 45. The Marine Colonel Becomes a War Criminal

*Sources:* Brig. Gen. Frank H. Schwable, USMC (Ret.), oral history (1983), Oral History Collection, Marine Corps Historical Center, Washington, D.C.; "Statement of Colonel Frank H. Schwable, 004429, U.S. Marine Corps," Sept. 25, 1953, PSB File 383.6 (POWs), Psychological Strategy Board Central Files, NSC Central Files, Dwight D. Eisenhower Presidential Papers, Eisenhower Library; General Lemuel C. Shepherd Jr. USMC (Ret.), oral history (1967), OHC; Gen. Gerald C. Thomas, USMC, oral history (1966), OHC; Maj. James Angus MacDonald Jr., *The Problems of U.S. Marine Corps Prisoners of War in Korea* (Washington, D.C.: U.S. Marine Corps History and Museums Division, 1988); N. C. Debevoise to Dr. H. S. Craig, June 11, 1953, PSB File 729.2 Psychological

Strategy Board Central Files, NSC Central Files, Dwight D. Eisenhower Presidential Papers; George S. Prugh Jr., "The Code of Conduct for the Armed Forces" and "Misconduct in the Prison Camp: A Survey of the Law and an Analysis of the Korean Cases," both in *Columbia Law Review* 56 (April 1956), pp. 678–707 and (May 1956), pp. 711–94; Paul M. Cole, *POW/MIA Issues:* Vol. 1, *The Korean War* (Santa Monica, Calif.: RAND, 1994); Chapter 8, Army Security Center, Fort Meade, Maryland, "U.S. Prisoners of War in the Korean Operation," 1954 mss. history, copy in Historical Files, U.S. 8th Army History Office, Yongsan, Seoul, ROK.

## Chapter 46. The Christian General at Panmunjom

*Sources:* Lt. Gen. William K. Harrison Jr., USA (Ret.), oral history (1981), Senior Officers Oral History Collection, U.S. Army Military History Institute, Carlisle Barracks, Pa.; D. Bruce Lockerbie, *A Man Under Orders: Lieutenant General William K. Harrison Jr.* (San Francisco: Harper and Row, 1979); Anne C. Loveland, *American Evangelicals and the U.S. Military 1942–1993* (Baton Rouge: Louisiana State University Press, 1996); William H. Vatcher Jr., *Panmunjom: The Story of the Korean Military Armistice Negotiations* (New York: Frederick A. Praeger, 1958); Sydney D. Bailey, *The Korean Armistice* (New York: St. Martin's Press, 1992); and the author's interviews and correspondence, 1995–2001, with Dr. Horace G. Underwood, Richard F. Underwood, Lt. Col. Kenneth Wu, USA (Ret.), Dr. John K. C. Oh (ROKA press officer), and Col. James C. Murray Jr., USMC (Ret.), UNC senior liaison officer. From the Communist side, Maj. Gen. Lee Sang-jo, KPA, and Maj. Gen. Chai Chengwen, PLA, wrote memoirs about the negotiations. An abridged, edited, translated, and annotated version of General Chai's *Banmendian Tanpan* (1989) appears in Xiaobing Li, Allan R. Millett, and Bin Yu, eds., *Mao's Generals Remember Korea* (Lawrence: University Press of Kansas, 2001).

# Index

# About the Author

ALLAN R. MILLETT is Maj. Gen. Raymond E. Mason Jr., Professor of Military History at The Ohio State University. His previous books include the best-sellers *A War to Be Won: Fighting the Second World War* (with Williamson Murray), *For the Common Defense: A Military History of the United States* (with Peter Maslowski), and *Semper Fidelis: The History of the United States Marine Corps.* He lives in Columbus, Ohio.